RS 200

FORD'S GROUP B RALLY LEGEND

GRAHAM ROBSON

RS200

FORD'S GROUP B RALLY LEGEND

GRAHAM ROBSON

H&S

Herridge & Sons

Published in 2020 by
Herridge and Sons Ltd
Lower Forda, Shebbear
Devon EX21 5SY

Reprinted 2021

Designed and edited by Spoon Media
www.spoonmedia.co.uk

Photography by Simon Clay
www.simonclay.com

ISBN 978-1-906133-95-5
Printed in China

CONTENTS

Introduction

I have been enthralled by the entire RS200 Group B project since the very first day that I learned of it. I was soon honoured to be asked to contribute to its launch and development, then for four amazing years in the 1980s I actually drove RS200s as my day-to-day road cars. Since then, I have been in love with this incredible car, and have finally found a way of assembling the full story of its career. So here it is.

Since the RS200 project was first revealed in 1984, and went hurriedly into production at the end of 1985, far too many myths and legends about its birth, its production and its qualities have grown up and been discounted – although a few have persisted. I am now happy to say that, as I was always involved in the life of this fascinating 200-off project, I hope I have been able to assemble a detailed chronicle of its birth, its design, its development, its production, and its short but distinguished career.

Now, at last, I have been able to compile and publish the true facts of where, when, why and how so much was done to make the building of just 200 phenomenal mid-engined, four-wheel-drive cars possible.

To compete with honour at the top level of the Group B rally category in the 1980s, any credible machine had to be conceived by a small, expert and totally determined group of people who really understood the sport, and who all shared the same ambitions. It was for those reasons that 'big business', though blessed with its massed ranks of finance experts, planners and marketing gurus, has rarely been able to match such visionaries. For those enthusiastic about Ford in motorsport, we must be grateful that Walter Hayes and Stuart Turner were able to assemble a small and dedicated team to turn a Good Idea into reality – and I have made enthusiastic mention of them in the acknowledgements section that follows.

> "The joy of firing up a car, to hear the irresistible clatter-tinkle-squeal-grunt behind my left ear as another wonderful journey was to begin"

In view of what I have already written, you would expect me to insist that the RS200 was probably the most outstanding example of what a Group B car could be – for it was not only technically very advanced, but it was very elegantly styled, very versatile, and it was brought from Good Idea to Available To Buy in very quick time. This is indeed so, but when writing this book I also wanted to emphasise that in many ways it was brought to the market against almost every possible obstacle – lack of time, lack of finance, lack of production facilities, and (at times) even lack of support from the great and the good of Ford itself.

Accordingly, this book aims to make it clear how much was expected of the tightly-knit team that did all the heavy lifting, how much was achieved by the sheer brilliance of engineers like John Wheeler and Tony Southgate, of can-do planners like Mike Moreton, how much willing work, consultancy and effort came from companies such as Cosworth, FF Developments and other suppliers, and how much time-consuming service followed from Bob Howe (Mr RS200 in so many ways).

Even so, it would still have been possible for the RS200 to be forgotten soon after its time in the spotlight was over, if stalwarts like Justin Smith – and the detailed information and research of his *RS200.org* website – had not matured and persisted.

For years to come, I know, I will still cherish memories as diverse as setting eyes on Car 001 for the very first time in March 1984; for having to thread my way through a London traffic jam on the day I collected my first road car; for enjoying the sight and sound of these peerless works cars on world championship rally special stages; and for the joy of firing up a car, to hear the irresistible clatter-tinkle-squeal-grunt behind my left ear as another wonderful day's journey was about to begin.

Were there any problems that the RS200 project encountered during its life in the limelight in the 1980s? Of course there were, but all were overcome, and none destroyed the reputation of what was, and still is, one of the most charismatic cars ever to carry that famous blue oval on its nose. I was proud to be involved with the car at the time, and I still am today.

Graham Robson

The RS200 was probably the most outstanding example of what a Group B car could be.

Acknowledgements

Although this is one of the most pleasant of duties for any author, it is usually very difficult to assemble a complete list of everyone who made this book – the entire birth, life and times of the RS200 – to be possible, authentic and complete.

Right from the start, therefore, I must quote what I wrote when I was finalising my complete history of Boreham, Ford's famous motorsport centre, which I described as a dream factory: *'Over the years a lot of people helped me to know Boreham, and its people, and without them I would never have tapped into the character, and charm, of the operation. In recent years, however, I interviewed almost all the important characters, whose insight made my job so much easier…'*

However, I must start by thanking several pivotal figures, without whom the RS200 project might never have matured, and without whom this book would certainly not have been written.

WALTER HAYES, Ford's vice president of public affairs, who was first to pick up the feeling within Ford that all was not well with the Escort RS1700T project, and who supported the RS200 from concept to final delivery.

STUART TURNER, ex-Motorsport director, later public affairs director, who answered Walter Hayes's call, conceived the RS200 'grand design', and lived with the project throughout the 1980s.

JOHN WHEELER, Boreham's chief rally engineer, who cooperated so well with Tony Southgate, and made sure that the RS200 was competitive from day one.

MIKE MORETON, whom I have often described as Boreham's Olympic-standard 'fixer', who not only steered the RS200 project through Ford's Byzantine approvals procedures, but also acted as project director in seeing the design of the road cars finalised, and then to see that production cars were all built at Shenstone, and reached their homologation date with destiny.

BOB HOWE, as far as the general public was concerned, was the individual who not only ran the arduous legislation and type-approval procedure, but then went on to sell every individual car. He was also the single Ford individual who drove more RS200 miles than anyone else.

PETER ASHCROFT, Motorsport manager throughout the 1980s, whose department at Boreham turned the RS200 from Good Idea to Winner, always with good humour, rarely with any signs of frustration, and always with the complete trust of all his workforce.

And then there were the people who helped me, sometimes with face-to-face interviews, sometimes with detail reminiscences, and always with a huge amount of Ford motorsport experience behind them…

Pete Arnold (of AMT), Tom Beck, Terry Bradley, Graham Dale-Jones, John Davenport, Keith Duckworth, Philip Dunabin, Matthew Grant, John Griffiths, Brian Hart, Terry Hoyle, Mick Jones, Mike Kranefuss, Mike Little, Karl Ludvigsen, Bill Meade, Gunnar Palm, Jim Porter, Charles Reynolds, Hamish Robson, Steve Rockingham, Justin Smith (creator and manager of *www.rs200.org*, the invaluable website in which so many RS200 memories are stored), Gordon Spooner, Sir Jackie Stewart, Andy Thorburn, John Taylor, Mike Taylor and Robin Vokins. There were others who I met along the way – technicians, RS dealer staff, even those patient people who occasionally (and I do mean occasionally) collected me and my RS200 from a place where it might have 'failed to proceed'. I never got to know those people well – and I salute them too.

Then, of course, there were the drivers and co-drivers – not only the heroes who used the RS200 in events in the late 1980s (Stig Blomqvist, Kalle Grundel, Mark Lovell and Roger Freeman) but brave test and development individuals such as Malcolm Wilson, John Taylor, Mark Rennison, and (later, of course) Gwyndaf Evans. We must never forget, too, that not only was (and is) John Wheeler a peerless engineer, but is also an extremely competent driver, as his performance in latter-day Slowly Sideways often proves. On the other hand, as far as is known, neither project boss Stuart Turner nor his competition manager Peter Ashcroft were ever tempted to drive an RS200.

At this point I would also like to thank all those people who helped me to amass all the colourful images that I have assembled to try to make this book memorable. A few (frankly of the happy snaps variety) came from my family, who often found the Robson 'endurance' car parked outside the family home. But the vast majority came from Ford's own photographic archive, where the team often went to great trouble to dig out some of the very rare and special images you will find in these pages. In particular, when I needed to illustrate the achievements of rallying RS200s in European Championship rounds, I was incredibly fortunate to receive help from Christophe Badau and Olivier Delhez of Belgium, whose archive made all the difference to Chapter 7.

"Their efforts to help me tell a full story have resulted in the birth of a lasting record that this magnificent car deserves"

Without help of all these enthusiasts, where could I ever have unearthed those rare studies of an Escort RS1700T platform, bare and ready for assembly; the highly restricted pictures of HRH Prince Michael of Kent getting a first-look at Car 001; and of the layout of a unique collection of components, semi-assembled on the Boreham workshop floor? And who else could have provided proof of the way that cars were prepared at Boreham, were test-driven in snowstorms in Wales, were assembled at Shenstone (not Reliant, of course), and were refurbished in such quantities at Aston Martin Tickford in Bedworth. Unhappily, Ford-USA closed down the aforementioned photographic archive in the 2010s, and the images were sent to the USA, where they are no longer easily available.

Finally, I would also like to salute supreme rallying chronicler/historian Martin Holmes, without whose help I would not have been to assemble the complete (if relatively brief) story of the fortunes of the RS200s in world and other events in the late 1980s.

My grateful thanks go to all those people, with the hope that their efforts to help me tell a full story have resulted in the birth of a lasting record that this magnificent car deserves.

Graham Robson

By Stuart Turner

RS200 foreword

As this book graphically illustrates, any project like an RS200 has its highs and lows. For me there was a personal high when we took the first prototype to the MIRA handling course and had a day of highly constructive input from Jackie Stewart. Towards the end of the session he beckoned me to get in the car with him, and when he winked at the engineers I knew what was going to happen – he was going to try to scare me with some quick circuitry, not realising that as a former rally navigator I would happily have sat there for hours.

The next day, Stig Blomqvist tested the same car over our rally handling course at Boreham, and he too invited me for a spin. So I was driven at speed by two world champions within 24 hours. Amazingly, my pay cheque still came through at the end of the month as usual.

"I was driven at speed by two world champions within 24 hours. Amazingly, my pay cheque still came through at the end of the month as usual"

On the other hand, a major low with the RS200 came one day when I was leaving for work, and I had to tell Ford bosses that the Group B 200-off rally category was being cancelled by the FIA, making our 200 expensive cars redundant. As I left, I told my wife Margaret that I'd probably be fired by the end of the day. Not so: the company could not have been more understanding and supportive. We took 46 cars to pieces so that we could, hand-on-heart, say that we had an adequate spares supply.

Soon, we even got a marketing lesson, when one customer took his RS200 to a Ferrari specialist to have luxury trim fitted. I popped in to see the result, and the MD queried what we were asking for the cars. I mentioned £49,950, and he said it was ridiculous. When I pointed out that we couldn't possibly go any lower, he explained that in that market a 50-something price tag was more attractive. "Put £3000 on the price," was his advice. We did... And sales went up.

The cars were still eligible for rallycross and did very well in that branch of the sport for some time, while to help owners of the road versions to know more about the product, we lent cars to a couple of people in the hope that their mileage would mount faster and thus reveal potential faults sooner than our customers.

One was an old friend I'd known since our early days competing against each other on UK rallies. I valued his wide knowledge so much that I used him as a sounding board several times during the development and manufacture of the RS200. His name? Graham Robson. And with such close involvement with the car, it's not surprising that he has written a book as absorbing as this.

Enjoy!

Stuart Turner

Timeline

January 1983 to July 1989

JANUARY 1983 Walter Hayes invited Stuart Turner (Ford-UK director of public affairs) to offer his thoughts about the possible future of Ford-of-Europe in motorsport.

17 FEBRUARY 1983 Stuart Turner submitted his thoughts to Walter Hayes, among other things suggesting that the C100 and Escort RS1700T projects both be cancelled, and that a new Group B rally car should take their place.

25 FEBRUARY 1983 Karl Ludvigsen left his Ford post of vice president, governmental affairs and motorsport, Ford-of-Europe.

MARCH 1983 Stuart Turner appointed director of motorsport, Ford-of-Europe, partly replacing Ludvigsen's position.

14 MARCH 1983 C100 and Escort RS1700T projects cancelled with immediate effect.

APRIL 1983 Turner visited Gordon Murray (Brabham F1 design chief), inviting him to take on the design job for the new Group B car. Murray turned it down.
Project planner/manager Mike Moreton visited Ford subsidiary Ghia in Turin, Italy, to discuss the styling for a new Group B car.

MAY 1983 Four respected engineer/designers - Mike Loasby, Tony Southgate, Nigel Stroud and John Wheeler - began working on proposed schemes for the new car, now coded B200.

JULY 1983 All four proposals were received, and studied. The decision was then made to merge the Southgate/Wheeler designs and go ahead.

SEPTEMBER 1983 Approval came to have the first prototype made. Work on the aluminium honeycomb chassis tub began immediately at ART (in Woolaston, near Northampton).

MARCH 1984 First prototype was completed, and shown to Ford top management and Prince Michael of Kent at a Ford office in Central London. Permission was given to complete five more cars, so that development and finalisation could proceed.

NOVEMBER 1984 The RS200, represented by Car No 004, was put on public display at the Turin Motor Show, after a launch in the Ghia HQ the previous evening.

APRIL 1985 All six prototypes had been completed. Much development, and initial rally preparation, was being carried out.

JUNE/JULY 1985 Ford took over the one-year lease of an empty ex-Reliant factory at Shenstone, near Lichfield, and immediately began attracting the skilled labour to assemble the 194 cars (not 200 cars, incidentally - for the six Boreham prototypes counted towards the necessary homologation total).

OCTOBER/NOVEMBER 1985 Assembly was in full swing at Shenstone, with all the revised BDT engines now delivered from JQF, with manufacture of four-wheel-drive transmissions in full flow at FF Developments in Coventry.

31 JANUARY 1986 After a detailed inspection by a team of FISA executives, Group B homologation was officially granted. Ford, incidentally, immediately adopted Car No 200 for its heritage fleet, and holds it to this day.

FEBRUARY 1986 Two works RS200s took part in the world championship Swedish rally. One of them, driven by Kalle Grundel, finished third overall.

MAY 1986 Although the RS200 was not involved in this series of events, a serious crash on the Tour de Corse rally led to the death of two Lancia works drivers, and was followed by almost immediate cancellation of future Group B competition by the sport's governing body, the FIA.

MAY 1986 Ford brought its use of the Shenstone factory to a close, emptying it of all RS200s, incomplete RS200s and component parts.

LATE 1986 Sales of RS200 road cars began, with Bob Howe running a one-man marketing operation at Boreham in Essex.

1987 AND 1988 Sales and deliveries of RS200 road cars continued. 2.1-litre RS200 Evolution cars (privately constructed, not built in a Ford factory) became dominant in UK and European rallycross.

SEPTEMBER 1988 Over 50 road cars remained unsold.

DECEMBER 1988 Last remaining cars sold. Three cars remained in Ford company ownership, including Car No 200.

JULY 1989 Final delivery of an RS200 to a retail customer. The programme was almost immediately brought to a close.

RS 200
RS 200

Above left: Sturdy seven-spoke aluminium wheels were standard. Competition cars had widened and sometimes split-rimmed alternatives.

Above right: Not much stowage space up front – a second spare wheel could be mounted there.

Left: A left-hand-drive road car in standard form, except for the red Recaro seats

Opposite: This car would have a unique high-tech structure, four-wheel drive and no-compromise engineering.

Chapter 1

Escort RS1700T The false start

The story of the RS200 project does not really begin with the first B200 design submissions of 1983, but with the unsuccessful car it was to replace – the Escort RS1700T. And even that car, if truth be told, was influenced by the legendary MkII Escort. If we therefore date the start of the investigation right back, it took no fewer than six years to urge Ford's world-famous Motorsport operation at Boreham to move from the 'why don't we...?' stage to the first impressions of what a four-wheel-drive rally car should look like.

This all started, really, towards the end of 1977, when Motorsport team boss Peter Ashcroft, his design engineer Allan Wilkinson and the team's works drivers had started to discuss Ford's rallying future. At the time Stuart Turner was not closely involved, for he had been promoted away from the Boreham/AVO operations in 1975, to run the company's prestigious public affairs division. We may be sure, however, that he was always consulted about what was to follow.

With a bigger competition budget available than in most of the previous seasons, the works Escort RS1800s were already seriously involved in events all round the world – in 1977 alone they had won the East African Safari, the Acropolis,

Boreham's very first proposed homologation special was the mid-engined GT70 of 1970. Only a handful of cars were produced before the project was cancelled.

When beautifully restored 30 years later, a GT70 prototype showed the lines of what a competitive mid-engined Ford rally car could have looked like.

the Finnish 1000 Lakes, and the British Lombard RAC (for the sixth consecutive year). It was only a run of bad luck that caused them to lag behind Fiat in the year's World Rally Championship stakes – and Peter Ashcroft was determined to win the title in the following years.

The best way to replace the Escort, they thought, was with a 'better Escort' – still with a front-mounted, in-line engine that drove the rear wheels. Ideally it would have more power, be lighter, and have better traction too. At this time, we should recall, four-wheel-drive cars were still totally banned from rallying. In any case, to meet FIA Appendix Group 4 regulations, for a new model to be homologated, a minimum of 400 cars would have to be manufactured within a 12-month period.

At this point there was an alternative suggestion within Ford – of developing a new car with transverse engine and transmission behind the seats, driving the rear wheels (really a further, and distantly related, development of the GT70 project, which had already been designed for Ford by an independent and multi-talented engineer, Len Bailey), but this did not find favour. The fact that team star driver Roger Clark had once described the GT70 as 'handling like a camel', and that Mick Jones once described it as 'the biggest heap of s**t I ever worked on' cannot have helped…

Because world championship rallying was taking up almost everyone's time in 1978, not much progress was then made until early in 1979, when Wilkinson encouraged Mick Jones's amazingly resourceful workshop team at Boreham to start work on the first of a new series of projects, the P1, or 'FiEscort'. This car was effectively an amalgam of Fiesta and MkII Escort thinking, which meant it could be speedily and, it was hoped, inexpensively developed.

Effectively this car would use a Fiesta cabin and much-modified floorpan, to which most of a MkII Escort rally car's front end (complete with 260bhp 2.0-litre BDG engine and its well-proven front suspension) was to be grafted. The basic difference, though, was that this was to be a front engine/rear-drive car, whereas the Fiesta was a transverse-engined/front-wheel-drive machine.

> "Roger Clark had once described the GT70 as 'handling like a camel', and Mick Jones once described it as 'the biggest heap of s**t I ever worked on' …"

Behind and underneath the modified Fiesta front bulkhead, there was to be a Fiesta-based floorpan/platform, while the transmission was to be a much-modified racing Hewland transaxle (a modified-type F1 layout coded FGB400) mounted in the tail, all matched to newly-developed independent rear suspension. By June 1979 a mock-up of this car was complete, and by August it was nearly ready for testing.

Unhappily, the active career of this, the one-and-only FiEscort, which was the true ancestor of the RS1700T, went

Above: Peter Ashcroft ran the Boreham motorsport department from 1972 to 1990, latterly being Stuart Turner's deputy on the RS200 project.

Above right: Charles Reynolds was Boreham's motorsport co-ordinator, and Peter Ashcroft's deputy, when the Escort RS1700T was originally conceived in 1980.

KARL LUDVIGSEN

Michigan-born Karl Ludvigsen was already a person with a significant motor industry record before he was appointed as Ford's vice president of governmental affairs and motorsport in 1979. As part of his duties, he took over from Mike Kranefuss, who was being moved to Ford's world HQ in Dearborn, USA, at the same time.

Having started as a designer at General Motors in Detroit, and serving in the US Army signal corps in Germany, he then spent time with General Motors, not only on engineering projects but in public affairs operations, before taking up automotive writing, especially concerned with motorsport.

By the 1970s he had become closely involved with several prestigious US and European magazines, then joined Fiat-USA as vice president of corporate affairs, before moving up to Ford-of-Europe, in Essex. It was there that his two most important projects – the development of the C100 racing sports car, and the Escort RS1700T rally car – took shape, but following a major policy change at Ford in March 1983 he left the company to further his own career in industrial consultancy, marketing, and writing a number of truly authoritative books. His motorsport responsibilities at Ford were taken over by Stuart Turner (who had been away from the sport from late 1975).

no further. At the time, in the autumn of 1979 Boreham was totally occupied in contesting the World Rally Championship: the team achieved second and third in the 1000 Lakes, first and third in Quebec, and a crushing 1-2-4 finish in the Lombard RAC rally – which tells its own story.

Not only that, but Ford's top management had already decided to pull out of world rallying for 1980 and 1981 at least – development, and the planned launch of an all-new front-wheel-drive Escort road car (the MkIII) was a big factor in this decision – so the media was told that Boreham would therefore close its doors, sell off all the 'old stock', and settle down to design new models. P1 (the FiEscort) was just one of that stock at Boreham, for which there seemed to be no immediate future, so the car was stripped out of valuable components, the remainder being sold off at scrap value, and the entity was never seen again.

RS1700T

Before Boreham finally started work on the car later badged Escort RS1700T, in 1980, a great deal had occurred, both within Ford and out there in the world of rallying. Notably, the sport's governing body, the FIA, had finally authorised the use of four-wheel drive in rallying (though when this was made clear in 1979 there were no such competitive rally cars on the market. The Audi Quattro would change all that in 1981…), and in 1980 proposals were enacted to change the format of Appendix J motorsport from Groups 1, 2, 3 and 4 to new categories of Groups N, A, B and C.

Not only that, but after Ford-Europe had effectively withdrawn from active motorsport at the end of 1979, also to start work on new models, its European team boss Mike Kranefuss had been promoted to Ford of Detroit to undertake similar responsibilities; a renowned journalist, Karl Ludvigsen, took his place in Europe. Although team boss Peter Ashcroft stayed on at Boreham, along with his capable and effective right-hand-man Charles Reynolds (and two of the team's star drivers Hannu Mikkola and Ari Vatanen were retained on contract), the rest of the staff (but not the mechanics) were either allowed to move on or be reassigned. Needless to say, Stuart Turner – whose influence was still always felt, even though officially in the background – was still in evidence.

Chief rally engineer Allan Wilkinson soon moved away, to take up a similar job with Toyota Team Europe in Cologne, which meant Boreham had to start a search for a new design engineer to take his place. In the meantime, one of Karl's first moves was to authorise Boreham to get rid of all but one of its existing fleet of MkII Escort rally cars – in fact, the records show that no fewer than 14 such cars, several of which had competed in only one event (the 1979 Lombard RAC rally), found eager customers – and another was to make a start on two major programmes. One was for the gradual development of a Cosworth-engined two-seater Group C racing sports car to rival everything that had so far been achieved by Porsche (this

In 1981, Karl Ludvigsen briefly asked for this Ghia-styled AC Ghia to be considered as the basis of a works rally car.

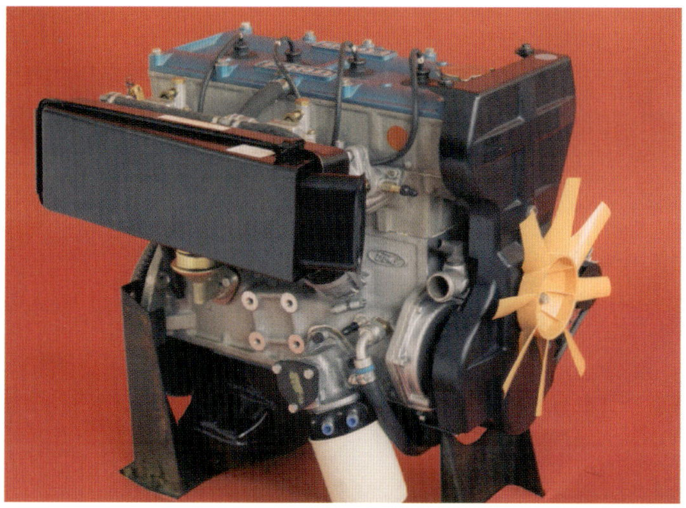

Left: Originally launched in 1970, with a cast-iron cylinder block, the famous BDA engine inherited an aluminium cylinder block from 1972. For the Escort RS1700T, a turbocharged version was developed.

was the C100 project), although it was never intended for this car to be designed, built or campaigned from Boreham. The other intention was for Motorsport at Boreham to conceive, build and develop a new world championship rally car, such that somewhere else in Ford's empire, or even outside the mainstream factories, the manufacture of 200 road cars could be completed, to allow Group B homologation to be achieved.

This project, incidentally, matured at the same time as the FIA decided to abandon the old Group 1, 2, and 4 categories, to replace them by new and, in some ways, more liberally-specified, Groups N, A, and B. Without going into too much detail for the moment, it is enough to explain that only 200 Group B road cars would have to be assembled to allow Ford Motorsport to return to the fray…

The first schemes for a new Group B rally car were laid early in 1980, but nothing was finalised for months – especially after Wilkinson left, which meant Boreham needed to find a new engineering design manager. In the Good Old Days, when Escorts were still relatively simple, though powerful, it was stalwarts such as Bill Meade and Mick Jones who could then have taken up the challenge. But this new project, somehow, would be much more complex to evolve.

Even at the time (and with the stillborn P1/FiEscort prototype experience now available), the basic idea was that a special new car should be based on the still-to-be-launched mass-market Escort MkIII structure and style, that somehow a front-engine/rear-drive installation should then be adopted and grafted into place, and that a turbocharged version of the well-loved BDA engine should provide the motive power. Because the budget for such a car was severely limited, the finance was certainly never available for a completely new platform/chassis to be designed – nor was the manpower available to deliver such a task – and although Brian Hart would have loved to supply his lusty own-design 2-litre Hart Type 420R engine in numbers (it had already proven its worth in Formula Two race cars), a lack of finance put paid to that too.

"No one could have realised, at the time, just what a cataclysmic and liberating effect it would have on the sport"

All these decisions were made by mid-summer of 1980, before a significant *Autosport* job advert appeared in which a new design engineer was to be hired, the in-line/front-

In the early1980s Boreham was concentrating on the development of the Escort RS1700T. This was the very first example of the unique chassis platform.

John Wheeler (right) and Ari Vatanen were firm friends and professional colleagues for years in the 1970s and 1980s.

engine/rear-drive layout had already been agreed, and at least one much-modified version of an Escort MkIII platform – with provision for the location of a propeller shaft, and accommodation for the Hewland rear transaxle – had been made. This, one should emphasise, came along soon after the four-wheel-drive Audi Quattro had already been launched, though no rally version of that all-new car was due to appear until the end of 1980, and no one could have realised, at the time, just what a cataclysmic and liberating effect it would have on the sport.

So, was it a mistake for Ford to persevere with a two-wheel-drive layout for its new car when Audi seemed determined to change the face of the sport in the near future? It seemed not, and even on reflection, most pundits are still ready to point out that no rival had even begun to think in terms of four-wheel-drive rally cars until 1981, by which time the Quattro had actually started winning. It is significant, for instance, that Lancia designed and developed its Group B Rally 037 as a two-wheel-drive car in 1980/1981 – almost in parallel with the Ford project – while neither Peugeot (with the 205 T16) nor British Leyland (with the MG Metro 6R4) even began to make any 4x4 plans until 1982.

Incidentally, it is not generally known that in the fullness of time there might even have been a four-wheel-drive

development of the RS1700T (John Wheeler had already schemed out what would have been needed in 1982, but his suggestions were rebuffed by management), while Vauxhall and Opel had the idea of doing the same thing with their existing, but conventionally-engineered, Chevette HSRs and Manta 400s.

Thus it was that a remarkable young engineer, John Wheeler, answered the *Autosport* job advert for a rally engineer, was interviewed at Boreham, and soon went on to lead the tiny team, where he would be mainly responsible for engineering the new car. John had already spent years working at Porsche, whose new 928 model just happened to have a front engine, rear transmission, and had a propeller-shaft torque tube connecting them. Does that sound familiar, or was it just a coincidence?

By October 1980 Wheeler had started his job at Boreham, as serious design work on a new car was ready to begin.

"There was the intent to do a new car," John told me many years later, "but as soon as I saw Allan Wilkinson's early schemes, I knew it was a non-starter – the driveline had a large-diameter propeller shaft, with all its inertia, which would not still be smooth at 9000rpm!

"Pretty soon, the team was convinced about using rear-wheel drive. We were looking at using 300 to 350bhp, so we chose to use a turbocharged engine. At this time, incidentally, we also did four-wheel-drive studies…"

Detail design went ahead with great urgency. The external style, carried out by Thomas Plath of Ford's design studio, included an extroverted rear spoiler, slots, louvres and bulges in the front end, and sizeable wheelarch extensions. But in this form it was never going to be an easy project to sell to management.

As Karl Ludvigsen, at the time Ford's vice president of Motorsport, later admitted, "In my opinion there was a fundamental misunderstanding of my arguments, which I made to justify the use of rear-wheel drive in rallying, when the company had just introduced a front-wheel-drive Escort."

Even so, Ludvigsen eventually gained an official go-ahead, and work on the new car forged ahead. It was not until mid 1981 that the project gained the pseudonymous title of Columbia – inspired by the launch of the first USA Space Shuttle of the same name.

John Wheeler has always been modest about his own input, though almost all the general layout was to his credit. "I used to scheme things out, and spend hours laying out the transmission and suspension installations, but I didn't draw it all up, not by any means," he said.

Much turbocharging work, of the BDA engine, was carried out by the Schrick company of Germany, Ford's contract race engineer Len Bailey did some details, and of course Hewland was much involved with the evolution of the transaxle. The Escort MkIII shell needed very significant front-end structural changes, while a completely new rear subframe was added to take the multi-link independent rear suspension.

"It was a very significant carve-up," John recalled, "which meant it was never going to be easy to build the production run."

That was the biggest problem. It was one thing to design the best rally car, but quite another to build the car in quantity –

Above: Sturdily engineered by Cosworth, the original 1.6-litre 16-valve BDA power unit had enough hidden development for it to become a 450bhp 1.8-litre turbocharged version for use in the forthcoming RS200.

Left: As fitted to the Escort RS700T, the BDT engine featured turbocharging. In modified and improved form, such engines would be adapted for use in the new RS200 project.

Boreham's engine-tuning and homologation guru John Griffiths worked hard on the RS1700T project for years – and is seen here while the car was testing in Portugal.

There was no visual evidence on the RS1700T that the car featured a front-mounted engine and rear-wheel drive.

even of only the 200 cars needed for Group B homologation. Peter Ashcroft couldn't achieve a solution with management, although Karl Ludvigsen should certainly have been able to do so. The project needed a personality who understood product planning, product legislation and timing – someone who could schmooze his way through all the important corridors of power within Ford. This was where product planner/project organiser Mike Moreton finally came onto the scene – but his appointment (in 1982) arrived perhaps a year too late to make a significant difference.

Technically, however, with the project concept approved, there were few shortcomings to overcome. Ford's homologation wizard John Griffiths, who also had a great deal of experience with engine development, was always involved in the turbocharging work, and recommended that the much-loved BDA be reduced to 1.78-litres and christened the BDT: according to the FIA regulations, the RS1700T could then go rallying as a '2.5-litre' at reduced car weight limits. To provide a quick comparison against the BDT, an early RS1700T prototype/test car was also to be fitted with a revised Hart 420R F2 engine – this particular unit being a normally-aspirated 2.4-litre unit with about 300bhp.

"But once we got the BDT running," John said, "we realised

just how much more torque we had..."

Other RS1700T features included provision for almost everything to be installed with a quick-change set of fixings, this including the five-speed gearbox (non-synchromesh dog 'box for works cars; synchromesh for road cars), independent rear suspension, large wheels and long suspension/wheel travel.

"We had huge wheel travel, which was good for traction. At the rear we also had fully-adjustable linkages – anti-squat, anti-dive, and toe-in control, so that we could always get the ideal set-up. Very minor changes could make a big difference to the traction."

There was also one major innovation, for a massive aluminium torque tube linking the engine to the rear-mounted transaxle was chosen, which meant a redesign of the Hewland FGB gearbox, which was packaged upside down to improve the weight distribution.

FGB? In typically agricultural Hewland language, they say FGB was an acronym for F*****g Good Box, for it had personally been designed by Mike Hewland himself, along with Mike Endean.

Positioning the heavy clutch/flywheel assembly, keeping the propshaft in balance at high speeds, and packaging everything proved difficult. So, drawing on his Porsche experience, John replicated what 'Weissach always did'. There were three intermediate propshaft bearings for what was really a long quill shaft linking front to rear.

When the project went public in mid 1981, only one definitive prototype – P7 – was up-and-running, and already

Because the Escort RS1700T engine produced 350bhp and a mountain of torque, Boreham made sure wide and grippy rear tyres were standardised.

A dedicated team was behind the RS1700T. All would be disappointed when the project was finally pulled.

As conceived in 1980/1981, the Escort RS1700T featured a modified MkIII bodyshell, an inline-mounted turbocharged BDT engine, and rear-wheel drive.

there were concerns about delays in the project. "We could always create the rally cars within Boreham's four walls," said John, "and we could have been rallying in 1982. But the production cars, well..."

Boreham clearly needed help, so over at Dunton, where the company's mainstream engineers had sumptuous accommodation and much equipment, Rod Mansfield's SVE team took up road-car development. It was originally decided that the 200-off production run was to take place at Saarlouis (the German 'home of the Escort' factory) but preparations were still not complete when the project was finally cancelled in March 1983.

Much of the prototype testing of the Escort RS1700T was carried out by Ari Vatanen.

"Although we got a lot of support from Karl Ludvigsen," John continued, "and Saarlouis was very helpful (the pilot plant was involved in making up low-cost press tooling for the special panels), this was always going to be a difficult project, to build 200 cars through the Ford production system."

Ludvigsen was more cold-blooded: "SVE put many fiddly hindrances in the way of the production car, but the one that stuck in my throat was on NVH (noise, vibration and harshness) grounds. I was sure that the Fiat Abarth people in Turin were not worried about that in the supercharged Lancia 037 they were making for the same reasons as us. The programme stalled, right there and then."

Although Boreham was often in despair over the delays, rally cars were very rapid in testing, and had tremendous potential. Yet the Quattro had already started winning.

From mid 1981 to early 1983 Malcolm Wilson (who did much of the testing), Pentti Airikkala, Markku Alén, Hannu Mikkola and Ari Vatanen had all driven the prototypes, in Wales and in Portugal, using actual special stages where times achieved by other rally cars were known, and could be compared.

Particularly in Portugal, the RS1700T was seen to be phenomenally fast – although John Wheeler's memory of the way that Ari Vatanen crashed one of the cars (the Hart-engined machine) when he was his sitting alongside as his riding mechanic, and all had to be rescued from a ravine, is the sort of shaggy-dog story that could enliven one-make club dinners for years.

By May 1982, incidentally, Wheeler had produced a long and closely reasoned analysis of what could be achieved with four-wheel drive, and what *should* be achieved on the RS1700T base. This paper suggested that the two-wheel-drive RS1700T would still be a potential winner on tarmac, but

Finally-developed RS1700Ts would have had these styling details.

would be uncompetitive (against the Quattro) on gravel and snow by the end of 1983.

'The success of the Audi Quattro has proved that even a relatively bad four-wheel-drive configuration could be made to work acceptably...'

John thought 200 of the rear-drive RS1700Ts should be produced, but that the prototype of a four-wheel-drive version, much-modified in almost every way (with the gearbox up front, perhaps), could be running by mid 1983, and rallying by the beginning of 1984.

"Ari Vatanen crashed one of the cars (the Hart-engined machine)... and all had to be rescued from a ravine"

He said, "'The four-wheel-drive option is an essential back-up for a large company involved seriously in motorsports."

Karl Ludvigsen remembered: "We went to FF Developments in Coventry, and fortunately the layout would adopt to 4x4 as well as rear-wheel drive. The final plan was to make around 300 and homologate both rear and 4x4 transmissions with the same basic car. But since you officially needed 400 manufactured – 200 of each variant – Ford management wouldn't stand for it."

What was not mentioned in the interview was a that a 4x4 conversion would have necessitated abandoning the original idea of using a Hewland-based rear transaxle, and an all-new main gearbox up front would be needed, placed between the driver's and passenger's legs.

Nothing, in any case, came of this proposal. "The reality was," John Wheeler said, "that what we had developed was right for seven-eighths of Ford's competition world, but wrong for the final eighth, which was the works team competing at the top level. That was the dilemma."

Even so, tests carried out in Mid Wales showed the RS1700T to be between three and five seconds per mile quicker than the best of the MkII Escorts and the rear-drive Opel Mantas – 15-to-25 seconds on a five-mile stage, which was quite a phenomenal improvement.

Even in rear-drive form, by the way, Wheeler was already studying an Evolution version – lighter and more powerful, with improved weight distribution, more of that weight moved

The RS1700T looked purposeful but lacked four-wheel drive.

Boreham took two cars to Portugal for test sessions in 1982 – one using the new BDT engine, and one a Hartpower 420R normally-aspirated unit.

STUART TURNER

Although Stuart Turner's best-selling autobiography was titled *Twice Lucky*, there was really no luck about his career. Already famous as BMC's competitions manager in the 1960s, along with Walter Hayes he was one of Ford's most influential motorsport characters from 1969 to 1990.

Turner initially trained as an accountant, broke into rallying at club level, after which his progress as a club magazine editor, a works co-driver, and the first rallies editor of *Motoring News* was logical.

Having won three national rally championship co-drivers' awards, and sat alongside Erik Carlsson when he won the RAC Rally of 1960, he became BMC's competition manager from 1961 to 1967 (when the Mini was at the height of its powers).

Head-hunted by Walter Hayes to join Ford Motorsport in 1969 (where he succeeded Henry Taylor), his ruthless methods, and a sure eye for publicity, stamped his authority on everything Ford tackled in rallying.

After becoming director of motorsport in 1970, he also managed the AVO production plant from 1972 until it was closed down in 1975. For the next seven years he then directed the fortunes of the public affairs department, before returning as director of motorsport, Ford-of-Europe, in 1983.

"His ruthless methods, and a sure eye for publicity, stamped his authority on everything"

In 21 years at Ford, he was a prime mover in the Escort RS1600/Mexico/RS2000 programme, in the MkII versions of those cars, in the Escort RS Turbo, the RS200, the Sierra RS (and RS500) Cosworth, and finally in the Escort RS Cosworth. On the other hand, it was Turner's decisive axe that killed off the Escort RS1700T...

Retiring from Ford at the end of 1990, he then turned to his next career – as a superb, and much-in-demand after-dinner and conference speaker, and was still enjoying this hobby as the 2010s ended.

backwards, better tyres and much suspension development.

In the meantime, Mike Moreton had finally arrived at Boreham. Moreton, the product planner who had once worked at AVO in the 1970s, and knew his way in, around, under and through Ford's complex new-car approvals systems, was really appointed too late to rescue what began to look like a doomed project.

"By 1982 Boreham was in trouble with the Escort RS1700T," Mike told me, "not knowing how to get it into production. Peter Ashcroft went to Stuart Turner (still at public affairs), and Stuart suggested me. Peter called me at Dunton and asked me if I was interested.

"Ford RS dealers were terrified at the prospect of having to sell these cars... £10,000 was acceptable. But within two years that figure had rocketed to £23,000"

"Well, I was, but it took me nine months to get in, nagging, pulling, pushing, persuading, cajoling, arguing – once I even lost my temper with Peter's boss, Karl Ludvigsen. I moved in during July 1982; there wasn't a spare office at first, so I sat in the corridor for a few weeks. With the RS1700T we tried all ways of making the 200 cars. We went to see Aston Martin, to Lotus and to Reliant to see if they would build the cars for us. We were beginning to get somewhere when Stuart Turner finally cancelled it. By then we had decided we would like to make the RS1700T at Lotus, and we were considering four-wheel drive."

Even so, it looks as if Ford RS dealers were terrified at the prospect of having to sell these cars. Originally someone had suggested a selling price of £10,000, which was acceptable. But within two years that figure had rocketed to £23,000, and further cost increases followed. It was unthinkable – this would make it by far the most expensive car in Ford's current line-up, where at the time the Capri 2.8i retailed at a mere £8125, and the top-of-the range Granada (the 2.8 Injection saloon) cost only £10,745. Ford faced the spectre of having to slash the proposed RS1700T selling price, and build cars that could therefore never be sold at a profit.

In hindsight, it seems that cancellation was inevitable. As everyone now knows, the RS1700T was abruptly cancelled after Stuart Turner took over from Karl Ludvigsen in March 1983.

"At that stage," Wheeler recalled, "we had 200 sets of body panels made, quite a lot of bodies in assembly, we had 200 engines made, and 200 synchromesh (road car) gearboxes made."

It was not until the project was cancelled that Boreham discovered that much of the machining for the main Hewland gearboxes was, at that time, still incomplete, so rushing the project through to have 200 such cars finished would have been truly problematical.

Although at least 18 prototype cars – or the makings of cars – had already been constructed (a handful still survive), from that day on, no further work was done at Boreham. Some cars were sent to South Africa, where ex-Boreham guru Mick Jones eventually turned them into winners in non-homologated events, and where Malcolm Wilson rallied them in the 1984 season, but they were never used in Europe.

By the early 1980s, of course, David Sutton's London-based team, sponsored by Rothmans, the cigarette company, had effectively become Boreham's arm's-length works team, but the cancellation of the RS1700T project crippled Sutton's future rallying plans, as he once told me: "Ford's Peter Ashcroft proceeded to knock us all sideways with some completely unexpected news. We listened in stunned silence as he revealed that the launch of the new, much vaunted Ford rally car, for which we had been waiting so eagerly for the previous two years, and that we thought was going to be ready in time for the next season, had now been postponed, indefinitely. For both Rothmans and David Sutton Cars, this was a real body blow."

Stuart Turner summed it up perfectly: "When Walter Hayes called me from Detroit in January 1983, he was not totally happy about what he saw. Telling me that he was picking up opinion that all was not well with motorsport in Europe, and what did I think?"

As you might expect, Stuart talked to a lot of people, listened, and eventually concluded: "I got an amazingly consistent response. I found that the Escort RS1700T, and particularly the C100, had absolutely no supporters. My paper to Walter, dated 17 January 1983, pointed out that '*We must accept that the new Audi will be a formidable competitor, and in 2WD form the RS1700T will struggle to beat it… Any car which, like the RS1700T, takes an eternity to come to life, makes me nervous*'."

Within a month of receiving this paper, Walter Hayes had moved decisively, persuaded his colleagues to move Karl Ludvigsen away from Motorsport, and also to persuade Turner to move back into Motorsport. Stuart returned to Boreham on 4 March 1983, and talked to Peter Ashcroft, Mike Moreton and Charles Reynolds, to see how far away the production of the RS1700T still was.

"My first task," Stuart recalled, "was to decide the future of the Escort RS1700T and the C100 racing sports car – both of them being Karl Ludvigsen's pet projects. Instantly gaining the reputation of Turner the Axe-Man, I decided that both the C100 *and* the Escort RS1700T projects would have to be

High-speed testing of an RS1700T prototype on a Portuguese special stage. The driver was Ari Vatanen.

WALTER HAYES

Between 1961 and 1989, when he finally retired from Ford, Walter Hayes was one of the most dynamic and enthusiastic supporters of all high-performance Ford programmes, whether it concerned motorsport or road cars. Yet, by his own admission, he was really a newspaperman and not a motor industry executive, and latterly a publicist rather than a motorsport administrator.

Already famous as an editor in the world of British newspapers, he joined Ford to revolutionise the company's public face. Originally in charge of Ford-UK's public affairs department, and soon the influence behind every motorsport programme, he modernised Ford's thinking in every way. It was Hayes who found the money to build the Boreham motorsport centre, who urged Ford to finance Cosworth's DFV F1 engine, approved the launch of the Escort Twin Cam, lobbied hard for the opening of Advanced Vehicle Operations, hired Stuart Turner as his new director of motorsport – and much more.

By the 1980s he had become vice chairman, Ford-of-Europe, and brought back Stuart Turner from the public affairs operation into Motorsport at Boreham, so that Turner could revitalise the operation and get the four-wheel-drive RS200 programme going. Later he kept the Sierra RS Cosworth in being when others had gone wobbly on it, and did more than most to make sure the Escort RS Cosworth went into production.

When he reached his 65th birthday he was obliged to retire, for that was a Ford global ruling, but he was not ready to forget about cars. One of his later tasks was to become Aston Martin's chairman, to get the DB7 project approved, and generally to revive yet another struggling organisation. When the time came to retire the Escort from top-flight motorsport, Walter was one of the most honoured in a glittering array of special guests.

Guru? Of course. Inspiration? Certainly. Influential top brass? Naturally. But also a deep thinker, a visionary, a motoring enthusiast – and a very important man. Without him, in our opinion, Boreham, as a motorsport centre, might never have existed, and after he died in 2000 it never seemed to be the same.

cancelled, there and then.

"I was genuinely sad that the RS1700T had to go. For more than two years Boreham had slaved away on the development of this car, but there was no chance of them carrying out a full world championship programme before 1984."

Accordingly, at a meeting of Ford's PSG (Product Strategy Group) on 14 March, Turner recommended that both projects should be cancelled immediately. After what he recalled as no more than a five-minute discussion, he got his way, without argument.

"As soon as I came out of the meeting I phoned Peter Ashcroft at Boreham, told him, and work stopped that very day."

Shortly afterwards, Ford issued a release stating that the two projects had been abandoned, and quoted Turner as saying, *'Having spent some time looking hard at our existing plans, I have become convinced that we are not moving in the best direction if we are going to resume our former position in international motorsport.*

'This does not mean we are giving up… Make no mistake – we shall be back, although not with the cars we have under development at the moment…'

When the news broke, there was much reaction in the press, some of it well-informed, some of it hysterical, and some of it quite unpleasant. But Boreham had already turned its attention to other projects. One of them, perhaps the most exciting of all, was the new RS200.

In the early 1980s, Boreham was concentrating on the building of Escort RS1700T prototypes – this showing three such cars under construction.

Engineer John Wheeler sometimes sat alongside the driver during high-speed testing of RS1700Ts.

Chapter 2

The big idea

I don't think I will ever forget the heady days that surrounded the birth of the RS200 project. Not that I was responsible for the design, or even the concept, of the new car – but I will always remember how I seemed to be involved in, or observing, the 'why don't we…?' discussions from the very start of it all.

Late one Friday evening in January 1983, in deepest Dorset, I was lazing in front of a roaring fire, with a snoring bulldog alongside me on the sofa, and a glass of the very best Scotch whisky to hand, when the phone rang. Because it was well after 10pm, I was certainly not expecting anyone to contact me. So I was amazed, puzzled and – soon – enthralled by the story that began to unfold from Ford's director of public affairs, Stuart Turner.

"The situation is too serious for niceties. We should have one key objective in motorsport: winning"

Stuart Turner (left) with Erik Carlsson.

At this point I should confirm that in many ways I was quite close to Stuart, and to most of the personnel at the Motorsport Centre at Boreham. Stuart and I had first met in 1960, when we were both active members of the British rallying co-drivers' 'trade union'. I had started writing rally reports for him at *Motoring News* soon afterwards, and had never lost touch when he pushed on through the competition boss's positions at BMC and later Ford. Not only had I continued to work for him on a variety of motorsport promotions (which involved opening the door for me to be able to ghost-write Roger Clark's autobiography *Sideways to Victory*, and also to write the first of several editions of *The Works Escorts*), I had also begun to take on minor assignments for Boreham.

Since 1975 Stuart had not been directly involved in running Ford's motorsport programmes but, through his boss, friend, and (in some ways) mentor Walter Hayes, he had never lost touch with what was happening, where, when and why. Which explains what happened in the days surrounding that phone call…

His opening remarks made everything that followed extremely clear: "This conversation is not taking place…" It was immediately followed by a long and detailed run-down of what had, was, should, and might happen in Ford's immediate motorsport future. The call lasted for more than an hour, and inspired me so much that the following morning I wrote a detailed resumé for him, and have kept a carbon copy of it, to this day.

This, however, is getting slightly ahead of what was already happening at Ford, so with Stuart's kind permission, I am now able to quote the opening remarks he made about the car in his best-selling autobiography *Twice Lucky:*

'I had never lost complete touch with motorsport because whenever Peter Ashcroft needed to make an important announcement, Public Affairs got involved, and we kept in touch as friends. As a result I knew that things were not going well at Boreham, but I was still surprised by what happened next. Once again, it was Walter Hayes who precipitated a change, but this time his phone call came from North America. He wanted advice….

'When Walter called in January 1983, he had been in Detroit as vice president of public affairs for Ford Motor Company Worldwide for nearly three years and retained responsibility for motorsport globally… He told me that he was picking up vibrations that all was not well with the RS1700T rally machine and the C100 sports cars. Would I talk to a few people and write him a note about it?'

Turner immediately set about a consultation process, where several people (and I was flattered to be one of them) were asked for their opinions, and to listen, then comment on what he was preparing to do about it. This, inevitably, would take several weeks to mature, but was soon seen to be central to Ford-of-Europe's entire motorsport strategy in future years.

In particular, and as already noted at the end of the previous chapter, the result of this forensic analysis was that decisive, abrupt (and, ultimately, successful) action should be taken, and that the two expensively-developing programmes that already existed – the C100 Group C race car and the Escort RS1700T rally car – should both be terminated.

But what followed would take a little time to evolve. Turner's initial note to Hayes, dated 17 January 1983, pointed out, *'I must be cutting across many company procedures in writing to you… but the situation is too serious for niceties. We should have one key objective in motorsport: winning… I think as a safety net we should commission in total secrecy, and outside the company the prototype for a run of 200 unique 4WD sports cars; if the RS1700T doesn't win then we should put a sports car into production at Lotus, Reliant or Tickford…'*

Although, by any measure, I was one of the least important people to be consulted about the need for a new rally car (it didn't have a name or project number at that point, of course), I am still proud that my response to that phone call, dated 10 January 1983, was to write a complete resumé of what had been said, mentioning several factors that I thought should eventually be adopted.

THE BRIEF

WHAT WOULD BE NEEDED FOR A NEW SPORTS CAR?

- It needed to be a purpose-built machine, not an existing modified production Ford.
- It needed four-wheel drive, so as to be able to beat Audi and Peugeot.
- It would need to have at least 400bhp.
- Two years, but no more, should be allocated for design, testing, development and the 200-off production run.
- Buy/hire/borrow/set up a small facility to build the 200 cars.
- Spend serious money on hiring a top-grade design engineer *and* on works drivers.
- Boreham should not be over-burdened with the development of the original design.
- Start legal homologation and legislation compliance at an early stage.
- Car size? Think of 1.7-litre or 2.0-litre turbo engines (BDTs, probably, but a Hart 420R perhaps) to allow the car to run at minimum weights in 2.5-litre or 3.0-litre capacity class form.

This head-on shot, taken low down in 1984, shows the distinct and obvious visual family relationship between (left to right) the Sierra XR4Ti, RS200 and Escort RS Turbo.

MIKE MORETON

As a planner, organiser and schemer, Mike Moreton had no equal. Many years ago, in a profile, I once defined Mike as a superb 'fixer', and although he thought this was a touch undignified, he never actually complained – for I reckon he was proud of that description. Whether it was in planning new AVO products or aiding and abetting Stuart Turner and John Wheeler to get cars like the RS200 and the Escort RS Cosworth approved, he was peerless. After working at Rootes in Coventry, and for Vauxhall in Luton, Mike joined Ford in 1966. Within two years he had hitched his star to Bob Howe, and became Ford AVO's product planner in 1972. After a period in mainstream product planning, where he wrote an influential paper suggesting that a special vehicle engineering department should be set up (eventually it was, but not until 1980), he was then seconded to Boreham to make planning sense of the Escort RS1700T project in 1982, although his hard work, in the end, was wasted.

He was an important mover and shaker at Boreham for some years after, heavily involved in the development of the Escort RS Turbo and Sierra RS Cosworth road cars, but in the meantime he became project production manager of the very demanding RS200 project, and the Sierra RS500 Cosworth that followed. It was Mike who takes much of the credit for settling on the Shenstone factory to build the RS200, and for running the entire operation there in 1985 and 1986.

In 1988 and 1989 he was one of the founding fathers of the Escort RS Cosworth, the others being engineer John Wheeler and director Stuart Turner, pushing it over every product planning hurdle, and finding a production home for it at Karmann in Germany.

He was then headhunted by Tom Walkinshaw to work at TWR in Oxfordshire, and his direct Ford connection was finally broken. In a decade at TWR he was project manager for the Jaguar XJ220, ran the Aston Martin factory at Newport Pagnell, inspired the planning behind the Aston Martin DB7, and still found time to advise Tom Walkinshaw on many other projects.

Mine was not the most important response, of course, but it was very flattering for me to realise that similar features were also to be proposed by the great and the good (who included Keith Duckworth of Cosworth, Brian Hart, Peter Ashcroft and John Wheeler from Boreham). In the meantime, Karl Ludvigsen, for whom I have always had the highest regard and still count as a good friend, must have known that something was brewing, and by the end of February he moved out of Ford.

Walter Hayes, for his part, had moved mountains, made such a move possible, and during February called Turner, effectively saying, '*We need you back at Motorsport. Now!*' Only days later, and after meeting with both the chairman of Ford-of-Europe (Ed Blanch) and the president (Jim Capolongo), Turner retained his sumptuously-furnished office on the sixth floor at Ford-of-Europe HQ in Warley, a suburb of Brentwood in Essex (the building has now been emptied and demolished), but effectively started to wear a new corporate hat. It was then, and immediately before the public announcement of his new appointment was made, that he started a series of meetings with senior colleagues, one of which was to begin to formulate the new Group B car, which he had begun to call B200.

> "It was not always as smooth to progress, and artistically as easy to finalise, as hoped"

One of his first collaborators was Mike Moreton, who was already based at Boreham and, until 14 March 1983, must have thought he was rather uneasily wearing two hats – officially he was diligently trying to help ease the Escort RS1700T into production (and this was proving to be a real struggle), while he had started working, in a clandestine manner, for Stuart Turner on the B200 project. Even before Stuart's appointment as director of European motorsports was officially announced, he had initiated a barrage of requests to me that his Ford colleagues could

The Boreham motorsport operation was based in this collection of buildings on the eastern edge of a Second World War airfield. Works cars were assembled, and operated from, the building placarded 'Motorsport' on the right of this aerial photograph, the parts supply department was in the centre, and many other cars, parts and equipment shared with other Ford departments were in the large building in the rear of that centre. In this study, the large tent was only there for a time, for an unstated special exhibition.

Although Boreham thought the Audi Quattro had an awkward four-wheel-drive system, the expensively-developed short-chassis S1 version was still a formidable competitor.

Jim Capolongo was the influential president of Ford-of-Europe when the RS200 project was conceived.

Ed Blanch was chairman of Ford-of-Europe when Walter Hayes and Stuart Turner persuaded him to give the go-ahead for the RS200 project.

not immediately satisfy – but that I might have a conduit to provide the information: could I find out how many Lancia Stratoses had actually been built? Could I acquire images and cutaway drawings of the Stratos, and the four-wheel-drive transmission of the Audi Quattro? Could I also suggest one or two supercar books for him to read, in order that he could learn more about modern trends? And more, and more. It was a rushed, but enthralling, time.

Once Stuart's new appointment had been announced, a few important characters began to join him in his speedy rush towards a solution to the Group B problem. Not only Turner, Mike Moreton, Peter Ashcroft and John Wheeler were involved, but technicians Bill Meade and Mick Jones had their own thoughts to add to the mix, while Andy Jacobson (chief of design for Ford-of-Europe) was also invited to set up links with Ford's Ghia subsidiary in Turin, Italy, which would almost certainly be asked to shape the final machine.

This, then, is the right time to spell out exactly how, why and when the RS200's attractive fixed-head coupé bodystyle was conceived – it took place, progressively, during the summer and autumn of 1983 – and to make it clear that it was not always as smooth to progress, and artistically as easy to finalise, as hoped.

Although Ford had a thriving design/styling operation of its own, with substantial studios located in Germany and at Dunton in Essex, in order not to get in the way of the heavy mainstream styling programmes it was decided that Ghia should be asked to tackle the job. As is explained in the panel on page 42, Ghia was a wholly-owned subsidiary of Ford-of-Europe, acted as the original styling consultants on most of the mainstream programmes, and was also effectively the company's skunkworks for limited-production projects like the B200.

It was Mike Moreton who became Motorsport's main conduit between Turner and Motorsport in the UK and Ghia in Turin, making several visits to Italy in the next few months, and often having to act as a mediator between company characters who all held very strong opinions, and sometimes disagreed completely.

Well before then, however, Stuart Turner's office at Ford HQ in Warley, Brentwood (he would not move that office to Boreham for another seven years) had become the epicentre of everything he hoped would result in Ford's whole approach to motorsport changing – and improving – in future years. Meeting after meeting saw his determination – and that of top bosses such as Jim Capolongo (Ford-of-Europe) and Sam Toy (CEO of Ford-of-Britain) – to get three new programmes under way. One was to be the Escort RS Turbo, a front-wheel-drive 'class car' intended mainly for 1.6-litre touring car racing; another was to be a powerful, re-engined, Sierra-based

Bill Meade was one of Boreham's stalwarts, who had been 'on the ground' since the early 1960s, and would have much to do with the building and development of RS200s.

machine intended to get Ford back to the peak of touring car racing; and the third, which grabbed everyone's attention, was to be coded B200, firmly intended to replace the stillborn Escort RS1700T.

Although Turner's over-optimistic vision was that B200 should be designed in 1983, put into production in 1984, and homologated by the end of that year, he soon realised that this timing forecast was not really feasible. None of his rivals – not even Lancia, whose Abarth-based motorsport team could move very quickly in those days – could meet the ambitious timing of targets like that. Later, as he quoted in his book, *'With luck I thought we might be back in world championship rallying by mid 1985.'*

Even before then, he began a whistle-stop visit to consult several greats of British motorsport, and within days of his appointment, I was honoured to be invited to see him, to stay overnight with him in Essex, and to discuss everything until the middle of the night. For me, that most momentous occasion came early, on 27 March 1983, and I hope I may now be allowed to quote some rather disjointed extracts from the post-meeting notes that I assembled:

'GST said that he had still not been to Boreham to sit down with Peter Ashcroft... He had already met Brian Hart and Keith Duckworth. Hart had already contacted Gordon Murray about designing the B200 car: Murray thought it could be a fascinating project, but was currently on holiday in Hawaii. GST thought there might be trouble in getting time out/permission from Brabham/Bernie Ecclestone to tackle the job.

'Duckworth had talked about his 4WD transmission proposals. Hart had mentioned the possibility of his own engine, in turbocharged form (but would have to move heaven and earth to get 200/250 engines built). GST also said he didn't want to get involved with FF Developments if he could help it.

'As to where the car should be built, he didn't really want to go to Lotus, was favourable to Tickford/Aston Martin, virtually dismissed TVR because they would have to stop building their own TVRs while this Ford contract was ongoing, and said that he was interested in having Reliant do the job. Reliant have much spare industrial capacity, and are looking for work.

'To design the car, he was looking for a nuts-and-bolts engineer to hold hands with "genius" Gordon Murray. AAGR suggested Mike Loasby (just out of work from the financially failing DeLorean project), and even mentioned Geoff Healey, but GST was obsessed with Oliver Winterbottom, who had done the TVR and was now back at Lotus...'

"It was in this sort of 'can-do, but do it now' atmosphere that the B200 eventually began to take shape"

It was in this sort of 'can-do, but do it now' atmosphere that the B200 eventually began to take shape in Turner's fertile brain, and I was honoured to be a part of it all – if only as an avid listener, as something of a court jester, and a person who would eventually remember almost everything that had happened at the time. Not that everything was going to be smoothly achieved, for only three weeks later Turner called me to confirm that 'the genius has taken the hook' (the genius being Gordon Murray) and wanted to do the project. He also told me that he personally was already working to a tight timetable, with his kitchen table in Essex full of timing charts every night. Yet only a week after that, the next call was to tell me that Murray had finally turned the job down, telling him quite truthfully that there was not enough spare time in his life, and that the Brabham F1 cars must come first.

Even by late April 1983, the evolution of the project was still only at the 'why don't we...?' stage, for no personalities had yet been hired, no metal had been cut, and no styling work had been carried out. More importantly, apart from Walter Hayes, who was still located in his Ford-USA office at Dearborn, none of the really-top management could yet visualise what Turner had in mind, for at that precise moment he had nothing to show them – no drawings, no mock-ups, nor any artists' renderings of what his new car might look like.

Again, this is where Robson-the-court-jester's talents came into play: *'3 May 1983: GST rang, asking for cutaway drawings/sketches of the AC3000 mid-engined car, to use to*

When someone asked a designer how to start shaping the RS200, a reply from the irrepressible Mick Jones was 'like this'. This was Boreham in 1983, when 'the car' literally consisted of a cut-down section of Sierra cabin, a couple of rally seats, and four suitable wheels placed in their correct wheelbase position, which had been borrowed from Escort RS1700T stores. That, incidentally, is an Escort RS1700T bodyshell in the background.

"give some ideas" to suppliers of the possible shape and size of the new car, even before it was designed. I also suggested sending GT70 equivalents, as well... Could I find picture and cutaways of the Lancia Stratos? he asked.'

I could, and I did. To this very day, perhaps, *Autocar* magazine and its archive can still not have every idea of how important it was to the swift progression of a paper study to an 'oh, you mean like that ....?' situation.

By the end of April – less than two months after his appointment – Turner's mind must have been a real maelstrom of ideas, disconnected thoughts, unrealised ambitions, and magnificent hopes, though the only two people who were functionally close to him at the time were his competition manager Peter Ashcroft, and the man who would become the RS200's project-managing genius, Mike Moreton.

As an example, these are the notes I made of a phone call received the day after Gordon Murray turned down the design job: *'GST rang, asking for my thoughts on names. He commented that in Italy Gianpaolo Dallara was well known, in Britain Lotus. Mike Loasby and Derek Gardner [ex-Tyrrell] were now in production car companies, John Barnard and Gordon Coppuck were F1 people, but there seemed to be a block from some people on the merits of Tony Southgate. He had already called Ken Tyrrell to talk about Gardner.*

'The intention was to get one mock-up sent to Reliant very quickly, for they would probably be building bodyshells (and maybe even the 200 cars), though other suppliers and specialists would be drafted in to produce components. Ghia would style the car and [at this time] Abbey Panels would

Building up a prototype bulkhead/chassis extension.

build the chassis tubs. If homologation was to be achieved by January 1985, work must be started very soon.

'Duckworth, he thought, would be doing the 4WD. Brian Hart, now a permanent consultant to Ford Motorsport, would certainly be involved, but GST was cagey about this. Hart's own four-cylinder 420R F2 engine was mentioned, but the problem would be to have 200 of such hand-crafted units actually manufactured in time.'

Time was pressing, of course, so at this point Turner decided to start what was effectively, if not officially, a design competition. Of all the names, and others, which had already been mentioned in his discussions with his business contacts, he would invite three of them to take part, to work closely to a brief that he would apply, from which a choice would actually be made.

When Boreham needed a few sketches to take to Ghia to suggest a start to the B200 project, Andy Jacobson's team at Ford Design produced a number like this. Ghia insisted it could do better – and eventually did.

Chapter 3

The design competition

Spring of 1983 had seen Stuart Turner start up the B200 project by approaching Brabham's F1 engineering supremo, Gordon Murray, to invite him to tackle the design job. But he had been hugely disappointed when Murray, who had originally been very enthusiastic about the challenge, finally turned him down.

At this point (to be accurate, May 1983) he made a speedy approach to Patrick Head, who was Frank Williams's F1 technical chief at the time, with a similar offer of technical leadership even if he was not to tackle all the engineering design work himself. Unhappily, even Stuart could not have been expected to know about everything happening in the motorsport industry at the time, so although he already realised Williams was about to dump the ageing Ford-Cosworth DFV engine from its future Formula One cars (in favour of a new turbocharged Honda power unit), he did not know that by this time Williams and Patrick Head were already working on what would be a rival Group B rally car concept – the MG Metro 6R4 – on behalf of Ford's biggest UK rival, Austin-Rover.

"This brief started with an underlined paragraph: **Key objective:** To produce an outright international rally winner. Nothing must be allowed to compromise this"

This was still a deadly secret to all but a very few, and even at the time of Turner's visit to Williams's headquarters in Didcot, Patrick Head received him courteously, discussed the provisional requirement and plans for the B200 project, made a few interesting suggestions about a general car/four-wheel-drive layout, but firmly refused to get more closely involved.

What is fascinating to recall is that although Austin-Rover had first started cooperating with Williams in 1981, and engineering design work on the definitive MG Metro 6R4 had begun in 1982, the original prototype was not finished until February 1983, the very same month in which Stuart Turner picked up the responsibilities for Ford's motorsport activities. Not only that, but it looks as if that single prototype might still have been at the Williams HQ (but firmly behind closed doors) when he visited. To this day he probably does not realise how close he was to discovering Austin-Rover's big secret before the rest of the world found out.

It was immediately after this rebuff that Turner reluctantly concluded he did not have time, and could not find the star designer by approaching candidates individually – and receiving rebuffs in more than one case – without his strategy becoming more widely known in Britain's motorsport industry. At that time, too, it seems he did not intend to involve Boreham, and chief design engineer John Wheeler, in the first discussions.

One of his problems, of course, was that the drawbacks experienced in getting the Escort RS1700T into production, and in finding ways (and people) of getting around that problem, were already quite well known, and there was certainly an air of caution – one might even say scepticism – in the air when he began his quest for a new rally car.

It was then that what we might call Plan B (one that, in the end, would prove to be extremely successful) began to crystallise, namely that having located several individuals who were not only well thought-of but seemingly available to take on the task, that each should be given an opportunity to pitch for the job, be given only a limited time to make a presentation on how they would lay out the new car, and would be paid (£5000 each is the sum still rumoured, but unconfirmed) for their efforts.

After carrying out further discussions with one or two of his most senior contacts in the industry, this quest was launched in mid May, with bids due to be called in at very short notice, at the end of June 1983.

To quote Turner's words in *Twice Lucky: 'I then drew up a designer's brief for the B200, based on my discussions with them and anyone else I could think of. I knew – or thought I knew – that what Ford needed was a four-wheel-drive sports car, of which 200 would have to be made, and on that basis I was ready for it not to be based on an existing or projected Ford road car.*

'This brief started with an underlined paragraph:

Key objective: To produce an outright international rally winner. Nothing must be allowed to compromise this.

B200 FMC

MIKE LOASBY

Mike Loasby was one of that happy breed of enthusiasts whom we now call petrolheads, who started driving an ancient Austin Seven while he was still at school in Monmouth (his friends there included Robin Herd and Alan Rees, founders of March). Apprenticed to Alvis in Coventry, he moved to Coventry-Climax (working on race engine design), then to Aston Martin as a development engineer, and later joined Triumph in Coventry, where he was involved in engine design for the six-cylinder Rover SD1.

Like other figures in the British motor industry, Loasby moved on again after a few years, becoming Aston Martin's director of engineering in 1976. It was then, in 1978, that he was headhunted by John DeLorean (who had grandiose, eventually fraudulent, plans to build cars in Northern Ireland), where he became the company's chief engineer, working directly with Lotus, which was reworking the original DeLorean car design.

Soon after DeLorean went into receivership in 1982, Loasby was made redundant, and then set up his own consultancy – the Midland Design Partnership – where as its founder/chief engineer he pitched for the design contract for the RS200.

NIGEL STROUD

Nigel Stroud, born in York in 1948, started his working life maintaining machinery on a 4000-acre farm in Wiltshire, before becoming a fitter at a Ford dealership in Buckinghamshire.

His motor racing career began in 1973 as production engineer at March, in Oxfordshire, after which he moved to Hesketh Racing at Towcester, working on design of F1 cars and the stillborn Hesketh motorcycle.

The Hesketh 308E was his first race-car design, and was followed in 1979 by the ATS D4. In a big move, from 1980 to 1982 he then became chief race engineer at Lotus, working on the Type 80, 87 and 88 F1 cars.

In 1983 Stroud set up his own design consultancy, NS Designs, and one of his first short-term tasks was to work up his proposal for the design of the B200.

To Nigel's great regret, he did not secure the main contract, nor did he ever again directly work with Ford Motorsport. In the next three decades he concentrated on other single-seater, CART/Indycar and long-distance sports car race projects, often as chief engineer, for companies such as AMG, Mazda, Reynard and Lotus.

'After this, other objectives stressed the need to make it simple to service and operate, to be safe, to have good driver visibility [NOT a lie-down racing position. Windscreen angle is critical for rallying …], to use standard Ford parts wherever practical and, ideally, to use developed versions of the cancelled Escort RS1700T's BDT turbocharged engines, for the majority of those units had already been manufactured, tested, assembled, and were in store at JQF Engineering in Towcester.

'Using these engines, we could claw back more than $1 million that had been written off in the Escort RS1700T's cancellation, which was bound to make me a little more popular with the number crunchers…'

> "Using these engines, we could claw back more than $1 million that had been written off in the Escort RS1700T's cancellation"

Although Turner had already approached Gordon Murray and been turned down, Williams F1 and also been turned down, and had considered inviting Lotus to do the job but decided not to take that plunge (it was only a year after the commercial and financial horrors of Lotus's involvement with the DeLorean project had begun to unravel in public), there was still much of the UK's vibrant motor racing industry available to him, and to Ford.

Accordingly, at that stage he decided to invite three individually very different engineers, all of them with impressive track records, to take part. What amazed many observers at the time was that at this stage Boreham's own top engineer, John Wheeler, was not invited to take part – though the reasons for that would unravel in the weeks to come.

The three heroes commissioned to fight for recognition with the concept of a new car were Mike Loasby, Tony Southgate and Nigel Stroud.

So far, so good, but as soon as Stuart Turner let it be known what he had in mind, Boreham's chief design engineer John Wheeler exploded with anger because he had not even been allowed to be consulted.

With Mike Moreton's permission, I would like to quote how Mike then saw the immediate result: *'John Wheeler came into my office, very deliberately shut the door, and then let rip, apoplectic with rage. Why hadn't he been asked to produce a design? He was so angry that he was determined to drive to Warley "right now", to see Stuart and resign. After half an hour he came down off the ceiling and we talked. I did my best to explain why he wasn't included, that we were deliberately looking for outside inspiration. But I couldn't convince him, because I could see that he was right, so I invited him to produce his own design, and to use my office to guard it from prying eyes. He did just that…'*

John's view, totally justified, was that there was no way that the three invited engineering consultants were close to modern rallying, so he readily agreed with Mike Moreton that he should therefore put up his own proposals and add it to the mix. To keep his proposal secret, and to distance it completely from the Escort RS1700T work that he was still frantically trying to complete, John set up a separate drawing board and working space in Mike Moreton's own office at Boreham, which (as the author experienced at the time) could easily be closed off from other areas of the building with a door that could be, and sometimes was, securely locked.

At the end of June 1983, each of the four designers were asked to present, and to explain, their paper vision of what they thought the B200 should be like. The jury comprised Stuart Turner, Peter Ashcroft, Lothar Pinske (Peter Ashcroft's opposite number at Ford-of-Germany Motorsport) and Mike Moreton himself. In addition, Mike Kranefuss (then based in the USA as Ford's motorsport supremo) had offered advice from time to time, while Gordon Murray was also invited to take a confidential look at what was proposed.

Before the identity of the chosen quartet was made known, by the way, it seems that the individual paper proposals were kept anonymous, although labelled – say, B200A, B200B and so on. John Wheeler recalled clearly that his own proposal was B200Z – even though there were not 25 other ideas ahead of it.

It was immediately clear that Tony Southgate and John Wheeler had gone furthest into the likely needs of a new world championship rally car – the accent being on 'rally car'. Of the other two designs, one (from Nigel Stroud) was a very competent study of what was likely to be a better race car than high-performance road car, while Mike Loasby's design was the opposite – in other words of a machine that would have been an excellent road car but might not easily be turned into a competitive competition car. The problem with those two designs was that their designers did not seem to be familiar with the eventual need for rally cars to be serviced

Audi took the rallying world by storm when it began using the turbocharged four-wheel-drive Quattro in 1981, then spent four more years making it faster and more specialised.

TONY SOUTHGATE

Tony Southgate was born in Coventry in 1940, completed his schooling at Coventry Technical College, and became an apprentice in the Dowty Group in 1956. After five years, and having already dabbled in club motor racing, he secured a junior design post with Lola Cars, and began a series of increasingly responsible links with the motor racing industry. Two years later, in 1963, he joined Brabham as a design engineer, but soon returned to Lola in 1964 (which, by then, had relocated to Slough, where work on the original Ford GT40 was forging ahead).

From 1967 to 1969, Southgate worked in California for Dan Gurney's AAR racing team (which produced Eagle F1 cars) before returning to the UK to become the chief designer of BRM. Thereafter he helped to set up the Shadow F1 team in 1973, next taking up the post of chief engineer at Lotus in 1976. Less than two years later he returned to Shadow, moved on to help found the Arrows F1 team in 1978/1979 (and became heavily involved in that company's design/ trademark dispute with Shadow), then joined the Theodore F1 team in 1980 as the founding technical director.

It was in 1982 that Tony became tired of F1 politics, set up links with John Thompson of TC Prototypes, and started his connection with Ford by working on improvements for the Zakspeed iteration of Karl Ludvigsen's Cosworth-powered C100 racing sports car. By this time he was also well used to the idea of working with aluminium honeycomb as a chassis material, so this was naturally included in his work on a new Alfa Romeo-powered Osella F1 in 1983.

In the winter of 1982/1983, Ford Motorsport provided Tony with a one-year contract to design a new-generation C100 racing sports car, and although such a MkIII Group C machine was ready and testing by March 1983, it was one of the projects abruptly killed by Stuart Turner, who had recently arrived as the director of Ford Motorsport.

Thus it was that Tony Southgate found himself without a project, while still being well paid by Ford. Soon afterwards (to quote Tony from his autobiography), *'I was well into what was probably the most demanding of all the competition car products that I have ever tackled, the most unexpected, and one of the most enjoyable…'*

That, of course, was the RS200 project.

JOHN WHEELER

London-born John Wheeler was always interested in automobile engineering but came to Ford almost by chance in 1980, after spending several years with Porsche in Germany. He was already a rising star in the chassis area at Porsche (including work on its racing sports cars) when, in 1980, he answered an Autosport advert for a job with Ford Motorsport at Boreham.

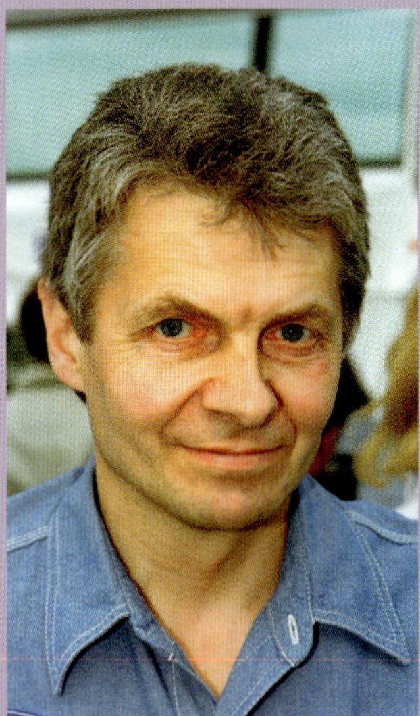

Along with independent design engineer Tony Southgate, Boreham's John Wheeler was one of the principal architects of the entire RS200 project.

Once there, he led the team that completed the design of the stillborn Escort RS1700T, and lobbied in vain for a four-wheel-drive version of that car to be developed; he spent time working out on paper how that could be done while retaining much of the work already completed on the existing car.

Later (and along with Tony Southgate), his concept for the RS200 evolved into the 200-off supercar, and after that programme came to an end he became chief motorsport engineer on the Group A rally-improvement programme of the Sierra RS Cosworth and Cosworth 4x4. From 1988 he ran the concept of the new Ford ACE (Escort RS Cosworth) project, later moving to Ford's SVE department at Dunton, also in Essex, in 1990, to usher that car into production.

A spell as Aston Martin's chief engineer, where he led the team that produced the DB7 V12 Vantage, was followed by a return to Ford's technical HQ at Dunton, where he spent the 2000s). He also worked on, and led, project teams at Ford-Germany, in Cologne, for the engineering of Focus RS road cars.

Having retired from Ford, Wheeler recreated his vision of the one-and-only Group S version of the RS200, which had been considered in 1986 – his personal car, which he owns and loves, it is often seen at classic events around Europe.

and repaired at the roadside, probably in the rain, often in the dark, and certainly against the clock.

In the meantime Lothar Pinske, although not likely to be directly involved in the RS200's motorsport programme (Ford-of-Germany was currently concentrating its efforts on circuit racing), had suggested that a well-known independent competition car engineering company, Dallara, should also be consulted; the idea was soon turned down because Dallara, being Italian, was thought to be too close to Lancia. Pinske also believed all the initial proposals looked too complex for rough-and-ready rally use. In later years, however, Lothar studied what Peugeot (with the 205 T16), and Lancia (with the Delta S4) had achieved at the same time, and apparently conceded that the various Ford proposals would have worked well.

"John Wheeler's scheme was preferred by most of the judges because of its designer's obvious knowledge of the requirements of rallying"

Having looked carefully at all four proposals, the high-level group of managers was in a quandary. To quote Mike Moreton: *'Tony Southgate was clearly a very accomplished designer, and his design was the best presented, showing a lot of vital detail, but more biased towards race than rally – it needed to be more rugged and able to cope with violent off-road treatment… As for John's layout and basic ideas, these were obviously well suited for a rally car, using all his know-how from the RS1700T and Porsche, but his draughtsmanship was not up to Tony Southgate's standard.'*

It seems that, right from the start, the judging panel was most impressed by John Wheeler's scheme, for although it was indeed to be a mid-rear-engined machine, with four-wheel drive, it was nevertheless engineered around the latest (and still new) Sierra frontal cabin, windscreen, doors (originally cut down in height) and roof, with obvious packaging benefits, and with strength and safety in mind. At that time, John

Even while Boreham was working on the concept of the RS200, Lancia was busily finalising its new Delta S4 design, which used the same intriguing combination of unit-construction tub/cabin with tubular front and rear chassis extensions.

was considering the use of high-grade steels, not composite materials – which were to come later in the programme.

The next step, apparently, was that John Wheeler's scheme was preferred by most of the judges because of its designer's obvious knowledge of the requirements of rallying, and the maintenance and on-event servicing requirements. However, Stuart and his advisors were keen on making an even more advanced – and perhaps more high-tech – machine, and suggested that John should get together with one of the other consultants to go ahead and make a finalised design out of a joint effort.

At this point John had already seen the other designs (the other consultants had been encouraged to contact him at Boreham when they were in the middle of their own product scheming) and was certainly most impressed by the proposal put forward by Tony Southgate. Not only that, but John was also convinced that the design of an entire car – whether his, Southgate's, or whatever – could not possibly be completed with his tiny staff. So to join teams (effectively to pool available man-hours) made a great deal of sense.

And so it was that Turner and Moreton decided to take the pragmatic course of trying to combine the best of the two designs, by instructing Tony and John to work together and establish a fully-engineered design. According to Moreton, *'They respected each other's talents – John was the logical chief engineer and Tony the creative chief designer.'*

By mid-July 1983, therefore, the die was cast, with work going ahead rapidly. At this stage there was no question of getting a car built, although Southgate had already persuaded Ford that the very first car should be manufactured by John Thompson's company, ART (Auto Racing Technology) at Wollaston, as this major expense would need approval from Bob Lutz at Ford-of-Europe level.

After a suitable interval, not only was the author privileged to see the four proposals, but on regular visits to Boreham in the summer of 1983 it became clear just how rapidly the RS200 project was taking physical shape. Outside the original Boreham workshop building (which had been completed in 1963, but whose modest offices were already full, and were quite incapable of taking the expanding team) a rather large Portakabin was placed in the car park, and it was here that Moreton, Wheeler and their most senior colleagues would live for the next two years.

Even so, as I make clear in the next chapter, it was never going to be easy to reconcile two sometimes different design philosophies, especially as there was a geographical conundrum to be solved. Although Tony was now working full-time, under contract, for Ford Motorsport, he worked from home in a village near Northampton, which was a considerable distance from Boreham. Meanwhile, construction of the first prototypes was to be located at John Thompson's premises in Wollaston, just ten miles east of Northampton itself.

Peugeot began working on the all-new mid-engined 205 T16 in 1982, a full year ahead of Boreham, and brought it into service during 1984. It was an immediate success.

Ghia – and setting the style

In the meantime, there had never been any doubt in Turner's mind that the styling of the exterior and packaging of the new RS200 was of great importance. It was not that the car needed to look good for rallying purposes (some of the car's rivals were hideous by comparison) but a pleasing style was essential from a marketing point of view, especially as 200 cars would eventually have to be manufactured, the majority of those being intended for sale to private purchasers.

Turner was always sure that the styling should be carried out by Ghia (Ford's distinguished design house, based in Turin), which already worked closely with Motorsport on what, how and why it should be asked to achieve. It all helped that Ghia's top man, Filippo Sapino, was not only an accomplished and artistic individual, but was also a great motorsport enthusiast. It was this last trait, in fact the only one, which would cause some friction between Ghia in Turin and Motorsport in Essex, in the helter-skelter months of summer and autumn 1983.

As already noted, the overall brief supplied to the four individual engineers in May 1983 mentioned styling, made it very clear that Ghia would be totally responsible for it, and that the following constraints would apply: *'The need is to make the car as simple to service and operate as possible, to have good driver visibility (NOT a lie-down racing position. Windscreen angle is critical for rallying…).'*

As he told us in his autobiography, Stuart Turner had already concluded that a unique shape would be needed for the car for three reasons:

1 He wanted a 'world car' that could be used by Ford outlets not selling European models.

2 It should be an ageless style, unaffected by mainstream model changes.

STYLING THE RS200, THE ITALIAN WAY

When Ford Motorsport set out to develop the RS200, it immediately chose to consult Ghia to develop the unique styling of this unique car. The prestigious Turin-based styling house had been absorbed by Ford-of-Europe in 1973, and had rapidly become what we might call the company's skunkworks.

Carrozzeria Ghia SpA had been founded in 1916, and initially prospered by producing stylish special coachwork for a number of Italian car makers. After the original factory was destroyed by Allied bombing in 1943, it was soon rebuilt in another part of the city, and from 1944 was controlled by Mario Boano and Giorgio Alberti. Boano moved on in 1953, after which Luigi Segre took control, and his company then expanded mightily.

Customers like Ford, VW, Chrysler, Renault and even Ferrari were prestigious clients, but after Segre died his shareholding was sold to Alejandro de Tomaso, who then went on to sell out to Ford-of-Europe in 1970. After all other customers' requirements had been satisfied, Ghia became a top-secret styling customer/supplier to Ford, one result being that the Ghia badge was a top-of-the-range symbol that was progressively applied to a whole series of Ford production cars from 1974 onwards, and featured on such cars until 2010.

Starting in the mid 1970s, Ghia began producing a whole series of prototypes, show cars, and even the final derivation of certain production machines, though many were never intended to be seen in public. In 1983, therefore, with the need to produce a striking style for the new RS200, and with very little time made available to think about the task, it was typical of the way Ghia was operating.

"The Turin-based styling house had rapidly become what we might call the company's skunkworks"

Motorsport's first approach to Ghia came in April, and after several phases of artistic development, the final (and eventually familiar) shape was agreed, on a full-scale mock-up, in December of the same year – only nine months later.

Ghia's task, therefore, was complete, for it would never be involved in building any of the RS200 prototypes, nor the production cars, as the project progressed.

3 It would be much easier to shift 200 cars if it was a unique shape rather than, say, a Fiesta with bulges and wings all over the place.

With this in mind, Turner pulled in a few favours, first of all approaching Andy Jacobson of Ford Design in the UK, and persuaded him to reassign one of his staff (Tony Catagnani) to provide preliminary theme sketches to be shown at management reviews, and also to Filippo Sapino at Ghia during Mike Moreton's first visit.

This came in April 1983, and although Sapino initially complained that Ghia was very busy with possible mainstream projects, he was very flattered about the approach, and very

Below: Technicians working on the nose of the original RS200 clay mock-up in the autumn of 1983. There was still work to be done to get the detail to their satisfaction….

Right: …. which eventually came when the shape of the radiator cooling vent was finalised.

enthusiastic about the challenge it laid down. It was, he said, just the kind of project that Ghia would enjoy tackling. Sapino then got down to the commercial realities, estimated that it would take between four and five months to progress from day one to management approval, and thought the entire job could cost about £200,000.

At this point it is worth comparing the styling career of the contemporary MG Metro 6R4, which went from being an acceptably-modified Metro shape to one that was totally different when it was actually seen in the public domain; a process that took well over a year. At the end of it all, the 6R4 might have been functional, but with all its different wheelarch extensions and a roof-mounted spoiler, it looked hideous.

By this time, of course, John Wheeler and Tony Southgate were working hard on the detail refinement of the mechanical design concept, not only with function but with safety and packaging in mind. They already decided on the wheelbase, the track and the overall width of the car they were detailing; they also wanted to be sure of the windscreen position to give the driver as easy a visual job as possible when rushing along unfamiliar roads and tracks. No one, the team drivers in particular, was ever likely to forget the trouble most of their colleagues had recently experienced in aiming the Triumph TR7 V8, or in somehow squeezing their way into the minuscule cockpit of the otherwise-outstanding Lancia Stratos. It is worth recalling that Wheeler had been involved in eight years of Porsche race and rally car design before he arrived at Boreham, while Southgate had just come through the trauma of what might have become Ford's definitive C100 racing sports car.

As described, Ghia was not asked to provide a style that would involve the completed mechanical layout being modified to suit the firm's artistic leanings. However, the deal offered was that when the winner of the design competition had been selected – forecast to be in mid July – the complete package information would be rushed to Turin, so that Ghia could then work its expected visual miracle before Christmas. Ghia, in fact, began work on the definitive style in September 1983 after Turner provided a detailed brief of what was expected.

In the meantime – during the summer of 1983 – Sapino's creative team spent time producing a sheaf of preliminary sketches, which Turner collected in Turin, having visited the Italian GP at Monza. Once back in Essex, he and Moreton spread out all the sketches, found they were very unexciting, and immediately called in Ford Design's Andy Jacobson for help and advice.

The result was that Jacobson himself was inspired to produce what they thought was a more suitable rendering (which, incidentally, featured a Sierra windscreen in Turner's preferred location 'in space', rather than the very laid-back screen of Ghia's original sketches) and Moreton was speedily sent back to Turin to reason once again with Sapino.

Work on the fascia/control panel layout moved ahead slowly in the autumn of 1983. This was just an early mock-up, within Ford Design, of what would later be adopted.

Stuart Turner's memories of that meeting have now gone down in history, in that he repeats the phrase whenever asked to discuss the RS200 project in print and in public: "Mike drew the short straw to go back to Turin, to tell Ghia that we didn't like any of their sketches. Even less tactfully, he took with him Andy Jacobson's sketch, which we all liked. I gather from Mike that Ghia's designers then hit the roof. Steam came out of their collective ears as they made it clear that what we had seen were only roughs, concepts, ideas – call them what you will – and were in no sense final proposals."

Mike Moreton confirmed this by relating that Sapino argued for about 20 minutes without giving ground. Apparently he refused point-blank, at this stage, to see his team produce a design that featured a relatively upright Sierra windscreen, because he claimed it would ruin the entire style.

'He would only do that,' Moreton later wrote, *'if told to do so by his boss in the USA. In front of Filippo I made a frantic phone call to Stuart, who in turn rang Filippo's boss in Detroit, who then rang Filippo to say, "Do it".'*

It was only then that any semblance of unity returned to what had become a very troublesome business. Although an outsider like the author cannot begin to understand that this sort of stand-off was normal at the top level in companies like Ford, there was huge relief when all the dramas were resolved and the true styling work could begin.

In the end, the style that Ghia inspired, produced, modified and refined, all to Ford's approval, incorporated a Sierra windscreen, and even the upper sections and glass of the Sierra's front doors. Ghia's work began by accepting

Above and below: Ghia's full trimmed and detailed full-size clay mock-up was originally decked out as a road car for display to Ford management, then as a competition car, complete with extra driving lights, split-rim road wheels, and a selection of sponsors' decals in place.

Left: Ford's top management inspecting the completed mock-up at Ghia's premises in Turin in December 1983; from left to right: Jim Capolongo, Ed Blanch, Mike Moreton, Stuart Turner, Filippo Sapino and Ken Kohrs.

Below: In December 1983, the RS200 mock-up was almost exactly in the form in which it would go into production, except that the panel behind the doors was black rather than in body colour, there were still no cooling louvres in the Perspex engine cover, and the rear moulding featured a rather anonymous outlet for the exhaust pipe.

(although never happy about it) that the general layout of cut-down Sierra doors, front A-pillars, and the Sierra windscreen position 'in space' was acceptable. It would revolve around a mid-engined chassis, which was to use a 99.6in/2530mm wheelbase, 59in/1500mm wheel tracks, and 225/50VR16in tyres on 8in cast-alloy road wheels. Just to emphasise this skeleton, Boreham's technicians placed a suitable mock-up on the workshop floor – cabin, doors and suitably placed wheels, no more and no less – had it photographed, and sent the images to Turin. Proof positive of this stratagem is reproduced on page 34.

Progress thereafter was swift, and within weeks the original full-scale clay model was beginning to look familiar to all RS200 enthusiasts, except that there was still no sign of the distinctive rooftop-mounted engine intercooler (which would not appear until actual prototype testing took place in 1984), and detail work would continue around the nose and tail.

In all this time Mike Moreton became the permanent conduit between Stuart Turner, the RS200 design team and the Ghia studio in Turin, making several trips before the job was done as Christmas 1983 approached. From time to time, he was accompanied by Stuart himself, by John Wheeler, Tony Southgate, Ken Atwell (whose small Welsh-based company would be invited to produce most of the GRP skin panels), and eventually by the two really big hitters of Ford-of-Europe – Ed Blanch (chairman) and Jim Capolongo (president).

In the meantime, however, and with the engineering work already getting into full swing, Stuart Turner was faced with leaping over the project's first big financial hurdle – to gain permission to build the very first complete prototype car. After this he would lobby for a further five prototypes to be constructed, and only after that could he hope to get board approval for 200 cars to be built.

To do so he would have to face up to several gruelling, top-level, presentations. The first, dated 20 September 1983, was to be in a meeting chaired by Bob Lutz in Ford-Europe's HQ at Warley in Essex. Lutz already had many years of top-management motor industry experience with BMW and Ford, had been a motorsport enthusiast during his time with Ford (latterly as chairman of Ford-of-Europe), and was then based at Ford world headquarters in Detroit, where he had reached the dizzy heights of vice president of Ford International Operations. Without his approval, and until he signed off a spending total of $293,000 US (Ford usually quoted capital sums in dollars in those days) there could be no further progress.

This, apparently, was a wide-ranging meeting, in which not only the RS200 project but the proposal for Cosworth to produce a brand-new V6 turbocharged F1 power unit (the all-new 1000bhp 1.5-litre GB, which subsequently appeared in 1986) was also discussed. It was only after a lot of persistent and hard talking that approval was given for a

The finished clay model in all its glory at Ghia, except for the existence of a petrol filler cap recess in the nearside rear part of the moulding. This would not survive the development period.

This was the original prototype, 001, being assembled, probably at John Thompson's workshops in Northamptonshire, early in 1984. Much detail change would follow the building of this car.

single car to be constructed.

Mike Moreton, so expert at this sort of lobbying process, presented most of the proposal/descriptive work in front of Ford's great and good, which, as he subsequently related, involved showing Ghia sketches of the style, overall engineering drawings of the car's layout, and a summary of the specification. It was good to know that at this stage the marketing, product development and public affairs departments of the company all approved of what was proposed.

A lot of design work (and styling at Ghia) had already taken place, which included a short, crudely-detailed, and 'why can't we....?' project by John Wheeler's team at Boreham, to build up a T88/Pinto-engined Sierra in which the front-mounted engine was installed at the proposed canted-over position it would occupy in the B200, to see if the lubrication system was still acceptable (which it was). Almost at once, John Thompson's Auto Racing Technology (ART) concern – in which Southgate was a partner – started work on turning good ideas and paper designs into a real car. Stuart Turner promised that the very first car would exist, and that it would be totally capable of running, by March 1984.

Stuart Turner later agreed to show the author some paperwork that followed this meeting, where a finance specialist, John Kaplan, made a formal request for funds to the board, stating, *'Assuming successful completion of the initial testing, it is planned to build five more prototypes. The additional expenditure of $580,000 will be included in the 1984 motorsport sales promotion budget.'*

Apart from the disappointing fact that, in his autobiography, Tony Southgate made the frequently-stated mistake of suggesting that RS200 cars *'were assembled at the Reliant factory'*, his book (*From Drawing Board to Chequered Flag*) gave an interesting insight into some of the restrictions surrounding the design competition, and I am grateful to MRP and its proprietor Howden Ganley for permission to quote from the appropriate chapter in Tony's fascinating book. At this point, too, I should stress that Tony was assisted considerably by Dave Amey in arriving at a very promising proposal.

"To emphasise this skeleton, Boreham's technicians placed a suitable mock-up on the workshop floor – cabin, doors and suitably placed wheels"

'I pressed on with designing the layout of the car,' Tony wrote, *'building into it some of the ideas that the experienced rally team members at Boreham suggested, mainly to do with ease of access and servicing – the suspension uprights to be removable in five minutes, the gearbox in nine minutes, that sort of thing.*

'I soon began to realise that my idea of a rally car was quite different from the idea of the people at Boreham. What the Boreham boys really wanted was a Sierra with tubular frames at the front and rear, and the old turbo Escort engine

somewhere in between. They couldn't visualise an aluminium honeycomb chassis frame. As far as they were concerned, it had to be sheet steel, spot-welded together, and capable of being bashed back into shape with a hammer in the event of an accident…

'The aluminium honeycomb chassis frame I proposed was received with great caution in the Ford camp. They were not convinced a material that light could take care of the loads handed out to a modern rally car…'

To speed things up, and to keep costs down, Southgate quickly realised (and was encouraged to make use of this fact) that it would be a great advantage to use as many off-the-shelf Ford production parts as possible. He soon settled on the front passenger area of the new Sierra as his donor car, and proposed that the windscreen, most of the roof sections, and lightweight cut-down versions of the front passenger doors would all be ideal. In the end, there were 117 Sierra components in the Southgate design.

And so it was decided, for from September 1983, Tony Southgate and John Wheeler had been brought together to work out the best possible combination of their proposals. All in all, they were soon ready to start releasing major sections of the design so that John Thompson's tiny team near Northampton could start building the car, and as soon as Bob Lutz's approval came through that process began.

Although Turner was determined to have the first car complete and ready to show to the decision makers, he imposed a near-impossible target on his tight-knit team. That first car, he insisted, must be ready by mid March 1984 – which was only six months from his success in achieving approval to design and build it. Although John had two or three other designers working for him at Boreham (working, incidentally, on the genesis of what would eventually be the Sierra RS Cosworth), and Tony relied a great deal on Dave Amey (another freelance who lived in Leamington Spa), all of them were insanely busy in the winter that followed.

The point should also be made, not because of any shortcomings that developed (which they did not), that Ford's mighty technical teams at Dunton, a few miles from Boreham, were never involved in the design and engineering of the car.

This was how the very first car, 001, was arranged, at Ford's Balderton Street premises in London, for management to view it in March 1984. It was the first of six prototypes that were to follow in the next year.

In this period, let it be emphasised, Boreham was actually providing expertise in the other direction, to Dunton, because John Griffiths, Bill Meade and Terry Bradley had all been seconded to SVE (Special Vehicle Engineering) in Dunton to work on the original Sierra RS Cosworth.

Not that the design of the car was already settled. "The reality," John Wheeler told me many years later, "is that the original engineering of that car was very unlike the car that went into production. When we showed the car to the board, it was not really finished but it could be driven – just. We took the car to Ford's Central London office/garage in Grafton Street, set it up in an upstairs room [which was kitted out as a temporary exhibition area, with drawings and images] and showed it off to Bob Lutz, Walter Hayes and others."

On that occasion, Lutz's meeting gave approval for five more cars to be constructed within the following year, for the design team had concluded they would immediately need two of the six cars for production development (and detail finalisation of the design), two to be allocated for rally proving and testing, and maybe for use in events in prototype form, and a final two for legal homologation work.

"When we showed the car to the board, it was not really finished but it could be driven – just"

Legal homologation? Ford always, repeat always, intended that the new car would go through the entire process of gaining type approval, which would allow the cars to be used without argument on the public highways of the world. One of the two cars was intended to go to an honourable grave by being hurled into a concrete block at 30mph, to meet the stringent crash test requirements governing integrity of the entire structure, and in particular to show that the steering column and its attachments were fit for purpose. This was done, and type approval (masterminded by Bob Howe with considerable input from Aston Martin Tickford) was finally achieved.

As an aside, it is clear that Austin-Rover decided not to pursue type approval for the MG 6R4 Group B car, precisely because it could not face up to the cost and aggravation of all the work involved. Which explains why the 6R4s were sold to private owners as incomplete kit cars, with a list of instructions as to how to make them roadworthy.

By this time, incidentally, authoritative estimates were that total investment in the programme would be about \$9.2 million (approximately £7 million at the current rates of exchange), which proved to be remarkably accurate when recalculated at the end of the programme in 1989/1990.

Building work on Cars No 002, 003 and 004 went ahead as soon as the first car (001) had achieved management approval. Meanwhile, the design team, allied at Boreham by

Peter Ashcroft's group (including those excellent technicians Mick Jones and Robin Vokins) concentrated on No 001 for initial testing, and immediately ran into all the problems that had been expected to crop up – suspension, steering, braking and other related details. In particular, the first car had been built with single telescopic suspension dampers all round, and it was from this point that the decision to use twin dampers took place, while at the same time the suspension movement geometry was thoroughly revisited and revised.

"We stripped it completely," John Wheeler recalled, "and totally redesigned the front and rear suspensions and related

Above and below: On the same day Bob Lutz had seen the original RS200 prototype and approved the building of five further prototypes, Stuart Turner was proud to show it off to HRH Prince Michael of Kent. Here he is seen with John Wheeler, and that is Prince Michael's equerry in the background.

BOB HOWE (1930 TO 2012)

How to summarise Bob Howe's remarkable career at Ford? Simply by suggesting that without him there might never have been an Escort Twin Cam, the RS family that followed might never have evolved, and in later years the RS200 programme would certainly have been submerged by red tape and a lack of salesmanship.

Yet there was no master plan. The young man who started his Ford life on the assembly lines at Dagenham eventually became a cost analyst in the new product planning department, lived with the birth of the Cortina range, and was much involved in making sure that the Lotus Cortina became a viable product.

It was then that Boreham's Henry Taylor called him to advise on a proposed new J25/Escort Twin Cam project – where to build it, how to build it, and what to include in the spec – so when Ford's Walter Hayes later needed to find a factory to assemble AVO products, Bob also got the research job, eventually became AVO's original employee, and ran its product planning operation for three years.

After a decade away in the service operation, he was then called back to Boreham by Stuart Turner, not only to guide the Group B RS200 through the legal minefield of type approval, but eventually to demonstrate and sell almost every car in the run of 200 machines. In the end it was Bob's allotted task to sell each of the road cars, which were stored at Boreham while this was going ahead, and for at least four years he used RS200s as road cars (as did the author), building up more miles than anyone else.

As an encore, he then got much involved in the type approval process of the new Escort RS Cosworth before repeatedly trying to retire, but often being persuaded to accept a range of special assignments at Ford until the early 2000s.

"Without him there might never have been an Escort Twin Cam... the RS family that followed might never have evolved"

Along the way, and afterwards, Bob was a delight to interview, and to provide reminiscences of Ford's greatest sporting period – for he was the sort of man who seemed to enjoy every assignment, forgot nothing of the excitement, and rather relished the fame he acquired along the way. For that, and for the sheer niceness of the man, when he passed away in 2012 he was very sorely missed; his long-term plans to complete an RS200 history, as he saw it, unfulfilled.

Mick Jones was one of the leading lights in Boreham's workforce in the 1960s, 1970s and 1980s. He led the team of technicians in developing the original RS200 prototypes.

structures. This was where Tony and I worked very closely together, because time was always a problem. As we progressed towards the final solutions, more and more work was done for us by Mike Pilbeam, who became responsible for most of the detail of the bodywork.

"We also worked closely with FF Developments, revising the transmission completely – the transmission we ended up with was by no means identical to my original schemes. I had originally proposed a four-wheel-drive system that incorporated a torque tube up to the front axle, but we decided to move the main box forwards to make one unit, which also gave more room for the passenger."

This work put a colossal load on the shoulders of a mere handful of capable designers, construction engineers and amazing can-do personnel, so during 1984 the decision was made to bring in Aston Martin Tickford (AMT) to look after the productionisation of the basic design. This meant that 200 cars could not only be built but would be acceptable in every way to the well-financed individuals and organisations who might then buy the cars. AMT was also responsible for producing the technical drawings for the production machine. It was a measure of the amount of work involved that John Wheeler still found it necessary to spend at least half of his working life up at AMT's Newport Pagnell plant, and that AMT had committed up to 20 engineers and managers to devote themselves to the job.

AMT was a separately managed subsidiary of Aston Martin itself, had separate premises, and employed an experienced group of design and development engineers who soon put

Immediately after its showing in Balderton Street, Car 001 returned to Boreham, where work began on making it ready for serious testing.

their stamp on what could, should and (they insisted) would be achieved in 1984 and 1985. One of AMT's outstations, incidentally, was an ageing factory complex in Bedworth (a town just five miles north of the city of Coventry). At the time this plant was busying itself with the batch production of the ultra-special Ford Capri Tickford coupés, and secret work was also going ahead for the carriages division of British Rail. Its involvement with the RS200 would not come until 1987, when a massive programme of refurbishment of the thrown-together Shenstone cars was to take place.

At this point it is time to introduce the name of Arch Motors into the fast-expanding group of contractors, for its already-great record of producing rugged and reliable chassis for racing cars (almost all of them, admittedly, being multi-tube frame types) made the firm ideal for producing the tubs and the multi-tube front and rear tubular chassis extensions that were being evolved. Arch Motors was also able to advise on every detail of adhesives and corrosion protection, which meant the RS200 was, and still is, one of the most robust Group B cars ever developed.

While all this was going on, and as soon as Car No 001 was back in one piece, a lot of high-speed driving and development began to take place, some of it on the various (and extremely useful) test tracks at Boreham itself. Testing also ensued at the British motor industry's proving ground at MIRA, just three miles north of Nuneaton, where there was an extremely useful, though rather serpentine, tarmac inner handling circuit on which the car's dynamics could be thoroughly assessed. It was there that, on three distinctly different days, F1 world champion Jackie Stewart visited and took part in the work that was proceeding. And it was there that the decision to finalise the use of twin, as opposed to single, telescopic suspension dampers at each wheel was finally made.

In a letter Jackie wrote to Walter Hayes in September 1984 (in other words, well before the car had been revealed to the public) he commented: *'The car, I think, has great prospects. Although there is still much to be done it has started off as a car with no apparent bad habits; the handling is extremely good for a first time running.'* And he would have further comments to make after he returned to drive the prototype, sometimes at truly high speeds.

Now it was fast approaching time to launch the car to the public, to make Ford's world rallying intentions clear, and to take another big step to turn a Good Idea into reality...

Another shot of Car No 001 after arriving back at Boreham from its viewing in London, where it was immediately stripped out for testing to begin.

Chapter 4

Technical analysis and prototype development

It had taken only a few months to turn the great idea into the real deal, but very little detailed design and engineering work had been completed before the famous meeting of September 1983 saw Bob Lutz give the go-ahead for a single prototype – just one car – to be built.

This, therefore, is the summary of what had already had taken place, and what would then take place, before Ford was ready to build 200 cars to gain Group B homologation.

In May/June 1983 Stuart Turner had invited four distinguished engineers to sketch out their ideas of what a 200-off B200 rally car should be like. At this time no more than a basic idea, all in his head, was what existed.

In July/August 1983 those suggestions, all laid out in brochures and estimates of timing plans, and of performance, were analysed. Two layouts – one proposed by Tony Southgate, and one by Boreham's own John Wheeler – were preferred.

Shortly after, it was decided to combine the best of the two designs (retaining the most significant parts of each), subject to gaining approval from top management for getting detailed work under way.

In September 1983, Bob Lutz chaired an important meeting at Ford-of-Europe's HQ in Warley, Brentwood,

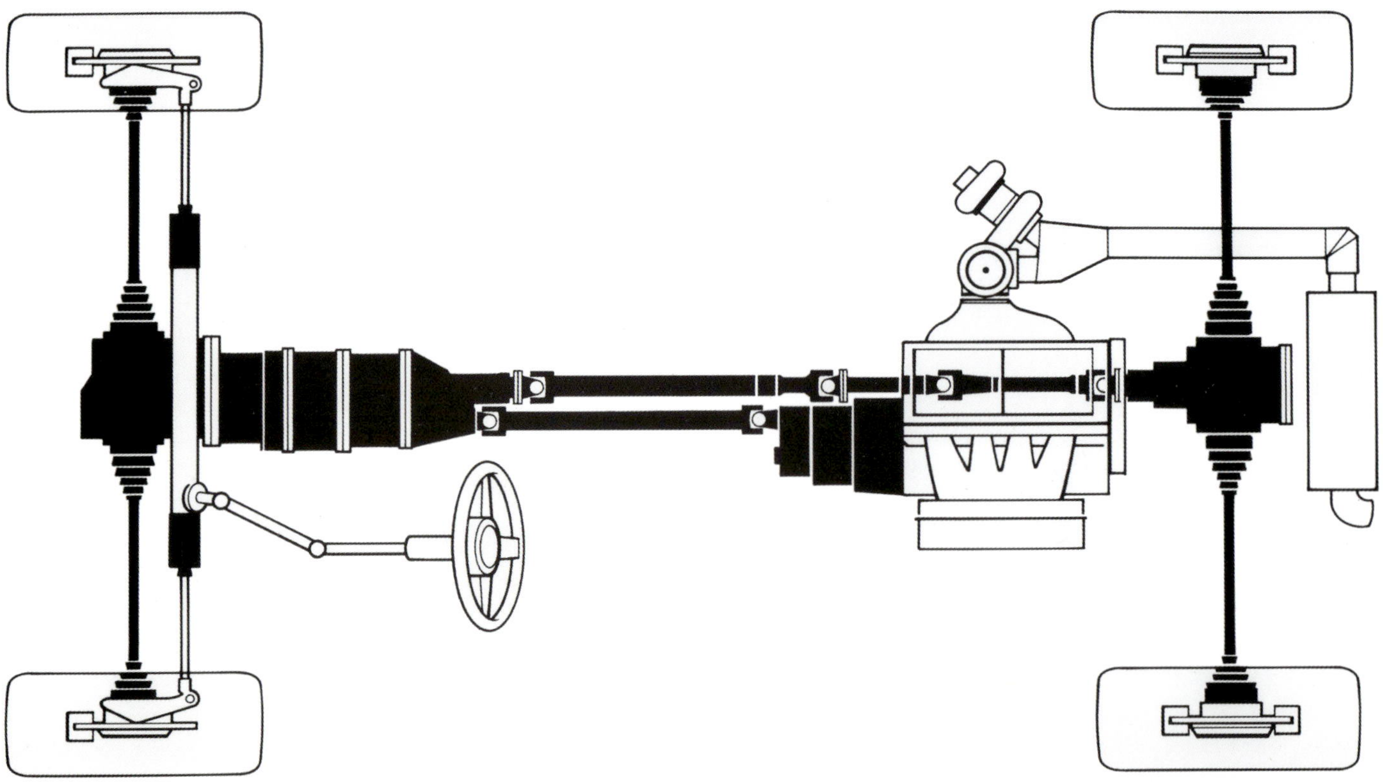

This diagram shows how the engine/transmission was laid out in the RS200 – with the engine and transfer box immediately behind the two-seater cabin, and with the main gearbox and front differential up front.

As finally made ready for sale, and complete with all details such as the extra tail lamps, which were normally hidden by the closed body moulding, this shot shows just how neatly integrated the final layout had become.

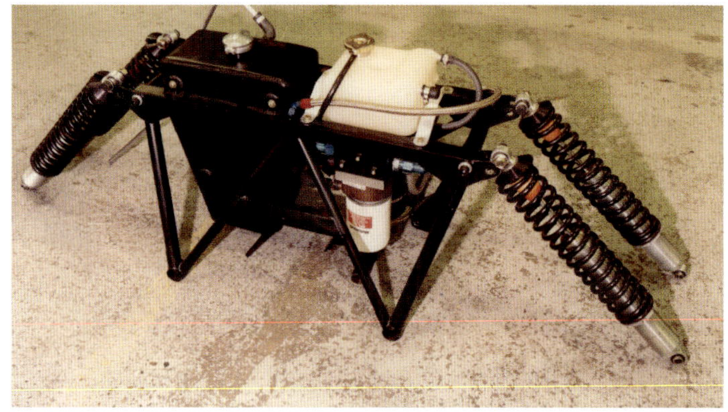

Above: The rear of the engine bay, showing there was little spare space left over. The way that the multi-tube rear chassis extension is fixed to the main tub is clear.

Top right: The partly-stripped-out rear of the engine bay/chassis/rear suspension layout, showing the way the engine was canted over to the right, the rear differential/axle housing was tucked away into the rear of the tub extension, and the fuel filler cap positioned near the rear bulkhead on the nearside.

Above right: The transverse tubular subframe fitted behind the engine was neatly detailed, not only to support the spring/damper units, but also to house the dry sump oil tank (black) and radiator header tank (white), both of which were accessed when the rear body moulding was lifted.

where the proposal was discussed – the result being that it gained approval and Lutz authorised the building of the first prototype.

At this meeting, Stuart Turner guaranteed that if he authorised work immediately, the first car would be completed – as a fully-functional runner, styled by Ghia – by March 1984. Once approval was gained at this meeting, Stuart once commented: "There was a great deal of lively debate, for some senior members did not understand rallying at all, particularly Group B, and wanted to spend all the money on the F1 engine programme instead." Serious design work got under way, certain long-lead priorities were identified, and assembly of that very first car began at John Thompson's premises in Northamptonshire, remote from Boreham or any other Ford facility.

Because much of the RS200's layout, its engineering, and the rationale behind it, was new to Ford, this seems the right time and place to analyse what, and when, major factors came into play. At all times, one must understand that Tony Southgate and John Wheeler were prime movers in it all and cooperated remarkably well, but both had significant specialised technical help from inside and outside Ford.

All of those consulted later made it clear that there was no way the original prototype could ever have been built at Boreham, and certainly not in the very compressed timescale available, without much expert help from outside consultants. John Thompson's part in building the first cars has already been emphasised, while at this stage the GRP body panels were produced (to a very high standard) by Ken Atwell in South Wales – who had already made his name with Ford in the 1970s by building the very best recreation GT40s that had ever been seen.

General layout

The Wheeler/Southgate design placed the engine in a north-south installation, in a mid/rear location behind the two-seater cabin. The BDT engine was still ahead of the line of the rear axle/rear suspension, slightly offset to the left side of the engine bay (but canted over towards the right to restore the left/right chassis balance, and provide more space for the fuel injection/inlet manifold side of the unit) with the clutch facing forwards.

The detail figures that confirm the above point were that the centre line of the engine crankshaft was 6in/15.24cm to the left of the car's nominal fore-and-after centre line, the cylinder block was itself leaning 23 degrees to the right, and the nose of the engine was 1.5 degrees down at the front. This was done specifically to allow the Monolok of the FF transmission installation, equipped with a pair of quick-to-change transfer gears, to align ideally with the shaft to the main gearbox itself.

The transfer box (the Monolok, named by FFD) was mounted directly ahead of the clutch housing, and from that point the primary propeller shaft ran forwards to mate with the massive FF/Hewland/Xtrac main gearbox, which was itself bolted to the front differential. Drive to the rear differential was then assured by a secondary three-piece propeller shaft from the main transmission package, which ran back in parallel to the original (primary) propeller shaft, and alongside the dry sump of the engine itself.

For clear and practical reasons, it was decided that the complex tub (see below) should not be engineered to have already-detailed fixings for many of the chassis components. Instead it would use sturdy multi-tubular steel subframes to surround the engine (at the rear), provide the mountings for the front and rear independent suspension assemblies and steering rack, and (again at the rear) enclose the cooling water tank and the engine's oil reservoir.

There was nothing novel about this approach, for similar installations had already been chosen by companies like Peugeot (for the 205 T16) and Lancia (for the Delta S4). If necessary, and in case of the consequences of a rally accident, it meant major parts of the chassis could be removed and replaced by new items.

To cover this, Ford's design colleagues at Ghia had produced a beautiful, but compact, two-seater bodystyle that cleverly used a number of the standard Ford components (which we can surely call fixtures and fittings) that were already available in numbers at tiny cost. This explains why well-informed Ford enthusiasts could recognise details like the proportions of the cabin, including the Sierra-type windscreen, pillars and front doors, the door furniture, some items in the fascia and instrumentation, the door mirrors, and the (Sierra) tail lamps.

As described below, however, it was also clear that the skin styling featured smooth lift-up sections front and rear, with space for the spare wheel (but no luggage if that was being carried) up front, and enough elbow room in the cabin for two people, but virtually no extra space for cases or bags. All the major body skin sections were moulded in GRP (glass reinforced plastic/fibreglass) on the road cars, though serious works competition cars tended to use exotic carbon or Kevlar material instead, this being a development programme that was intensifying until FISA announced the imminent death of the Group B category. Naturally, it would have made no financial sense for Ford to use carbon-fibre panels for sections on the road cars.

Chassis/platform

As is clear from the drawings and images displayed in this book, the RS200's structure was somewhat of a halfway house between a self-supporting tub and a separate chassis. The centre section featured aluminium honeycomb (Ciba-Geigy 5052 technology) aramid, light alloy and fabricated steel sections (the basic technology of which had originally been brought to this design by race-car specialist Tony Southgate), while front and rear suspension, steering, and the engine/transmission assembly were all mounted onto sturdy multi-tubular sections securely fixed to the front, and rear, of the two-seater passenger cabin.

Much of this layout was originally evolved around the original Southgate proposals, and his impression was that the Boreham team had wanted to retain a welded-up steel chassis/cabin section (a desire and an impression that he rapidly eliminated). Already well-established in a motorsport career, in which he had been involved in the design of several very notable and successful cars – all the way up to race-winning F1 machines – along the way, Tony had engineered multi-tubular chassis (for Brabham in 1964), aluminium monocoques (for Lola in 1965), aluminium honeycomb (for Theodore in 1982) and an aluminium honeycomb monocoque (for the second- and third-generation Ford C100s of 1982 and 1983). He was therefore comfortable with the idea of utilising what was effectively a honeycomb platform, to which a front bulkhead was attached. A standard Sierra windscreen was used, and the door assemblies, which – although they would be of a more exotic material – would be closely based and shaped on the front doors of the newly-launched Sierra, though not as deep as those of the Sierra itself.

The basic centre section/survival pod was therefore totally

Car No 001, as hurriedly finished and ready for showing to Bob Lutz and senior management in March 1984. Many details would change in the following months – for instance, the intercooler was mounted in the engine bay, on the left side, there was a cover over the spare wheel (which was later abandoned), and only one spring was mounted at each side of the rear suspension.

The front end, almost completely assembled. There was not much room for stowage up front – there would be a spare-wheel-shaped recess behind the cooling radiators (for a second spare to be carried on arduous rallies), so some luggage could be carried.

With the rear of the car partly disassembled, it was easy to see how the large transverse alloy plate at the rear of the tub was vital to the sturdy setting-up of the rear suspension. A close study of the plate shows that the two co-designers, John Wheeler and Tony Southgate, had built in a choice of inner mounting pivot points so that the geometry of the system, and the available wheel movement, could be changed rapidly for different types of terrain.

influenced by Tony Southgate, though Arch Motors, which got the contract to supply all 200 of this vital section of the cars, had much to do with the productionisation, simplification, and reduction of costs that made it not only more elegant but more cost-effective too. Amazingly, in 1985/1986 when the time came for Ford to start building 194 RS200 road cars at Shenstone in a great hurry, Arch never let the side down, for (as the images clearly demonstrate) there always seemed to be enough platform/tubs available for the simple assembly process to begin.

With pre-event motorsport preparation in mind, and with the possibility of side-of-the-road service and major repairs having to be made, the ability to drop the transmission units down after mountings had been loosened, and also for the rear axle assembly to follow the same procedure, was always a factor.

"The suspension of this car was laid out, and detailed, so as to be as adaptable as possible, to take account of stage surface conditions"

A full tubular steel roll cage was to be standard on every car, this being bolted, not moulded, into the structure of the car as it took shape. Although the structure of the tub reached all the way to the nose of the car (this was thought essential if the car was to pass the obligatory 30mph barrier crash test – and the test proved the worth of that decision), a substantial tubular steel front subframe not only held the water cooling radiator, but also provided the top mountings for the twinned spring-damper units. Similarly, at the rear of the chassis there was a tubular steel cage, which surrounded the engine, supported the water and oil reservoirs, and also provided pivot points for the inner mountings of the rear suspension.

This may sound unnecessarily complex to some people, and if the RS200 had only been intended for use as a road car, that might have been a justified opinion. However, when it was explained to the doubters that the rough and tumble of world-level rallying might suddenly impose a ten-to-15-minute window on service crews to work some sort of repair, adjustment or replacement miracle, it made a great deal of sense.

Suspension

John Wheeler always emphasised why, and how, the suspension of this car was laid out, and detailed, so as to be as adaptable as possible, to take account of stage surface conditions, and whether or not the track was rough and damaging or smooth.

John always made the point – and continues to do so to this day – that race cars (the type with which Tony Southgate was a total expert) were specifically detailed for a task that always involved going fast on a super-smooth tarmac surface, as close to it as reasonably possible, and therefore with very limited wheel travel. In contrast, a successful rally car required a much greater range of wheel movement (bump and rebound), along with the possibility of raising or lowering the entire structure of the car, depending on the surfaces over which it was to travel. Think of extremes like the tracks of the East African Safari, and the tarmac stages of the Tour de Corse (or Monte Carlo where snow was absent) to get the picture. Southgate, although bowing to superior experience on this point, later wrote that, *'John was totally convinced about this, but I am still scratching my head. The total suspension movement was eight inches, basically four inches of bump movement and four inches of rebound movement.'*

The cars had what one might flippantly call conventional supercar suspension, by coil spring/damper units with double wishbones, all linked up to front and rear anti-roll bars, along with rack-and-pinion steering. Yet the actual installation was more sophisticated, in detail, than one might expect. For one thing, there were twin coil-over-telescopic-dampers at each corner of the car, with each Bilstein-supplied damper including an adjustable coil spring platform for height, which could be screwed up or down to lift, or lower, the entire car if required.

There was the possibility that the cars could run with single spring/damper units at each corner, but it was during the first concentrated high-speed testing of the first car (where Jackie Stewart was closely and expertly involved) that it was decided to finalise the installation to feature two coil-overs instead of single assemblies of telescopic hydraulic dampers at each corner. For motorsport purposes, incidentally, each spring/damper unit could be removed from the car in a matter of seconds and substituted by another, which meant that the handing could be changed from hard to soft or vice versa, but this was not the prime reason for such an installation.

In 1983/1984, the idea of having remote oil reservoirs for dampers and struts was still a pipe-dream for the future (Ohlins was apparently the pioneer, its invention involving remote reservoirs following shortly after the RS200 car was finalised), so Ford still had to rely on its regular supplier, Bilstein of Germany. Since John Wheeler was convinced that the RS200 needed to be supreme in rough going, where the suspension would have a hard time, he realised that damper oil and gas temperatures would inevitably rise considerably, and therefore he was looking for an increased volume of damper fluid; not only that, but there would be occasions mid-event where softer springs would be preferable to hard springs, and in motorsport conditions would need to be changed at a moment's notice. In addition, there was alternative provision for affixing the inner wishbone mounting points in different locations, so as to give a choice of further settings on rally cars to cater for rough or ultra-smooth conditions.

Except that the emphasis was always on suspension performance (rather than making sure that they always worked silently, without squeaks and bangs) the chosen systems performed well, together with the conventional anti-roll bars front and rear, and the steering gear itself. If there was a valid criticism (which was only valid on road cars, and not on rallying machines) it was that the steering (a lightly-modified Sierra unit) had relatively high gearing, and therefore the steering wheel efforts at low speed were quite high.

To complete the line-up, seven-spoke alloy Speedline wheels with 8in rims plus 225/50VR16in Pirelli P700 tyres were standard, allied to 11.2in/285mm ventilated disc brakes front and rear, with conventional split-circuit hydraulic action.

As finalised, the independent rear suspension featured twin Bilstein telescopic dampers at each corner of the car.

Engine

Ford's Motorsport team could rightfully congratulate themselves on the way they were able to rescue, adapt, improve and recreate all the BDT engines originally destined for use in the Escort RS1700T. But modifying those power units, getting the specification right for the RS200, and building up the requisite quantities was never going to be a simple process.

Although the history, heritage and worldwide use of the legendary Ford-Cosworth 16-valve, four-cylinder BDA engine family is well-known, the evolution of the ultimate turbocharged types, in which Cosworth was never closely involved (Cosworth's founder, Keith Duckworth, was intellectually opposed to forced induction of any type, dismissing turbocharging as 'providing a second engine'), and

As finalised for installation in the RS200, the turbocharged BDT engine had its inlet manifold and fuel supply on the left side of the car (the left side in this shot too, which was taken from the rear), and the turbocharger on the right.

has not previously been outlined in great detail. Here is how that derivative, later known as the BDT, came to fruition.

As far as one can see, the first turbocharged BD power unit to have a Ford or Cosworth connection was developed (independently of Cosworth or Ford-UK) in the late 1970s by Zakspeed of Germany, originally for use in one of its racing Escorts but then most notably applied to ultra-specialised Capri-based cars for use in the Group 5 German championship of the period. Zakspeed used two types and sizes of BD-family engines in the Capris, both being based on cast-iron rather than light-alloy cylinder blocks. One, of 1427cc, produced up to 460bhp at 9000rpm; the other, of 1746cc, produced 600bhp at 9000rpm. Even before Boreham took an interest, the two types had already achieved great and spectacular success between 1979 and 1981.

> "One, of 1427cc, produced up to 460bhp at 9000rpm; the other, of 1746cc, produced 600bhp at 9000rpm"

Ford-Germany and Cosworth had both taken a benevolent interest in these engines at the time, but neither was closely involved in their design and development. In view of what followed, it is important to know, therefore, that although Zakspeed did much of the design and packaging work, the German tuning specialist Schrick was much involved, along with KKK (which provided the turbochargers).

In the meantime, however, Ford-UK and Cosworth had been dabbling with turbocharging since the mid 1970s, there being a BDL project, originally of 1425cc, but later apparently replaced by a BDG-sized 1975cc unit. The latter engine produced 364bhp at 8100rpm, but neither company had any settled idea of what it should be used for, so its development was abandoned.

Then, in 1980, the idea of using a turbocharged BD power unit for Boreham's new-generation Group B car (which became the Escort RS1700T) began to mature. Simply, this was because the normally-aspired BDG, as used in the obsolescent rear-drive Escort RS of 1979/1980 appeared to have reached its limit at about 270bhp, yet Boreham wanted to run with up to 350bhp in its new-generation turbocharged machine, to make it truly competitive. In 1980 and 1981, therefore, with Boreham controlling much of the work but with Cosworth (however reluctantly) increasingly involved in testing, in casting or forging new components, and in providing the myriad of other components required, what became the definitive BDT engine began to mature.

At Boreham, John Griffiths and eventually Graham Dale-Jones had much to do with the administration of the project, Schrick of Germany was closely involved (its existing Zakspeed involvement was invaluable), and a search of surviving Cosworth historic material shows a constant flood of correspondence and advice flowing between Peter Ashcroft and Cosworth's then-managing director Alf Vickers. Originally, in 1981, it was agreed that Cosworth would first provide ten prototype sets of material for the RS1700T project, and eventually provide all 200 sets of production material (though the firm had still not agreed to assemble the engines themselves). By the spring of 1982, when the RS1700T programme schedule was already showing signs of slippage, Cosworth agreed to provide up to 50 sets of material per month to a chosen engine builder when the production button was finally pushed.

Although the agreed specification of the 200 BDT homologation engines was virtually settled in the next few months, it was not until later in that year, it seems, that batches of components were readied for delivery. By that time, the Escort RS1700T project timetable had slipped even more, and the location of production had not finally been settled, though it seemed that the cars would eventually have been assembled at the huge modern Escort assembly plant in Saarlouis, close to the German-French border. In the meantime, the BDT engine assembly contract was awarded to Jon Fisher's JQF Engineering business, whose main workshops were in the grounds of Lord Hesketh's mansion at Easton Neston in Towcester.

After the RS1700T project was cancelled, all 200 near-completed engines were apparently securely stored at Hesketh's Potcote farm, and according to ex-Cosworth manager Mark Parish (who started working at JQF in late 1983) they were all dutifully turned over (had their cranks rotated, and a little oil circulated) every month.

That, really, is the end of the rather mysterious early career of this engine, for it is definitely recorded that when the RS200 project got under way, it was soon decided that these carefully-stored engines would be used, albeit suitably refreshed and modified.

When the time came to finalise the specification of the engine for use in the RS200, there was a new director at the helm – Stuart Turner instead of Karl Ludvigsen – who had a different idea of the capacity class in which Boreham's Group B should compete. Because the cancelled Escort RS1700T was meant to run in the 2.5-litre class, the BDT engine (complete with the mythical multiplication factor of 1.4:1 imposed by FISA's regulations for forced induction) had used a 1778cc size, which was deemed equivalent to 2489cc of normally-aspirated engines. Stuart Turner, on the other hand, had higher ambitions, and wanted to run the RS200 in the 2.5-to-3.0-litre class, which meant a slightly larger and more powerful engine could be used.

As a vital feature in the design of the RS200, therefore, it was decided to modify the existing stock of engines by slightly enlarging their cylinder bores (to 86mm) during the re-engineering process, so they measured 1803cc (or – according to FISA's formula on turbocharged engines –- 2524cc).

This meant that, when the time and opportunity came, and because the current homologation rules still allowed it, their capacity could eventually be enlarged even further – as an example (which was theoretically possible, not carried out on this car using the standard cylinder block), on the BDT engine a bore increase to 90mm would have allowed the actual size to go up to 1975cc (in FISA terms 2765cc). The 90mm bore block was already familiar to all normally-aspirated BDG users, as it had already been used in hundreds of Ford Escort RS competition cars built in the 1970s.

For the RS200, however, not only were the RS1700T engines stripped out to have their cylinder blocks slightly modified, they were also treated to revised dry sump installations, and had the turbochargers and inlet manifolds redesigned and repositioned, more widely separated than before, on opposite sides of the engine.

The final position of the air-to-air intercooler, very neatly and elegantly placed atop the rear of the car's roof panel, allied to hidden tubes carrying compressed air from the turbocharger (at the right-hand side of the engine bay), on to the inlet manifold side of the engine (on the left side of the engine bay) was not how it was originally intended. On Car No 001, but not on any subsequent prototype, the intercooler was placed in the engine bay, effectively behind the left-hand fuel tank/seat position.

The initial idea was to keep the passage of air from turbo to intercooler to inlet manifold as short as possible, but as engine bay heat was soon found to be a problem, the intercooler radiator was then moved to the roof where, by definition, it

BD ENGINE SIZES – 1970 TO 1986

The original Cosworth BDA evolved round the use of a Ford Kent Crossflow cylinder block, but as the years passed, this connection became more and more tenuous.

As time went by, these were the different sizes of engine used in high-performance Fords, both road and competition types:

TYPE	USAGE	BORE X STROKE (MM)	CAPACITY
BDA	RS1600 road car	80.97 x 77.62mm	1599cc
For homologation purposes Ford usually quoted this as:			
		80.97 x 77.72mm	1601cc
BDT	Escort RS1700T	85.4 x 77.62mm	1778cc*
BDT (second type)	RS200	86.00 x 77.62mm	1803cc*
Not titled	RS1800 road car	86.75 x 77.62mm	1835cc
This was not a Cosworth development, but by Brian Hart. It never carried an official BD-type suffix.			
BDG	race/rally engine	90 x 77.62mm	1975cc
BDT-E	race/rally engine	90 x 84mm	2137cc*
This last type had a completely different cylinder block casting from other, earlier, types.			

*For use in FIA-authorised competition, the regulations calculated that turbocharged engines had their capacities increased by a factor of 1.4:1. Accordingly, the following engines officially ran with larger capacities, as follows:

1778cc - when multiplied by 1.4 = 2489cc

1803cc - when multiplied by 1.4 = 2524cc

2137cc - when multiplied by 1.4 = 2992cc

COSWORTH AND BRIAN HART – THE ENGINE CONNECTION

Although Brian Hart was never a Ford employee, in the 1970s and 1980s the commercial and technical links between his company and the works team were close, cordial, and extremely successful. Later, into the early 1990s, his company became a subsidiary of Cosworth (with obvious Ford connections) but this arrangement was short-lived, and a divorce occurred long after every connection with the RS200 project had ended.

In the beginning, Brian Hart had started his working life as an apprentice at the de Havilland aircraft company in Hatfield (where he first met up with Mike Costin, who would soon move on to Lotus, before later becoming a founder/partner in the Cosworth business) and stayed there for six years. After working with his father in the motor trade for a short time, he eventually decided to combine life as an engine builder/tester at Cosworth, from 1961, with being a racing driver, at which he rose to the top level of British and European F2 racing.

After moving to Northampton with Cosworth for a short time from 1964 to 1965, he then concentrated on being a racing driver who could also build and prepare race engines in his spare time, until 1969 when he set up his own business – Brian Hart Ltd (BHL) – as an engine builder, tuner, development specialist and small-time manufacturer, locating it in Harlow New Town, north of London.

"Brian Hart combined life as an engine builder/tester at Cosworth, from 1961, with being a racing driver, at which he rose to the top level of British and European F2 racing"

Because he concentrated on Ford-based Cosworth FVA F2 power units, and the rather different Cosworth-BDA that followed, he soon came to the attention of Ford's motorsport centre at Boreham. It was not long before he decided he should retire from race driving, and become a development engineer and – most importantly – design engineer instead.

Prosperity, new work, a rising reputation and the inspiration to develop his own engines instead of other peoples' soon led Brian, together with his brother Tony and – soon – John Lievesley, to work on more ambitious projects. The first was the aluminium cylinder block for the Ford BDA engine – which eventually allowed such 1.6-litre engines to be expanded to the full 2-litres that Escort runners desperately wanted. The next was the design, manufacture and development of the Hart 420R F2 engine of 1977. Both would have a direct influence on the Boreham-inspired Ford Escort RS1700T and – equally important – the turbocharged BDT engine that would power the RS200.

Brian Hart's connection with Ford, with Motorsport, and with the two Group B cars covered in this book was always close, but at this stage one should recall that it was after the RS200 project came to an end, and when Brian's hope of supplying BDT-E power for the Evolution cars was abruptly cancelled, that BHL was taken over by Cosworth, and remained a Cosworth subsidiary until 1989.

BHL then returned to a financially precarious independent existence, somehow managed to produce all-new normally-aspirated V10, V8 and similar engines, before being absorbed by the TWR organisation at the end of 1997. This arrangement then survived only until 1999, when the business was closed down.

was faced with a welcome blast of cooling air, over the roof, at all times. If it had been allowed to go ahead, the 1987 Evolution version of the car (or the Group S derivative of the type that might have taken its place) would have seen the intercooling radiator moved, yet again, towards the rear of the engine bay, along with a much shallower (but still Ghia-approved) cool-air slot in the roof to feed air down, across the engine, to reach it.

Development work in the meantime had allowed significantly more power to be extracted from the 1.8-litre engine, where it was concluded that the homologation run of road cars would use turbo boost of up to 0.82 bar, while the ultimately tuned works engines would run with 0.78 bar. In both cases, engine behaviour was to be controlled by Ford's own EEC-IV electronic engine management system. To keep this cool enough, incidentally, the black box was to be mounted inside the passenger cockpit, immediately behind the seats.

As about to be released in the Escort RS1700T, road cars would have had 200bhp, whereas the original works rally specification would have included a 350bhp package. But two years later, for the RS200, the road car rating had risen to 250bhp, while the full-house competition cars had at least 420bhp. By the time the RS200 reached production, 300bhp or 350bhp tuning packages were already available for road cars. By mid-summer 1986 some of the rally cars had up to 450bhp, and more was apparently on the way when the programme was cancelled.

Laying out the transmission

This was the centre point of the new car's entire layout, and rationale, for even in 1983 – when the B200 project was no more advanced than lines on paper, or still locked away in Stuart Turner's fertile imagination – it was always assumed that the new-generation mid-engined rally car would have four-wheel drive. Originally, it seems, Boreham was not enamoured of the idea of working with FF Developments (the problems the works team encountered with 4WD rallycross Capris in the 1970s were still sadly remembered), and for a time it was thought that Cosworth (which seemed to be omnipotent at this period of automotive history) might be asked to tackle the job instead.

But by 1983, time, technology and (of primary importance) Ford's mainstream and motorsport engineering links with FF Developments (FFD) had improved considerably. In particular, Rod Mansfield's Special Vehicle Engineering (SVE) department had grappled successfully with FF's evolution of four-wheel drive for the Sierra XR4x4 road car, and Boreham had come to terms with the merits of FF's viscous-coupling differential/axle package. So before the Southgate-Wheeler cooperation got under way in earnest it was clear that FF Developments would be the favoured supplier, and basic design engineer, of the RS200's complex transmission.

At first, however, the four engineers all tasked with

suggesting how they would tackle the installation had their own ideas. In his autobiography, for instance, Tony Southgate noted that, *'My design consisted of a mid-mounted, single-turbocharged, four-cylinder Cosworth BDT engine, placed fore and aft but offset to the left. The gearbox was alongside the engine, driving forward to the front wheels, and rearwards to the rear wheels.'* This, however, was soon abandoned as detail engineering design got under way.

Although the RS200's definitive transmission package, as finalised, was very neat, it was by no means the first car to have been laid out in that manner. Bill Munro's splendidly-detailed book on FF and all its achievements (*Traction for Sale*) spelled out how far back in history HFR (Harry Ferguson Research) and (to follow it) FF's expertise had originated, not only on laying out successful four-wheel-drive systems, but in designing and evolving many of the details that made them unique. The very first of their rear/mid-engined systems, complete with two propeller shafts and with the main gearbox and transfer box up front, seems to have been designed for a new 1.5-litre BRM single-seater F1 race car in 1962 (that is, 21 years earlier), and it was the BRM company's test car that took the concept further in an F1 machine coded P67, where its V8 engine was placed behind the driver's seat, while the main transmission was alongside the driver's legs.

This partly disassembled display of the complex FF four-wheel-drive system included the clutch and transfer box in a casting immediately ahead of the engine.

As laid out for inspection (and to help in the compilation of the owner's manual) this is how the engine was bolted up to the clutch housing and transfer Monolok gearbox, and it also shows how the second propeller shaft would eventually be lined up to one side of the engine.

FF DEVELOPMENTS – AT THE HEART OF THE RS200'S LAYOUT

It is clear – it was always clear – that without four-wheel drive, the B200 project would not have got beyond the 'why don't we…?' stage. Further, once Ford elected to go ahead with the car, there was no easy way and no know-how for it to engineer such a system. Eventually the choice of FF Developments was almost a given, and no one seems to have regretted making it. But where and how did FFD (as it was soon affectionately known throughout the motor industry) come into existence?

The story really started in 1950 when the irascible and dogmatic tractor tycoon Harry Ferguson set up a company called Harry Ferguson Research Ltd, where the principal characters were Major Tony Rolt (who had spent several frustrating years in Colditz as an Allied prisoner of the German Nazi regime) and Freddie Dixon (a spectacularly extrovert British tuning expert), along with Claude Hill, who had previously worked for Aston Martin. Originally, the tiny business was based in Redhill, but a move to Coventry followed in 1953.

HFR at first concentrated on four-wheel drive, new engine projects, and a people's car – Ferguson hoped to sell concepts to one or other of the large companies that made up the British motor industry – but as none of these grandiose schemes found favour, HFR gradually began to concentrate on four-wheel-drive systems, in layouts that eventually became known as the Ferguson Formula.

By the late 1960s, cars and vans as ambitious as the Coventry-Climax-engined P99 single-seater racing car, Indianapolis 500 race cars, 4x4 conversions for a number of Ford Motor Co products, the Jensen Interceptor FF of the late 1960s, and a great deal of consultancy for the rest of the world's industry saw HFR grow and grow… Until Major Rolt decided to break away, and to set up his own new concern.

"When the time came to develop the RS200 (and in the separate case of the Sierra XR4x4 and Sierra Cosworth 4x4), it was inevitable that FFD should be an integral partner in the evolution of these very significant cars"

Thus it was that an organisation called FF Developments, still based in Coventry, was set up in 1971, and grew steadily – both in size and in its reputation throughout the industry. It was FFD that was closely involved with Ford throughout the 1970s and 1980s, not only in building transmissions for the infamous Capri rallycross machines, but also the Capri and Zephyr/Zodiac road car programmes.

When the time came to develop the RS200 (and in the separate case of the Sierra XR4x4 and Sierra Cosworth 4x4), it was inevitable that FFD should be an integral partner in the evolution of these very significant cars. FFD continued to expand and prosper after that – and was eventually voluntarily absorbed by Ricardo in 1994.

As to the four-wheel-drive installations, and their components, for which FFD became justifiably famous, when no-holds-barred Group B cars were developed by the world's most serious teams, FFD was almost, but not totally, a go-to contact. Certain cars developed in secrecy, and never used in motorsport, have still not had all the details of their transmission layouts revealed, but in addition to the Ford RS200 one can certainly mention the Lancia Delta S4, MG Metro 6R4, Opel Manta 4x4 and Peugeot 205 Turbo 16 Group B cars.

P67 was unveiled in July 1964, was entered, and practised unsuccessfully, but did not start that year's British GP in the hands of Richard Attwood. It did not race again in BRM's hands, but later achieved success, and fame, when owned and driven in hillclimbs by Peter Westbury.

To quote Bill Munro's comment on the similarity between P67 and RS200, he told me, "The critical differences are in the actual components and the order in which they are assembled. The BRM has a Monolok [transfer feature] attached to the front of the gearbox, with the centre diff behind the gearbox and all three parts in unit but separate from the front diff. In the RS200, the gearbox and VC centre diff are in unit with the front diff. A bit of an Eric Morecambe job, if you like – all the right bits, but not necessarily in the same order."

"Versions of the VCs were quickly adopted as optional equipment for cars needing snatch-free limited-slip differentials"

In the meantime, in the late 1960s, and while the company was still Harry Ferguson Research (not yet FF Developments), chairman Tony Rolt had been introduced to a magnificently quirky plastic material whimsically known as Potty Putty, but more scientifically known as a polymer that contained a visco-elastic liquid silicone. Rolt and his chief designer, Derek Gardner, soon concluded that this was an ideal basis for use inside a limited-slip differential – and thus the ubiquitous VC (viscous coupling) was born. Once sufficiently developed, the new assembly was patented in 1970, well before HFR had a product whose principals could be stolen, or copied, by any of its rivals.

Once introduced to various works motorsport teams, versions of the VCs were quickly adopted as optional equipment for cars needing snatch-free limited-slip differentials – especially front-wheel-drive competition machines such as the Ford Fiesta and Ford Escort RS1600i. And by the time the RS200 was conceived they had already been adopted for future use in thousands of still-secret Ford Sierra XR4x4 and Granada Scorpio 4x4 production cars.

By 1983, therefore, when the first B200 technical sketches were made, complete with a mid-rear-mounted engine and four-wheel drive, FF Developments was already being considered as the principal contractor to produce the detail design, and to arrange the manufacture of all 200 (plus spares) production units of that transmission.

Robin Price, who would head the team that eventually completed this job, recalled, "Tony Southgate originally came to see us at FFD with a piece of paper with a drawing of four

Still partly disassembled, this is where the FF assembly fitted into the structure, immediately alongside the left-hand seat, and close to the rear bulkhead.

Everything mysteriously connected with the front differential, the main Hewland/Xtrac gearbox and the centre differential fitted into this complex casting.

wheels, a gearbox, a four-wheel-drive unit and an axle at each end. It was almost a kid's sketch, a cartoon. He had put two arrows in a line to '4WD unit'. We were told (by Ford) that they had to use as many bits available to hand as they could, so that's how we made it."

Even so, it was never going to be easy, for FFD was neither given a free hand to look after every detail, nor an ultra-generous financial budget. Indeed, both FF Developments and Boreham were unhappy with the situation they uncovered when the mass of Hewland/Escort RS1700T hardware handed over in mid 1983 was found to be still unfinished, and a great deal of extra machining would be required to make any of it useful in the new RS200 transmission.

Not only that, but they rediscovered that the gearbox, complete with its VW-type synchronisers that Hewland had adopted, and with an unmodifiable dimension of only 3.00in/7.62mm centres between the alignment of the main and secondary gear shafts would no doubt be acceptable for the unmodified RS200 road cars, but would need considerable change (even replacement) before a full-house rally car could use it with impunity.

Even so, the transmission layout, with the 3.00in fixed centre dimension between main and layshaft, was substantially improved during the competition programme, and the rallycross specials, complete with a reputed 650bhp-to-700bhp from the 2.1-litre sprint version of the 2.1-litre BDT-E engine, used similar substitute transmissions designed by Mike Endean (whose skills were already being established with what became the world-famous Xtrac concern) and showed just what a formidable four-wheel-drive car the RS200 had become.

As to the 2WD/4WD feature of the transmission that was to be found on serious competition derivatives, but not on the ordinary road-car versions of the RS200, it was to be controlled by a small extra gear lever that would be positioned on the transmission tunnel in the cockpit, mounted very close to the main gearbox lever itself. This lever also allowed the centre differential to be locked, so that it was no longer able to vary the distribution of torque from front to rear wheels.

"Those with other-worldly driving talents could drive anything very fast and not worry too much over the details"

Today, of course, deep-thinking designers like John Wheeler and, of course, FF-Ricardo would be able to do things differently, but this feature, let us not forget, was designed in 1983/1984 when electronic control was still not available, nor even invented. At the time, two-wheel-drive rally cars such as the Lancia Rally 037 and Toyota Celica Twin-Cam Turbo (and the Ford Escort RS1700T, of course) were still capable of winning events in some road and track conditions, often defeating the crudely-engineered four-wheel-drive Audi Quattro in the process, while the Quattro was already proving itself to be supreme on icy, loose and other combinations of slippery going.

Ford, therefore, wanted to cover all bases, by making it possible for the RS200 to be driven in four-wheel drive or rear-wheel-drive states, with no diminution of its capabilities. Specifically, all three differentials in the RS200 – front, centre and rear – featured epicyclic gears, and used viscous control limited-slip differentials.

The front and rear differentials featured 50/50 per cent torque splits to each individual wheel. It would have been quite possible to provide the centre differential with 50/50 front-rear control of torque as well, and in that case a VC feature would not be needed. However, in certain conditions the ability to lock up the action of that centre diff outright was thought to be an important bonus. Incidentally, the works rally cars had a 46/54 front/rear torque split, which was radically different from that provided on normal road-going RS200s, which was 37/63.

Incidentally, such details had been established only after a lot of testing of individually different set-ups had been assessed, and Boreham's engineers agreed that some drivers were very analytical indeed, while others – those with other-worldly driving talents – could drive anything very fast and not worry too much over the details...

This, in John Wheeler's wise words, was only the beginning of what would probably have been an increasingly more sophisticated works system, though there was never any thought of making significant changes to the original FF design for road cars, which was finalised in 1985.

Bodyshell and fittings

Although it caused great controversy at first, when Ghia was originally extremely reluctant to style a two-seater coupe around the windscreen/bulkhead/doors/upper roof panel of the Sierra, it was always something about which the team was totally happy. For all the obvious reasons connected with packaging, visibility and intrinsic safety it was ideal, and there was ample space for tall and even rather sturdy drivers and passengers to remain comfortable (as the author found on long journeys).

Incidentally, even with the sizeable intercooler scoop installed on the rear of the roof panel, and with the sizeable rear spoiler incorporated into the body moulding aft of the tail, the drag coefficient proved to be about 0.40, and slight downforce was always developed, even as the car reached relatively high speeds.

Even so, because it was meant to be a single-purpose two-seater coupé, with motorsport rather than long-distance touring in mind, there was little spare space in the cabin to store luggage of any type – though what it had was still a major advance on minimalist cars like the Lancia Stratos. Whereas the original car featured cut-down Sierra doors and a standard windscreen aperture, a series of engineering changes meant these did, in fact, become entirely special before the production run was initiated, not least because the doors were finally made from special lightweight mouldings rather than from cut-down pressed-steel panels.

Not that it was all straightforward. The story goes that when production quantities of the plastic screen surrounds

HEWLAND – GEARBOX SPECIALISTS

Hewland Engineering Ltd is a specialist engineering business, originally based in Maidenhead, England (but years later relocating to White Waltham, just a short distance away), and was originally set up by Mike Hewland in 1959. From the very beginning it specialised in the design and manufacture of transmissions for use in racing cars.

The company's first products were rear-mounted transaxles (all intended for use in mid/rear-engined racing cars) based around modified VW Beetle transaxles, whose casings were light alloy and very robustly detailed, with specially designed and manufactured four-ratio forward gear clusters. Later, five-speed and six-speed derivatives were also made available.

From 1963 a series of larger, and more robust, transaxles were designed, all having new purpose-designed light alloy casings. By the end of the 1970s, one or other of this big range could cope with torque inputs up to 600lb.ft, and when the time came for the Escort RS1700T to be designed, a Hewland-supplied rear-mounted transaxle (the gearbox combined with the final-drive) was chosen.

When the RS1700T was cancelled, the incomplete run of engines and transmissions was kept in store, pending the birth of a new contender (the RS200), which explains why major elements of the Hewland/Escort RS1700T could be used.

Once an RS200 was in regular use, the engine bay soon became grubby, as this shot of one of the author's 'endurance' cars demonstrates. The rusty tubular device across and above the exhaust silencer is actually the jack. There is an engine in there somewhere!

and the roof panel were finally available, the screen aperture seemed to be slightly under-sized, so rather than have the plastic mouldings re-tooled, the screens themselves all had to be lightly ground to fit the hole exactly.

Although the production cars differed from the first prototypes in many detail ways, the basic layout of the bodywork, as finalised with Ghia, never changed. The exterior, what we might call the general envelope of the machine, involved only four moving panels – a massive front-end moulding, the two passenger doors themselves, and an even larger rear moulding. In case anyone therefore thinks this made it simple for the car to be engineered, one should point out that Ford Motorsport and Aston Martin Tickford agreed, at an early stage, that consultant competition car engineer Mike Pilbeam should be hired to look after the finalisation of almost every aspect of items such as fixings, hinges, latches and connecting brackets.

Except for the material from which they were finally made, the door assemblies were mainly equipped with Sierra fixtures and fittings, which explains why the fourth of the road cars used by the author (Car No 192) for long-term transport from 1988 to 1991 had electric window lifts, which he believes to have been unique on primary-build cars, though others have been retro-fitted in more modern times.

The design and layout of the cabin was almost all to the credit of Ford Design at Dunton, for at the initial styling phase Ghia had been tasked to concentrate purely on the line and character of the car's exterior, and was not involved at any time in the detail of the interior. Even at the very genesis of the project, it was decided to make the interior cleanly-detailed and functionally up-to-date as if it was to be like any other of Ford's million-off passenger saloons. So as soon as he knew the project was going to be serious, Stuart Turner contacted the top man in Ford Design, Andy Jacobson, and invited him to have his staff style and engineer the interior. From the very start Turner made it clear that the RS200 was to be available in left-hand-drive *and* right-hand-drive form; as far as is known, the other fully-blown rival Group B cars – certainly the Peugeot 205 T16 and the Lancia Delta S4 – were built only with left-hand drive.

The result was that John Hartnell and Ian Callum were both asked to take on the job of laying out the cabin, which

EXTRA TAIL LIGHTS

When Ghia completed the styling of the original RS200 in 1983/1984, the large lift-up rear section of bodywork housed the number plate recess, which was flanked by a pair of unmodified current-shape Sierra reflector/stop/turn indicator tail-lamp assemblies at each corner. This was the arrangement installed in the first handful of prototypes (six in all), of which Car No 004 (as described fully on page 132) was the machine put on show at the Turin Motor Show in November 1984.

On the original prototypes, when the tail section was lifted, the engine and all of its related rear suspension and fluid tanks was displayed, and the engine bay was closed off at the rear by a transverse structure linking upper and lower wishbones to the chassis tub, and the tubular superstructure that linked up to the rear of the passenger roof panel.

However, by the time most of the testing and type approval had been completed in summer 1985, it had all changed where the transverse multi-tubular steel tube arrangement housed the engine's dry sump oil tank and provided support for the (second, if required) spare road wheel. Plus, lo-and-behold, out of sight of the rest of the world until the rear body panel was lifted up, a pair of extra tail/turn-indicator lamps, which were bolted to a transverse steel tubing, had been included.

So what was going on? The need for this extra installation had been unearthed by Bob Howe at an early stage of his work in securing type approval and legal approval for every market in which the RS200 was due to be sold. As an expert product planner who had already been involved in project work on cars such as the Escort Twin Cam, Capri 2.8 Injection and Escort RS Turbo, he had unearthed a German requirement that if the tailgate was lifted when the car was stationary at night, at the side of a public highway, then it should still be showing the necessary display of red tail lights to traffic that was about to overtake.

Incidentally, the need to use such extra lighting clusters did not involve Boreham in any extra unwanted capital expenditure, for they were apparently located after a study of the wide range of electrical equipment used on Ford's latest commercial vehicles unveiled suitable candidates.

they did very briskly and successfully. Their brief, naturally, was a little restrictive, for as well as being expected to produce something smart and functional, it was also made clear to them that they should use as much as possible as had already been developed for one or other of Ford's current models. Since the RS200 doors were to be based on Sierra items, the door furniture almost designed itself; some of the steering column switchgear, handbrake mechanism, heater outlets and vents and other controls were carefully and successfully lifted from that and other newly-announced Ford cars.

Project manager Mike Moreton later recalled that this duo produced a whole series of attractive layout proposals, which were always constrained by the requirement for the panel layout to be simple, as the rally car derivatives would no doubt be considerably altered to suit their special needs. John and Ian therefore produced some very attractive styling ideas, all of which were essentially practical in their detail, and after several wood and clay models had been offered up for approval, the final one went into Car 001 (though not all the switches, knobs and dials had a function at the moment the car was unveiled…).

> "When the car had to be refuelled (and as the average road-car consumption was rarely better than 20mpg, this meant it happened often), the entire rear moulding had to be lifted up and propped open"

Incidentally, and just to show that Ford wanted to make this a practical, versatile and appealing machine to those not intending to use it in motorsport, provision was made in the centre of the fascia for fitting the same type of radio/cassette unit as a Ford dealer would normally fit to a Fiesta, Escort or Sierra. Although cabin noise levels inside an RS200 were by no means as low as those of mundane models, such a fitting was eminently usable – the author having such devices on each of the four cars he ran on a long-term basis. Rival Group B cars did not have such a civilised installation.

As originally sold, the road car was equipped with a pair of figure-hugging rally-style seats, which were best suited to slim owners with athletic figures, but quite a number of cars (including those habitually driven over long distances by the author) were fitted with wider and more comfortable seats that had a Ford Escort RS Turbo heritage, and could even be re-trimmed with leather covers by Strattons. Although in March 1984 the very first car was shown to Ford's top management while fitted with full-harness sporting-type safety belts, the homologation run of 1985 to 1986 would have normal Ford-type three-point/inertia-reel belts.

All this equipment was separated from the fuel tanks and entire engine bay of the RS200 by a sturdy rear bulkhead behind the seats, in which steel, aluminium honeycomb and carbon fibre were all present. Twin low-mounted fuel tanks were standard on the road cars (hidden from view under the rear bulkhead, effectively behind the occupants' bottoms), the left-hand tank being of 16.2 imperial gallons/74 litres, the

Partly stripped out, this is the work-in-progress instrument panel/fascia of the RS200 road car, this being a left-hand-drive machine with the optional 2WD/4WD control gear lever also ready for installation alongside the main gear lever.

right-hand tank of 9.2 imperial gallons/42 litres.

To keep the external rear body moulding as simple as possible there was no exterior filler neck, so when the car had to be refuelled (and as the average road-car consumption was rarely better than 20mpg, this meant it happened often), the entire rear moulding had to be lifted up and propped open – it was hinged high up on the rear passenger bulkhead – as the filler was on the nearside of the engine bay, and when the rear moulding was down it was completely hidden from the outside world. Because this manoeuvre also exposed the engine and its various add-ons, need one say that it usually caused a stir at fuel stations, where other motorists often rushed across to see what was involved, and often attracted the sort of hackneyed comment from bystanders that RS200 owners soon learned to ignore.

The engine bay, need one point out, was rather full of machinery, manifolding, components and tanks. It was therefore logical to find that the transverse tubular chassis structure at the rear of the engine itself also cocooned the massive engine oil tank (the engine had dry sump lubrication, of course) and the engine's water-cooling header tank alongside. There was no external indication to the driver as to how much oil was in the system, and when checking it also helped if one recalled that the result depended on whether the engine was running or not.

This, then, was the settled specification of the cars built in the production run at Shenstone, and the entire process of completion had been a supremely changing business to the team. The challenge of building all the homologation run against the clock was going to be equally as demanding.

Chapter 5

Going public and building the cars

By the autumn of 1984 the existence of a brand-new Group B Ford project was something of an open secret in Britain's tightly-knit rallying fraternity, but – amazingly – no reliable sneak pictures or accurate summaries of the mechanical specification had yet leaked into the specialist press. More than one attempt had been made to snatch spy pictures of a car on test at Boreham airfield, but they were taken with ultra-long lensed cameras from outside the limits of the airfield, and revealed very little of the detail.

The rather breathless news piece published in *Autocar* on 24 October 1984 (for which the author, who had links with the magazine at that time, was not responsible) was typical. The copy suggested that the bodyshells of the production car would be supplied by Reliant (a sweeping statement, only partially true), body moulds would be from Ghia (wrong), the basis of the car was a 'monocoque chassis' (only partly true), power would be supplied by a transversely-mounted turbocharged BDA engine (wrong again – it was not, of course, transversely-mounted), it would have about 200bhp (wrong – it would go into production with a 250bhp power unit), and there would be a long radiator mounted in the transverse rear body spoiler (also wrong).

"If it had been a schoolroom exercise, that pupil would have gained an A for effort, but probably a C-minus for content"

If it had been a schoolroom exercise, that pupil would have gained an A for effort, but probably a C-minus for content.

Ford, nevertheless, took note of all such forecasts and, with four prototypes now completed, and based at Boreham, elected to show the newest of these RS200s in public for the very first time – choosing to do so at the international Turin motor show (rather than the British NEC exhibition), which opened in the first few days of November 1984. Not only was this a brave, and publicity-conscious move (the RS200's style, of course, was by Ghia, which figured strongly in Turin's motor industry at the time), but on that occasion it also allowed Ford to make a bigger flag-waving exercise out of a less-than-exciting production car display. The only other show novelties were two Ghia-styled Ford-USA one-offs, in which few of the media were interested.

Opposite page: In 1984 and 1985, endurance testing of the RS200 was unrelenting – this being Malcolm Wilson on one of his long stints on Boreham's loose-surface track.

At last, it seemed, launching the new car at the Turin show was an enormous relief to all concerned at Ford – not only for Boreham, but for major suppliers such as JQF (engines) and FF Developments (transmission systems). The new model could now be seen in public without disguise, and could begin a serious road-proving exercise on normal roads to check out its endurance. One of the precious cars – No 004, only recently finished as a road-car type, suitably spruced up, and not yet road registered – was therefore flown out for that great occasion.

It was at this time that the author became even more closely linked to the development programme than he had already been – first by advising on a suitable base for road testing to begin in public, and then by getting started on the compilation of the owners' service manual, which the company thought essential even for marketing a car of which only 200 examples would ever be made. In the meantime, my four-page analysis of the new RS200 had already appeared in *Autocar*, where all the rumours and pre-launch mistakes were finally laid to rest.

It was also a great privilege to be asked along to join the small motorsport group who flew out to Turin to be involved to the private press launch, which occurred at the Ghia HQ on the evening before the show itself. Having travelled to the private-aviation side of a still under-developed Stansted airport, we then flew to Turin in an executive-equipped Ford Air (yes, really) BAC 1-11 jet, which took only two hours.

This, however, was not a caviar-and-champagne journey, for the moment the BAC-11 got off the ground and the safety belt signs had been extinguished, yet another series of meetings began to take place. PR boss Walter Hayes was seen conferring with Stuart Turner about his forthcoming speech at the launch of the car in the Ghia workshops, John

"Members of the British specialist press were fast enough to criticise Boreham for taking so long to develop the previous Group B car – the Escort RS1700T – and then to cancel it"

Getting day-to-day endurance mileage on to the RS200 (prototype 001) was a snowy, gloomy and sometimes hazardous job in Wales in January 1985. At that time the car was not road registered, which explains the trade plates. The location seems to be Bwlch-y-Groes.

Wheeler, Tony Southgate and Peter Ashcroft were animatedly discussing the engineering problems that continued to arise, while Mike Moreton found time to corner the author about the way that preparing the car's paperwork – the manuals – should proceed.

The launch in Turin, an evening affair, was a great success, though a few members of the British specialist press were fast enough to criticise Boreham for taking so long to develop the previous Group B car – the Escort RS1700T – and then to cancel it, commenting that it made Ford late in evolving a 'proper' four-wheel-drive Group B car.

Even so, Stuart Turner, at his best when speaking off-the-cuff in front of a crowd of car enthusiasts, shrugged it off in his own inimitable way: "When I made my pitch, one journalist asked why I had changed my mind about Group B and about four-wheel drive – both of which I had scorned at one time. There was only one thing I could say, and I did: 'It was one of the most damn fool comments I have ever made'."

By this time Tony Southgate, and Ford Motorsport, had decided he had done an excellent job on the car, so he was released to get involved in future projects in his own distinguished career. As Tony later wrote, *'I had enjoyed the project very much indeed. It had been a great challenge for me, and a clash of two cultures – me, the circuit racer, and Ford Motorsport, the traditional rally men. Ever since, I have had a great respect for the rally world and what they achieve, and for the drivers, who are all quite mad – either that, or stunningly skilful.'*

In retrospect, it is a pity that Tony ascribed so little to John Wheeler's part in the concept and execution of the RS200 project (John's name is mentioned only twice in Tony's seminal autobiography), for the two had cooperated well in an advanced and rather rapidly-completed scheme.

For interest, Tony's next assignment was to work with Tom Walkinshaw's TWR organisation, and to design Group C Jaguars that would go on to race remarkably successfully at Le Mans and around the world.

After having flown the RS200 prototype back to Boreham – it was a completely functional car, and was meant to work for its living, which it began to do so as soon as it was unloaded – almost the next decision to be taken was to commit one car to a lot of day-to-day public-road motoring. It was one thing, Ford concluded, for John Wheeler and Tony Southgate to have come up with the design of the most ideal Group B car that could be afforded, but it was quite another to assume that it would work for a long time, over long distances, and in various conditions, unless Ford did not build up the mileage to prove it. Driving it round and round the Boreham airfield runways and taxiways was never going to be the total answer, for their surfaces were far too smooth, and far too familiar to the drivers, for that.

But where should the open-road motoring be based? Boreham realised that using the expanse of East Anglia's roads was surely not the answer (they were too fast, too busy, too well-surfaced, and not hilly), even though it might have been possible for the test car (or test cars) to be returned to Boreham every evening. Apart from the fact that most of these roads were too full of other traffic, once motorsport's enthusiasts found out where the favoured routes were they would be out in their numbers with cameras – which might be flattering, but not always convenient.

The Boreham motorsport complex in its heyday, showing not only the layout of the workshops, but the airfield and its runways, plus the custom-built loose-surface circuit that was useful for so many projects.

It was then that Boreham's ingrained expertise, and experience, swung into action, and it was decided to set up a base at a lovely old-fashioned but rally-friendly hotel called the Wynnstay, in the centre of the Welsh town of Machynlleth. Not only was that hotel big enough for Ford's needs, with suitable garage areas that could be commandeered, but over the years it had been an enthusiastic host of any number of RAC rallies, and its helpful and friendly staff knew just what motorsport was all about. Not only that, but for out-and-back endurance runs, there were demanding routes north, east and south of the town (but not to the west, for that was the Irish Sea). Incidentally, although world-famous forestry rally special stages such as Dovey and Pantperthog were just up the road from Machynlleth, there was never any intention of using them during this phase of the programme.

The big advantage, too, was that during the winter (it was in 1984/1985 that Boreham needed to see some mileage built up) that part of Wales was lightly trafficked and almost devoid of tourists, so the RS200 would not necessarily have

to fight its way through traffic and camera-toting enthusiasts for much of the time.

Thus it was that Car No 001 was sent to Wales, with a small team of technicians to build up their experience of the car. As can be seen by the pictures that survive of this period, the Welsh weather was wintry, to say the least, so although much could be learned about the car's capabilities in cold, wet, snowy and often downright unpleasant weather conditions, there was no chance to assess just how good it was going to be when hot and summery conditions (in Europe) would be encountered.

According to John Wheeler's enthusiastic memory, it was a time when not only he (and his team) was trying to release the myriad number of drawings needed to get the road cars ready for production – and for the first major steps of developing a works rally specification – but there was no doubt that in technical and specification terms Car 001 was already beginning to lag behind. The front-end style, for instance, was as originally shown to management (via Ghia) in March 1984, and not the design shown to the media at the Turin show several months later. The front and rear suspension needed to be reworked in detail, as did the structure around the rear of the engine (it would be changed from a light-alloy

Multiple F1 world champion Jackie Stewart worked hard with Boreham on refining the high-speed habits of RS200 prototypes. Here he is seen in deep technical discussion with John Wheeler after yet another intensive session at MIRA.

Boreham management and senior technicians taking a few minutes' break from building and developing RS200s in 1986. From left-to-right: Bill Meade, John Wheeler, Andy Thorburn and Mark Deans are in the front line-up, and driver Mark Lovell is at the rear.

Malcolm Wilson not only did much of the high-speed testing of RS200 prototypes but also drove the first car to its maiden victory in the Lindisfarne rally of 1985.

John Wheeler discussing RS200 development with Robin Vokins (in the car), who took over from Mick Jones when the latter moved out to Ford-of-South Africa.

Even in pre-event testing at Boreham, crash helmets were worn.

In 1984 and 1985 triple F1 world champion Jackie Stewart took an active part in high-speed driving development of the RS200. Here he is seen at MIRA during 1984, discussing a handling set-up with John Wheeler – note that on this occasion there are two dampers but only a single coil spring on the rear suspension, and the car is running on split-rim road wheels.

sheet to a multi-tube layout).

Some attention was also given to the positioning of spare wheels. Whereas road cars and rally cars (in most but the roughest conditions where impact punctures were likely) only needed to carry a single spare wheel, in events like the East African Safari and the Acropolis rally, it was often wise to carry a second spare. This explains why there was a spare-wheel-shaped plastic housing in the extreme tail, and another up front under the lift-up bodywork panel. In later years, when the author was running RS200s as day-to-day road cars, the front-end recess was ideal for carrying luggage, as there was very little spare space in the cabin.

The roof-mounted intercooler, however, was already in its final position, and work was still going ahead to try to improve the engine bay flow of cooling air. Amazingly, the awful cabin heater was already known to be lacking in refinement and performance, but even in the depths of winter it was not thought to be a problem on which much valuable time should be spent.

"Rival companies had bent the rules and got away with this strategy in the past, but it was no longer possible, or commercially acceptable"

Having hived off work on the detailing of the bodywork to Mike Pilbeam, and with Aston Martin Tickford already hired to do much of the productionisation of the rest of the car, Boreham could not only begin to pay more attention to the world championship rally specifications, but could also try to finalise the choice of a site to build the production run of these machines. To those who were privileged to visit Boreham at this momentous time, there seemed to be more and more RS200 activity in the workshops, and out on the test tracks, though this was also the time in which work was starting on the evolution of an Escort RS Turbo rally car project, and on first thoughts about the new Sierra RS Cosworth, which had just been revealed to the public at the Geneva Motor Show.

The sixth and last of the prototypes was completed, and set to work, at the end of March 1985, and as Car No 002 was about to meet its end in the compulsory 30mph barrier crash test, this meant five cars were now in use, either as road-car development machines, or for rallying. Much mileage was built up in shuttling cars between Boreham, MIRA and Aston Martin Tickford in Newport Pagnell, where Jackie Stewart spent three full days on high-speed handling tasks, and the patient and hard-working Malcolm Wilson repeatedly drove cars for hour after hour on the various test circuits at Boreham.

While all this was going on, and as the entire RS200 project took shape, and was completed, in a very short period –

Car No 003 being shaken down at Boreham by an unidentified driver in the autumn of 1984. Visually, it is close to the ultimate specification except for the different front-end styling detail, and the fact that there is no Ford badge on the nose.

short, that is, by contemporary motor industry standards – the biggest miracle was that Ford Motorsport managed to organise the how, where and when of the production of the 200 cars (six prototypes plus 194 true production machines) needed to achieve sporting homologation without causing organisational and financial chaos to the rest of the Ford-UK empire. Looked at from the very beginning – from the 'why don't we...?' moment in March 1983 – it was always the biggest problem the entire programme would have to face.

Even after the bare bones of the new car's layout had been agreed and the first prototype was taking shape, and when Stuart Turner, Mike Moreton and John Wheeler settled down to turn the great idea into a feasible programme, they had not finally chosen, nor gained approval, as to how and where the cars would be built. They all realised, of course, that a mass cheating or smoke-and-mirrors exercise could not even be considered, so 200 real cars would have to be created, and be seen to exist. Unscrupulous rival companies had bent the rules and got away with this strategy in the past, but it was no longer possible, or commercially acceptable, for Ford to cheat like that.

At this time, the contemporary FISA system of Group B homologation would include a detailed inspection of the cars being assembled (the inspection group would always include at least one sharp-eyed personality from a rival rallying concern), with the visual evidence needing to be backed up by suitable paperwork and computer programmes, and the stock of components, to prove that point.

There was no question that things had changed considerably in recent years. In the good old days of the 1960s and 1970s, homologation of new competition cars was often claimed on the flimsiest of evidence, such that an intention to produce 400 Group 4 cars (the elite of rallying at the time) was often believed to be acceptable at a time when only a handful of complete cars existed (although a solemn written assurance of production would always be formally provided by a company's top executive). The extreme example of this practice had probably come from Vauxhall in 1976, when the new 16-valve Chevette HS (later a direct and partly successful competitor of the Escort RS1800, as it happened) was approved when only

Someone was bound to do this! A prank, set up by a Ford contractor, to remind people of the links between Ford Motorsport and Reliant.

two such cars had been completed, one of which started (and promptly broke down) on the RAC Rally of that year. That, of course, is an even more extreme case than was achieved by Alan Mann Racing in the mid 1960s when Ford-USA hired Mann to run USA-engineered V8 Falcons in the Monte Carlo Rally of 1964. Mann specified a version he thought could win (and it nearly did), his own Byfleet-based company built 14 cars and achieved Group 2 (1000-off) FISA recognition on the basis of a solemn letter from Ford in Detroit saying that this model existed, it was in the showrooms, and the necessary quantities were assured.

Even Lancia, which always committed the resources (and the motorsport ambitions) to do the job properly, was not averse to massaging a few figures and a few dates along the way. As an example, when the sensational mid-Ferrari-engined Stratos achieved homologation on 1 October 1974, Lancia swore blind that 500 cars had already been built – yet many years later an irrefutable Bertone statistic revealed that only 141 cars had been completed at that point. The fact that more than 500 Stratoses were eventually built made most people forgive them.

By 1985, however, FIA had considerably tightened up its procedures and the inspection of numbers being built. Audi (with the Quattro Sport), Lancia (Delta Integrale) and Peugeot (205 Turbo 16) had all been open and honest in their dealings, so there was no longer any question of a sizeable manufacturer getting away with any sleight-of-hand. Ford certainly had to plan to do the job properly, to build all the cars and get them counted by a certain date. As I have already made clear, Stuart Turner's original optimistic timing forecasts had to be abandoned, but soon after the RS200 had been unveiled, and received so enthusiastically, at its launch in November 1984 (when only four cars – all prototypes – existed) everyone in Ford Motorsport hoped that the figure of 200 complete cars could be reached before the end of 1985. At this point Ford-UK was still convinced the RS200 would be a loss-making programme, so it was decided that a mere 194 (and that figure is significant) should be built as production cars, leaving the existing six prototypes to make up the numbers.

Below: Who decided to commemorate the RS200 connection with an ex-Reliant factory by producing this cartoon?

"There was never any likelihood of RS200s being assembled alongside the company's notorious three-wheelers"

In earlier chapters I related the process in which a search for a suitable assembly site was in people's minds from 1983, when nothing more than a B200 acronym existed and a 'why don't we…?' strategy had taken root. It is also worth repeating that although the Reliant company was a front-runner for the assembly job, it was mainly because there had already been much lobbying from that concern (it was over-staffed, and badly needed work at the time). I should emphasise that there was never any likelihood of RS200s being assembled alongside the company's notorious three-wheelers, or even close to the much more respected Scimitar GTE sports coupés of the day.

In the end, though, perseverance paid off (notably in fighting off Lotus), for it was a redundant Reliant factory and a number of its skilled workers (who would otherwise have been jobless, and who had an enviable record of producing high-quality fibreglass bodywork and of being demonstrably

Left: Reliant was not only noted for producing three-wheeler cars. In the 1970s and 1980s the company also made smart, fast, and capable Ford V6-engined 'sporting estates' called Scimitar GTEs. It was this ability that made them prime candidates for producing much of the RS200's bodywork, and for lending redundant workers to Ford to produce RS200s.

very keen to take on the task) that won the job. By that time it had become clear that demand for Reliant's relatively high-priced Scimitar was falling away (the elegant sporting hatchback would die of old age at the end of 1986), so the firm's entire business was busily being contracted back into its original premises in Tamworth, and a complete and geographically separate factory at Shenstone had become available, and was already empty.

And so it was that the production run of RS200s found itself a home in Shenstone. Once again, I need to emphasise that although the Ford RS200 production cars – all 194 of them – were originally assembled in a factory with previous Reliant connections, Reliant, as a concern, had virtually nothing to do with the project management of this prestigious operation itself. Although Reliant had once used the building in Shenstone (mainly as a plant stuffed full of machine tools, where engines and transmissions were manufactured), there was absolutely and utterly no Reliant managerial presence, or evidence, on that site in 1985 to 1986 when RS200s were being manufactured in a project controlled by Mike Moreton for Ford-UK.

And yet, to this day, pictures and comments continue to appear in other publications (books and magazine articles) and on the internet, of brand-new RS200s being lovingly assembled in surroundings fondly captioned as 'a Reliant factory'...

Reliant, originally a humble maker of three-wheeler cars and light commercial vehicles, had been set up by Tom Williams in 1935, with a small factory in Tamworth, Staffordshire, a few miles north east of Birmingham. It was there that the first Reliant four-wheeler (the Sabre sports car) was announced

This was September 1985, the early days of RS200 production at Shenstone, with two completed cars at the top of the shot, and several newly delivered chassis tubs on the simple assembly lines. Things would get busier in the weeks that followed.

in 1962, and where the smart Ford-engined Scimitar sports coupé was revealed in 1964.

For many years Reliant three-wheelers took shape around remanufactured 1920s-design side-valve Austin Seven engines, but from 1963 the company announced its new and cute little own-design overhead-valve 600cc engine. Although castings were sourced from specialists, final machining of components, and assembly (along with much other machining of parts) was located in an ex-military production factory in Lynn Lane, Shenstone village, close to the railway station. This was ceremonially opened, with a flourish, by F1 world champion Jim Clark, in November 1963.

While working with *Autocar* in the 1960s the author paid several visits to Shenstone, which was three miles due south of Lichfield, and about seven miles west along the A5 from Reliant's Tamworth HQ. The building was, it seems, originally set up as a munitions plant during the Second World War, and had a large and airy floor space of 61,000 sq feet (5700 sq metres). By the 1980s, Reliant had expanded its original operations to both sides of the A5 trunk road (cars, bodies and trolleys of equipment were regularly seen being pushed from one side of the road to the other, which could

SARDINIA TEST DRIVES

It can only have been Ford's defensive irritation at the controversy caused by the RS200's rather belated entry into production that caused the company to invite a few privileged members of the specialist press to sample prototypes of the RS200 in Sardinia in September 1985. This, incidentally, was in the same month as another RS200 prototype car contested – and won – its very first entry in a rally, a great occasion that is described in some detail in Chapter 6.

This Sardinia event, in fact, was an add-on occasion to the European-wide press sampling of the brand-new four-wheel-drive versions of the Granada/Scorpio range, for which the twisty tarmac roads (and a few loose-surface tracks) of Sardinia, in the Mediterranean, had been chosen. Boreham, one would think, really had enough to do when concerned with getting an RS200 ready for its competition debut in the UK, but somehow two of the six prototypes – No 3 (B888 CHK) and No 4 (B690 CEV, the machine originally shown to the world at the Turin Motor Show) – were slightly refurbished, stripped of all their test equipment, and despatched to the island, where they were in the safe and capable hands of John Taylor.

Even though both cars were already well-worn, and had been driven for many miles in their hectic prototype lives, Ford thought it was justified to unleash a few journalists – not to drive, in most cases, but usually to sit alongside Boreham's nominated drivers. Because the specification of the road cars had virtually been settled by that time, both were approximating to the performance and character of what the (very limited) public would be able to buy, though the quoted power output was still stated to be 230bhp (not 250bhp, for performance tuning was still going ahead) at 6000rpm.

Mike McCarthy treated *Autosport* readers to his views in the issue of 26 September 1985, made the usual mistake of crediting the entire design to Tony Southgate while ignoring John Wheeler completely, then wrote, *'At first I sat next to John as he conducted the car along some fastish A-type roads, and then a nice dirt road that had been comprehensively ruined by some heavy rain… The dirt road showed that, under all that road-going skin, the RS200 is a rally car at heart. Put it this way: I wouldn't have even dared to show [this track] to a Ferrari 308, much less driven on it in one, yet Mr Taylor had the little RS200 flowing smoothly and undramatically – well, as undramatically as you can be in a bucking, roaring, bumping, shaking rally car on what was effectively a fast special stage – as if he was on a well-surfaced minor road.'*

Much of the rest of the report concerned the car's character, in particular the behaviour of the clutch, which was a twin-plate metallic device at this stage (*'road cars will have something much less performance-orientated'*).

'I stalled it. In fact just about every time I tried to pull off from rest, I stalled it. Having Mr Taylor sitting next to me didn't help: the harder I tried, the worse it became. Such embarrassment. The technique in fact was to trickle off with as little throttle as possible, then give it some welly when the clutch was engaged. Once on the move then, the whole car comes alive…

'Summing up, and bearing in mind the cars we drove weren't the final thing, what impressed me most about the RS200 was its lack of fuss and drama: for a rally homologation special it made a superb road car, while for a high-performance road car it makes a quite astonishing rally car.'

Autocar's comments, as one might expect from this magazine (there was no byline to the piece so we do not know whose opinions they were), was a little more subdued, and included the oft-repeated howler that it was Reliant building the road cars at Tamworth. One of the two cars sampled was reported to have already completed *'over 50,000 mile of stage and other test driving'*, which was hard to accept, particularly as neither of these machines had been built to rally-car standards, and neither was more than nine months old.

"What impressed me most about the RS200 was its lack of fuss and drama: for a rally homologation special it made a superb road car, while for a high-performance road car it makes a quite astonishing rally car."

All this, however, could be forgiven, by this extract: *'The strongest impression was made as we tore up the rough road, a heavily rutted, hard-gashed yellow ribbon into Sardinia's hard hills. We were not bumped badly; it rides astonishingly well for a rally car and not at all badly by any standards given the surface. It was truly remarkable, this ride, compounded of exceptionally long wheel travel – we didn't bottom once – though we ought to have done – allied to the right springs and damping.'*

It was this trip alone, one feels, that finally convinced the specialist press that Ford Motorsport was serious about its new car.

be a rather hazardous operation), but with business in decline the company needed to rationalise its commercial operations. Accordingly, the Shenstone plant became redundant, was closed down, and remained empty for some time until Ford acquired a one-year lease in 1985.

Ford, although operating the RS200 project independently, took on a number of ex-Reliant employees (particularly those who had become skilled in assembling Scimitar sports cars) as contract assembly staff in the RS200 period (another reason for the false rumours about Reliant involvement), but while Reliant supplied many of the RS200's fibreglass external body mouldings, the firm was never directly involved in whole-car manufacture. After the RS200 assembly project was finally completed in mid 1986, Ford would once again vacate the premises. The building still stands but is now occupied by a company totally unconnected with Ford, Reliant or even with the British motor industry.

Although it was Stuart Turner who had originally conceived the idea of producing the RS200, it was Mike Moreton who headed up the small but experienced team who made it possible to change the good idea – already superbly engineered by John Wheeler and Tony Southgate – into a viable production entity,

In September 1985, Ford sent two RS200 prototypes (this car is 003) to Sardinia, where they took part in a press evaluation of several other cars; John Taylor was the chauffeur on all these runs.

where almost 200 highly-complex cars were assembled (and were seen to exist by FIA homologation inspectors). More than anyone it was Mike (whose career is summarised on page 32) who managed the Shenstone plant, and after many frustrating setbacks and delays made it certain that the great mass of RS200s would be lined up and ready to be counted on 31 January 1986.

Ford planners had been looking forward to this day for many months, but it was not until April 1985 that they first set foot into the Shenstone site, whose principal factory floor was yawningly empty. With Moreton as the boss, he soon appointed two long-term Ford managers, Mike Goddard and Ivor Joynes, to be respectively responsible for parts supply and quality control, while among the management team of mainly seconded ex-Reliant employees it was Trevor James and Gerry Wilmott who were prominent assets. Boreham's Bill Meade and Terry Bradley, recently released from SVE at Dunton to return to Boreham, were swiftly reassigned to work at Shenstone.

First of all, it was necessary to lay out what we might basically call an assembly line, although at Shenstone they were simple guidance tracks for major trolleys to use; there would be absolutely no elevated tracks, cranes, jigs or welding equipment involved. On the other hand, there was ample space to set up a seven-station assembly sequence, along which the trolley-mounted tubs would first be placed, and which would be pushed forward as the next major addition was needed. Not only that, there was plenty of space under the same roof to stack all the parts as they were delivered from other sources – and, as it happens, there would be enough space for all the completed cars to be lined up for inspection by the FIA inspectors.

"Each and every one of the cars would originally be painted in a standard Ford Diamond White"

Before this simple but efficient operation could swing into action – slowly at first, but with increasing frenzy as November 1985, December 1985, then January 1986 loomed – contracts needed to be placed, and deliveries had to begin, of everything needed to turn fresh air into complete cars.

Above left: One of the first assembly procedures at Shenstone was to lower the engine and its associate clutch and transfer box housing into the chassis/tub. This also shows one of the twin fuel tanks hidden away under the sloping lower section of the rear passenger bulkhead.

Left: Andy Rouse drove this RS200 on the Beaujolais Run of 1985, from Bordeaux to London – a non-competitive run, but great publicity for the project.

Central to the entire car, of course, was what we all called the tub, which (as described in Chapter 4) allied metal pressings to aluminium honeycomb, carbon composite and Kevlar mouldings, along with simple pressed-steel items, and the ability for the roll cage and the front and rear subframes to be added as assembly went ahead.

The main platform-making contract eventually went to Arch Motors, already well-respected in the motorsport industry, which had grappled successfully with the repeated manufacture of multi-tube chassis before turning to this more complex type of structure. Its factory location was in Coventry, about 30 miles from Shenstone.

When Ford decided to place a contract to make all the fibreglass body panels, it made eminent sense to choose Reliant, which had literally made tens of thousands of GRP mouldings in previous years. Not only that, but Reliant could also produce the cabin mouldings (which looked like Sierra components but most certainly were not), and could provide them all painted to a high standard. Each and every one of the cars would originally be painted in a standard Ford Diamond White hue, simply because it was thought (correctly, as it happened) that almost every one of the rally-specification machines would eventually be plastered with a sponsor's livery and other trade decals. In later years, proud owners

Some of the production cars tucked into a corner of the Shenstone factory, ready to be counted by FISA inspectors on 31 January1986.

RS200 assembly at its height, at Shenstone, in January 1986.

sometimes had their cars resprayed and recoloured.

In fact, a tiny handful of completed cars were eventually put on sale in alternative colours – this taking place after the chosen machines had been in stock, still unsold, in Diamond White, for some time – but only to an individual request. The author's fourth car (No 192), for instance, had originally been built in white, but before delivery it was resprayed in Ferrari Rosso Red. As far as it is known, this was the very first non-white RS200 road car to take to the public highway, in late 1988.

"When the final inspection took place at Shenstone there were still cars that had no transmission installed"

As already described and analysed in early pages, the engines manufactured for the cancelled Escort RS1700T had been stored carefully while the new car was being designed, but nevertheless had to be thoroughly re-engineered – not only had the cylinder bores to be opened up slightly, but new inlet manifolds, fuel rails, exhaust systems and turbocharger locations had to be produced. JQF Engineering was capable of meeting this challenge, and was able to be well ahead of the needs of the simple assembly lines of the RS200.

In contrast, FF Developments had never before had to tackle such a major contract, and needed to make substantial investments in its production facilities in Coventry. For many of the intricate machining jobs involved, FF had to recruit other companies in the incredibly capable engineering 'Mafia' that still thrived in Coventry. Admitting it was almost more than the company could tackle, FF said there were occasions when supply was only just ahead of Shenstone's demand – and when the final inspection took place at Shenstone there were still cars that had no transmission installed.

As to the rest of the car – wheels, tyres, brakes, steering gear, electrical items, and more and more and more – was concerned, it needed all of the team's experience and expertise to keep manufacture going ahead. Once again to quote Mike Moreton's wise words: *'Time seemed to fly by and the situation became frantic, chaotic and very difficult. Parts were being delivered, but in random order, making it extremely difficult to build anything. It became a nightmare getting suppliers to make what we needed at the right time, and emergency meetings took place at all hours of the day and night.'*

EVOLUTION CARS

No sooner had the RS200 programme been wound down than magazine 'evidence' began to circulate about so-called Evolution cars, which Ford built in 1986/1987. More than 20 cars had been built, it was rumoured, some of which were to have been used as the basis of what Ford had planned to prepare for use in 1987. This, in fact, was total nonsense – for although more than 20 VIN numbers were allocated, VIN plates were never printed, and no such cars were originally registered by the DVLA in the UK or when cars were exported to overseas customers.

Only one such prototype car (No 012), with an authentic 2.1-litre Hartpower engine, was built by Ford Motorsport at Boreham (and was originally seen in Martin Schanche's hands in the Bettega Memorial Rallysprint of December 1986). However, as time passed, more than 20 such cars were granted provisional VIN numbers. How, when and why this was done is best explained by quoting from an RS200 Club newsletter of the period, written after I had stepped down, though even this includes anomalies: *'It was Motorsport's intention to build 20 cars with a much revised chassis, with alloy subframes and the 2137cc Brian Hart engine.'*

This is not true, for Boreham had neither the intention, nor the facilities, to build any but its own works fleet. Because the lease of the Shenstone premises had been relinquished, any such cars would have had to be built by asking a trusted contractor to tackle the job. The chosen contractor, in the fullness of time, was Gordon Spooner Engineering, of Witham in Essex, which had successful, cordial, and long-term links with the works team.

'The cars would have carried new VIN plates numbered 201 to 220. The decision was made to reconstruct 19 cars (VIN 012 was already built as a prototype Evolution machine)... Ford did, however, allocate on paper only, the VIN numbers 201 to 220 against the VIN number actually on the cars...'

As a result, 20 'paper upgrades' were agreed (as detailed in the table to the right).

It is understood that several further Evolution cars were also built, rescued, restored or recreated by private owners (please make up your own minds about the most suitable description of each of those machines), but none had direct factory involvement.

ORIGINAL CAR NUMBER	EVOLUTION VIN ALLOCATED
012	201
146	202
174	203
087	204
097	205
098	206
099	207
145	208
081	209
153	210
101	211
168	212
070	213
084	214
105	215
106	216
096	217
083	218
084	219
086	220

Although Ford first occupied the Shenstone site in April 1985, it was high summer before even the first two completed cars – logically numbered 007 and 008 – were ready for dispatch, their departure to Boreham being delayed for some time; they were meanwhile located to one side of the production line, which proved to be ideal as very real on-the-hoof examples of what had to fit, and where.

Those two cars, incidentally, were destined for important careers – 007 as a rally development car, and 008 as the paradigm of the production of road cars that were to follow – although neither was registered until October/November 1985.

Series production eventually got under way around October 1985. Ford archive images show one side of the big hall was devoted to two parallel equal-purpose tracks, with assembly starting around the painted and corrosion-proofed Arch underpan/tub. As they were slowly pushed along the angle-iron guide tracks, the cars took on the roll cage, then the mid-rear-mounted engine was craned into place from above, followed by the addition of the main transmission/four-wheel-drive assembly from the underside of the front, after which

Two publicity gimmicks for the price of one. In 1985 Ford put a works rally car on a trailer, and had it towed by a concept prototype of the next-generation Transit.

The date was 31 January 1986, and the entire production run of RS200s was lined up inside the Shenstone factory complex for inspection by the FISA homologation team. Count them if you can – remembering that a number of other cars had already left for Boreham, and for more specialist preparation. Note that a considerable number already have the extra 'bat ears' added at each side of the intercooler roof scoop.

the basic cabin structure was added.

The bulky front and rear body mouldings were added towards the end of this process, and (to be brutally honest), with much of the early cars' interiors not yet available, they were then pushed into the side of the assembly hall to await their arrival. In the meantime, supplies of those mouldings, engines, transmissions, and many of the 2000 individual parts (which included wheels, tyres, fuel tanks, electrical goods, brakes and much more) began to flood in, and to fill the plentiful space to one side of the assembly lines.

"Everyone agreed that the last batch would probably have to be thrown together"

Way back in the spring of 1985 when Ford had first started moving into Shenstone, it was hoped that the entire production run would be completed by the end of the calendar year (which would have enabled sporting homologation on 1 January 1986), although even then it was clear that FIA inspectors might not be able to see all 200 cars in ready-to-go condition. Yet it was not to be, for (as Austin-Rover found with the rival Metro 6R4 project) there were times when the line was stopped, waiting for vital parts to arrive.

One oft-repeated story (which sounded like a good wind-up until the author had a chance to see the evidence on a visit to Shenstone) concerned the late delivery of some welded-up suspension parts, a shortage which had led to a manager and his estate car being sent off to the supplier to pick up a new batch. On the way back to Shenstone the car had to stop and be hurriedly cleared of the components, which had been loaded when freshly welded, and were busily setting fire to the car's rear carpet!

Immediately after homologation was approved in 1986, Boreham took a development car down to the Nardo high-speed track in the south of Italy for extended flat-out test runs.

Although it rapidly became clear that the 200 cars could not be completed until early 1986, Stuart Turner and Mike Moreton concluded that they needed to convince the homologation inspectors that all was well, and that the specialist press needed to see the factory. Accordingly, the very first FISA inspection took place at Shenstone on Monday 13 January 1986, when the first 60 completed cars were lined up for scrutiny, at a time when it was also known that a number of cars – prototypes and off-line machines – were already known to be at Boreham where full-house rally-car preparation was under way. A facility trip for the press, potential owners and Ford-based car clubs followed – although it (attended by the author) had to be arranged on a weekday evening, so that the then-frantic assembly-line activity should not be disturbed.

Many major components (exterior body mouldings mainly) were already stacked up in the spacious assembly hall, and it was clear that the honest intent was to get the entire run completed as rapidly as possible. With the tempo rising all the time, the possibility of completing the 200 cars by 31 January was becoming a probability, as the hundredth car was then completed just three days later.

Even so, everyone agreed that the last batch would probably have to be 'thrown together' (rather than carefully assembled, and made completely functional) to meet the deadline. Ford was not ashamed about this – especially as the rival team, Austin-Rover, had been known to have similar problems, and after the cancellation of Group B in mid 1986 would eventually be obliged to sell off a number of incomplete MG Metro 6R4s.

As is now well known, and is clearly proved by the unposed images taken at the time, the second and final visit came on Friday, 31 January 1986. The FISA inspection team had already visited the Boreham motorsport facility on the previous day, and now wanted to see evidence that all the run of road cars had been completed. As they had done with rival concerns, they were prepared to accept the fact that some of the cars were still by no means complete. On the other hand, all of the cars on show had complete structures, bodyshells, engines and (apparently – but not in detail – transmissions), and looked impressive when lined up.

Even though it had seemed spacious when Ford moved in during the previous year, the Shenstone plant was nevertheless not large enough to accommodate all the cars at this inspection, so apart from the batch that had already been relocated to Boreham, it must have been a great relief to Mike Moreton to discover that some cars could actually be parked outside, under snow-covered tarpaulins.

The resulting display (seen in the image on page 83) was impressive to say the least, and although I defy anyone to count the number of cars in the shot (the line-up seems to stretch to the horizon) it was certainly enough to convince the authorities that the car was now well-and-truly able to pass the 200-off figure, and Group B homologation was granted there and then.

Ford was tremendously relieved to achieve this, and made sure the workforce could be gathered together to enjoy a champagne toast before they dispersed for the weekend. This, however, was not the end, but the end of the beginning.

Even so, there was quiet satisfaction among the management in bringing what was a complex project to a satisfactory climax – especially when the earlier trauma of the failing Escort RS1700T was still on their minds.

It was no wonder that Stuart Turner immediately wrote to his top boss, Bob Lutz, with these words: *'200 RS200 cars were counted by the motorsport authorities 2 years and 4 ½ months from getting approval to start the first prototype, which must be some sort of Ford record. Austin-Rover took over a year longer with the Metro 6R4.'*

Nevertheless, much more remained to be done to get the entire project completed. Not only had the machine to start a winning career in rallying, but the selling operation needed to begin.

The Ford caption for this 1986 shot states 'RS200 at a police test day', which was a subtle nudge that the brand-new Sierra RS Cosworth was fast enough to match an RS200 on the A12 close to Dunton. But police in an RS200? We think not – where would they put their helmets, and surely the blue-flashing bar mounting would interfere with air getting into the roof-top intercooler?

In November 1984 Ford issued this remarkably detailed cutaway drawing of the RS200, as it was ready for production. This was done when the prototypes were still running on split-rim alloy wheels, and when the hidden inner extra tail lamps had not been added to the specification, but is otherwise extremely representative of the 200-off run that would follow.

Chapter 6

Rallying – the works effort in Britain and overseas

The RS200 made its competition debut in the 1985 Lindisfarne Rally, using the rugged forests of Kielder. Using Car No 005, Malcolm Wilson won the event outright, and gave the team (and himself) a great boost.

The RS200 could not start its serious rallying career until Group B homologation was achieved, and because the 200-off build programme did not begin until the summer of 1985, this meant the first major events could not be tackled before the 1986 season had begun.

In the meantime, testing, development and finalisation of the cars continued flat-out at Boreham, with much of the emphasis falling on the road-car specification. At that time only two of the original six prototypes – No 001 and No 005 (registered B55 CHK) – were rally-specification machines, and they had been testing for much of 1985 on the various tarmac and loose-surface tracks at Boreham, and occasionally on clandestine trips to stages in Wales, with Malcolm Wilson at the wheel.

Soon after completing the first works RS200, Ford Motorsport introduced it to one of the much-loved collection of older cars – this being the famous outright winner of the 1970 Daily Mirror World Cup Rally of 1970.

The very first two cars to be assembled at the Shenstone factory in the late summer of 1985 were No 007 (registered C98 FHK; a left-hand-drive rally-specification machine that was soon shipped south to Boreham for works preparation to take place) and No 008 (later given the number B200 COO), which was originally a right-hand-drive road car, built to satisfy every legislative requirement.

However, even by the beginning of September 1985 it was becoming clear that completion of the 200 cars (and the compulsory FIA inspection that would accompany this achievement) could not be guaranteed in time for approval to come on 1 November, and to allow works cars to take part in the Lombard RAC that month. Not only did this give the specialist media much to write about, to whinge about and to comment upon, it was also a great deal of embarrassment to Ford's PR machine and the hard-working team at Boreham.

The fact is that one, maybe two, cars could have been prepared at Boreham to take part in the Lombard RAC but, as Ford PR man Steve Woolmington commented in *Autosport* regarding road car production, *'The problem has been getting the parts together, and having them in the right place at the right time… It would be silly not to say that we have had one or two problems.'*

Austin-Rover, the big rival concern, was having similar problems with getting 200 MG Metro 6R4 Group B cars ready, but its timing was just far enough ahead of Ford to make sure that they could compete in the Lombard RAC Rally.

It was the galling fact that the 6R4 was just ahead of Ford in the race for Group B recognition, and that the Metro had already appeared in minor British events, that finally persuaded Boreham that the RS200 needed to appear and compete at least once – anywhere that the competition was of a sufficiently high standard to make it credible, and where homologation was not yet a factor. Happily the Marlboro

B55 CHK
3
speedline

Early days in the test programme for the new RS200. This was mid 1984 when Car 001 was the mule carrying out much of the hard work. Even at that point, the intercooler had already taken up its definitive place on the rear of the roof of the car. That is Malcolm Wilson talking to engineer Andy Thorburn at the rear of the car.

The cockpit of this early rally development car (probably Car 005, in 1985, before it tackled the Lindisfarne rally) shows the general layout of the controls, a temporary location for the handbrake lever, and the placing of the extra 2WD/4WD control lever alongside the conventional gearstick.

THE BOREHAM FLEET – WORKS CARS AND PROTOTYPES

From 1983 to 1986, the Motorsport centre at Boreham concentrated on RS200 design, development and rallying, but as soon as Group B came under sentence of death in 1986 its attention was redirected to new Sierra-based programmes. After this, RS200s were seen more and more often at Boreham, for all the road cars were eventually stored, sold and usually delivered via Bob Howe's one-man operation, based from an office on site.

This is a full listing of the cars that came under the direct influence of Boreham's motorsport team in those years, either as Boreham-based works cars or as quasi-works cars prepared by Ford's favoured preparation specialists, and run in Europe:

VIN NUMBER	REGISTRATION NUMBER	YEAR BUILT	NOTES
001	B200 FMC	1984	The original LHD drive prototype, and the first car shown to management, but not the media. The registration number was a fake, for show only.
002	Not registered	1984	The second car, also LHD, used for prototype development, culminating in the compulsory barrier crash test in 1984. After this, of course, it was never rebuilt as a functioning road car.
003	B888 CHK	1984	A development road car, LHD, in 250bhp form.
004	B690CEV	1984	The car originally launched at the 1984 Turin Motor Show. LHD, a road car.
005	B55 CHK	1985	The first full rally-spec car, used by Malcolm Wilson to win the Lindisfarne Rally of 1985.
006	B340 CAR	1985	A hard-working road-car prototype, briefly used by Mark Lovell in two British rallies (Citroen National, and Skip Brown) in 1986 before eventually being sold to Diabolique Motorsport in Portugal, where it became a donor car for that team's other rally car (VIN 072 and the identity of the two machines effectively became merged).

The above were the six original prototypes. Except for the cars listed below, the remainder of the production run (194 identities) were originally completed at Shenstone, before being re-prepared at Boreham or at Aston Martin Tickford in Bedworth, near Coventry.

VIN NUMBER	REGISTRATION NUMBER	YEAR BUILT	NOTES
007	C98 FHK	1985	A rally car, used for practice/test/development.
008	B200 COO	1985	Although carrying such a registration number as to make one assume it was a works rally car, this machine was a standard RHD road car, used for a time for demonstration purposes.
012	C200 LWC	1986	Rally car, used on the Welsh Rally of 1986, then for testing and reconnaissance, then intended to be the first Evolution/Group S car. Also used in the Bettega Rallysprint in Italy, in December 1986.
014	B200 YEV	1986	Rally car, one of the first full-house rally cars to be completed at Boreham in the autumn of 1985. Competed in five events in 1986: Sweden, Portugal, Circuit of Ireland, South Sweden and the Audi Sport.
015	B200 YOO	1986	Rally car, completed and prepared at Boreham in autumn 1985. Competed in four events in 1986: Sweden, Portugal, Circuit of Ireland and the Audi Sport.
061	C200 JJN	1986	Rally car (used by Stig Andervang in Europe), prepared by Mike Taylor Developments in Yorkshire. Very successful and intensively used. Made the trip to India for the Himalayas event. The car was damaged on the 1986 RAC Rally, but was later repaired.
062	C200 KHJ	1986	Rally car, prepared and run by Mike Little Preparations' Carlisle-based team. It became Mark Lovell's very successful machine, in which Mark won the British Rally Championship of 1986. It competed in no fewer than seven events during 1986: the National Breakdown, Welsh, Scottish, Ulster, Manx, Audi Sport and RAC. It caught fire and burnt out completely on the RAC Rally. The crew – Mark and Roger Freeman – were not injured, but the car was a total loss. Even so, it is believed to have been recreated in later years, though it contains none of the original car's components.
063	C200 KWC	1986	This rally car (for use in Switzerland) was prepared by Mike Little Preparations in Carlisle. It started its career in May, when (as detailed in Chapter 7) it suffered a total and fiery accident in which driver Marc Surer was seriously injured, and his driver killed. The car was completely written off.
064	B200 XVX	1986	Rally car. Along with its sister (No 065) this was the first of the truly heavyweight or rough-road cars to be prepared at Boreham. As such, and as driven by Kalle Grundel, it competed in the Acropolis Rally of May 1986, and the RAC at the end of the season.
065	B200 AYD	1986	Rally car. This was the sister car of No 064, which Stig Blomqvist drove on the Acropolis, the RAC and the Bettega Memorial events of 1986.
067	C200 HVW		Rally car (used by Robert Droogmans in Europe). Prepared by Mike Little Preparations, apparently a lighter and more specialised tarmac alternative to Car 069 (below), only occasionally seen with its correct registration on display, and sometimes standing in for car 069/C200 MNO and carrying that car's identity.
069	C200 MNO	1986	Rally car (used by Robert Droogmans in Europe). Prepared to approved Boreham specifications by Mike Little Preparations, it enjoyed an extremely successful season, in which Droogmans emphatically won the Belgian Rally Championship.
072	C440 BHV	1986	Rally car (mainly used by Joaquim Santos in Europe) originally supplied direct from Boreham. Badly damaged in the horrific accident on the Rally of Portugal in March 1986 (analysed in Chapter 6). The car later went on to record several outright victories in Portugal.

John Taylor, based at Boreham, was an invaluable (and capable) member of the RS200's test and development team throughout the programme, and was the private competitors' major link with Boreham as use of the cars began to spread.

Lindisfarne Rally, a qualifier for the second-level British Shell Oils/Autosport Rally Championship, was due to take place on 7 September. Not only that, but Austin-Rover had decided to enter the MG Metro 6R4 (with Tony Pond to drive it) in the same event – so there was a chance of real competition between the two new British Group B cars.

Shell Oils/Autosport Lindisfarne Rally – 7 September 1985

Although Boreham had been frantically busy with the ongoing development of the RS200 project (Ford's mainstream design and development HQ at Dunton was never remotely involved in this job), in the summer of 1985 the team had neither the time nor the spare chassis/tubs to start building up a fleet of works cars – that would come later, during the winter of 1985/1986. Accordingly, when the decision was taken to enter Malcolm Wilson and his co-driving partner Nigel Harris in an RS200 into the Lindisfarne Rally, there was only one car they could use – No 005 (B55 CHK). At this very moment, incidentally, rumours began to spread that Wilson had tired of waiting for the RS200 to be ready, and was frustrated by Boreham's refusal to award him a world championship programme for the future; it was suggested he had received a lucrative offer from Austin-Rover and was all set to join the rival team for 1986.

Building on all the previous testing, for the Lindisfarne the revised car ran with a slightly enlarged aperture for the water-cooling radiator in the nose, and there was as yet no sign of what became known as the 'rabbit ears', which would eventually be fitted on every rally car at each side of the roof-mounted intercooler moulding to channel more cooling air into that component. On this car, on this occasion, there were no cooling vents in the top of the front moulding.

> "In the five forest stages during the afternoon, the RS200 ceded just six seconds to the Metro, with Wilson insisting that he was no longer running flat-out"

At this stage the 1.8-litre engine had been boosted to produce between 380bhp and 405bhp, and although Austin-Rover claimed to have more than this in the Metro 6R4 power unit there seemed to be little difference in the results. The diagonal striping on the flanks was already present, but there was little evidence of technical partners elsewhere on the paint job.

It was to be a wet and slippery day spent mainly in the Kielder Forest complex, ideal for both teams to see just how good their cars actually were, and (privately, if not for public consumption) to see whose pre-event hype had been closer, or further, from the truth. On the first two stages, run on the crumbly tarmac of the Albemarle Barracks, the Metro built up a 12-second lead over the RS200 – but this was only the beginning.

Wilson then set out on the first forestry stage to reduce the deficit, and things almost immediately went wrong. Flying off the loose-surfaced track in front of a crowd of spectators (which included several influential press-men), he needed their brawn before he could regain the track, lost up to 40 seconds, and dropped to sixth place. Fortunately for him, the car's chassis was not damaged, and although the GRP bodyshell was slightly scarred at the front, that was the only evidence of an off.

In the next two hours the dramas continued and intensified. The Metro 6R4 suffered braking problems, the RS200 caught up some of its deficit but arrived at a service point after six stages with a nearside rear wheel completely lacking any trace of a tyre. This had been caused by a high-speed blowout, which had caused the car to limp slowly through the last five miles. The result was that a rear driveshaft also had to be changed and, because there was time (the phrase 'one became used to this in 1986' comes to mind) the main gearbox was also changed – a process that took a mere 15 minutes, and would be good practice/training for the next season.

With seven stages to go in the afternoon session, it was now very much of a game-on situation – until, that is, the 6R4 suffered lengthy delays in rectifying its braking problems, and was stalled by several minutes at the next time control. Even so, Wilson was not about to cruise to victory. Having set two of the first six fastest times before the lunch halt, he then set two more fastest times in the afternoon session, eased his way back to cruise through the final Albemarle tarmac stages, and made the entire Boreham crew (and hundreds, it seemed, of Ford-backing spectators) happy too. All in all, in the five forest stages during the afternoon, the RS200 ceded just six seconds to the Metro, with Wilson insisting that he was no longer running flat-out.

And that, for the time being, was that, for almost immediately Ford let it be known that it had conceded that it could not possibly be ready for the Lombard RAC Rally (preparation of a second car had not yet begun at Boreham, and there was no sign of the 200 cars being completed before the first days of 1986).

The good news was that the team then retreated to get on with more intensive testing, though the bad news was that it was soon clear that Malcolm Wilson would leave Ford to take up a team position with Austin-Rover, driving the Metro 6R4. This defection was even more damaging than it seemed at first, for not only would Wilson no longer be available to drive the RS200 in public and in private, but he would also arrive at Austin-Rover (based at Cowley) with his brain full of knowledge about the RS200's then-known strengths and weaknesses.

The further good news, though, was that Jim Porter (Roger Clark's long-time co-driver) was re-hired to join Ford as Boreham's team coordinator, which would bring real experience, stretching back two full decades, to add to the promise of the new RS200 programme.

Malcolm Wilson won the 1985 Lindisfarne Rally outright on its competition debut, even though he went off the track at one point, and suffered punctures along the way.

Car 005, having just won the Lindisfarne rally of 1985, follows a factory-owned GT40 on parade at the Brighton Run of November 1985.

Pre-Lombard RAC Rally - November 1985

Having said Ford would withdraw from public use of its RS200s before homologation was achieved, Boreham soon changed its mind, and elected to send one car to take part in a light-hearted pre-RAC Rally press day at Blidworth Forest, close to the start (in Nottingham) of the 1985 event.

Stig Blomqvist and Kalle Grundel (who had both signed up to drive world championship cars in 1986) both turned up to drive the hard-working Car No 5 (B55 CHK), which had won the Lindisfarne Rally.

It might not have been a serious head-to-head contest but, to quote *Autosport* magazine: *'As Blomqvist proved while acting as chauffeur for the winner of the BBC Top Gear/ Radio Times RAC Rally competition, the car is indeed quick. Stig's first three runs were all timed at 1 minute 21 seconds and, by the end of the day, only Grundel's Peugeot 205 Turbo could equal it, the Metros of Tony Pond and Malcolm Wilson being just 1 second slower.'*

Numedal Rally, Norway - 18 January 1986

As part of their pre-Swedish outing, both team drivers worked hard on testing and familiarisation of cars in the weeks leading up to the event. In that quest, Stig Blomqvist took his recce car (carrying the registration number B690 CEV) to compete in the Numedal Rally of Norway in January 1986, where homologation was not required.

In deep snow, and running first, Blomqvist's RS200 floundered while acting as the event's snow-plough, finishing well down on the first stage but being fastest on every other stage. Although this event could never be described as serious, Stig was nevertheless pleased to finish second overall.

Right: Even after the RS200 programme was complete, John Wheeler always kept in touch with Stig Blomqvist, who was not only a world-class driver but a patient and thoughtful test driver too.

Stig Blomqvist had already won the World Rally Championship before he signed up to drive for Ford in RS200s. His co-driver, Björn Cederberg, did not join him in the team.

Kalle Grundel (right) and his co-driver Benny Melander posed atop a prototype RS200, immediately after signing up for the works team in 1986.

Swedish Rally – 14 to 16 February 1986 (World Rally Championship contender)

Recognising it would probably not gain Group B homologation by the end of 1985, Ford was obliged to miss out on the first international event of the 1986 season, the Monte Carlo Rally, and instead elected to enter two cars – for Stig Blomqvist and Kalle Grundel – in the Swedish Rally, which was due to start from Karlstad on 14 February.

The decision to abandon any chance of competing in Monte Carlo was not only taken on the pragmatic grounds that the cars might not be homologated in time, but also that team boss Stuart Turner did not want them to appear for the first time on that world-famous event in case a disappointing performance brought bad publicity with it. The fact that precisely those circumstances afflicted Austin-Rover's two MG Metro 6R4s on their debut surely proved the point – for their much-hyped outing was spoiled by one car being eliminated in an open-road accident after completing only six stages, the other suffering an engine failure the following day.

By January 1986, therefore, Boreham had already commissioned four rally cars, two of which were used for practice, testing and training in snow-afflicted Sweden, and two being brand-new machines. A lot of pre-event testing

In January 1986, this pre-Sweden shot shows the two brand-new works rally cars being prepared at Boreham. A service van – a Transit barge – is in the background.

There was not an inch of wasted space in the front compartment of the car, ahead of the windscreen. The battery was not at all easy to reach, and there was a totally functional scoop behind the water radiator to channel hot air out through the bonnet louvres. Road cars had an extra plastic container on top of all those chassis items – or a second spare wheel could be carried in that position.

and development had been completed during the winter, and the works team was quietly confident that they would be competitive at once.

For the Swedish Rally, the cars used were No 014 (B200 YEV) of Stig Blomqvist/Bruno Berglund, and No 015 (B200 YOO) of Kalle Grundel/Benny Melander.

Both were left-hand drive, of course, and were kitted out with the whole range of extra pieces that had already been proved by testing, practice, and also by Mark Lovell's first tentative appearances in non-championship British events. Not only did both cars have the 'rabbit ear' air intakes on the roof, at each side of the intercooler housing, both were fitted with the hot-air exit louvre in the front bonnet panel, so that fresh air could continue to circulate around the water radiator in the nose. At first the front end of the cars looked exactly like those of the 200-off homologation cars, with the addition of a pair of low-mounted free-standing Hella driving lamps. However, as this was naturally to be an ultra-cold event, with snow guaranteed for the entire route, the central decorative body striping moulding across the front of the radiator was finally removed. One of the frankly stone-age fitments carried on this event was a stout shovel clipped to the rear chassis subframe of each car – presumably just in case the car went off a track and needed to move a lot of snow in a short time. Shell provided the fuel and transmission fluids, while Pirelli supplied the tyres – as indeed both would throughout the season, and seasons to come.

Engine development work, headed up by Graham Dale-Jones, had continued at Boreham throughout the autumn

With homologation finally granted, Boreham could unleash its works RS200s into world championship rallying. On a wintry day at Boreham, John Wheeler, Andy Thorburn and Robin Vokins, along with some of the mechanics who had just completed the machines, pose with the two cars that would shortly start the Swedish Rally.

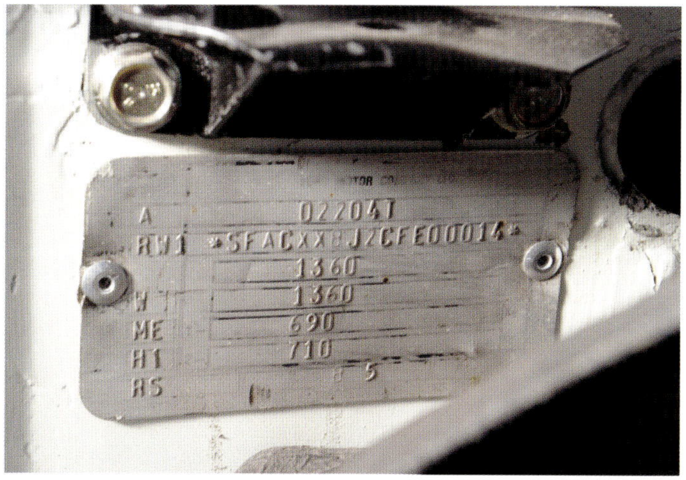

The authentic VIN/identification plate of Car No 014, one of the small and select group of works cars prepared at Boreham in 1986.

Extra air intakes could be (and often were) fixed at each side of the intercooler housing, helping to channel even more fresh air into the engine compartment.

Kalle Grundel, almost unknown to British Ford fans before he joined the team for 1986, put up a fine performance in the Swedish Rally, setting five fastest stage times, six second-fastest and nine thirds on his way to third place overall.

'The office' – totally functional but by no means luxurious, this was how one of the works fleet was equipped in the 1980s.

The engine bay of a works RS200 competition car was full of kit, but everything had a purpose. Note that the turbocharger itself is well clear of anything that could be affected by the heat.

and winter of 1985/1986, and although the standard size of 1803cc was retained, the engines were running with a maximum of 1.5 bar of boost, rated at 420bhp, with 325lb.ft of torque, which made the cars competitive (if not yet superior) to the principal competition. In fact, because the weather on this particular Swedish rally was cold even by Scandinavian winter standards, the air was more dense, and pre-event the engines were tending to run at up to 1.8 bar boost, so much work went ahead on the night before the start in a partially successful attempt to solve it.

With more to come, clearly it was going to give the all-new five-speed main gearbox a hard time – as the works team and its principal associates were soon to find out. Both drivers chose to run with a 37/63 front-rear torque split in the four-wheel-drive layout.

Because there had yet been little time to get down to the detail of weight saving, the two cars were a little heavier than Peter Ashcroft's team would have hoped – the official weighbridge recording of 2597lb/1178kg for Stig Blomqvist's car, and 2522lb/1144kg for that of Kalle Grundel.

To support this full-blooded effort, the Boreham posse amounted to no fewer than 47 individuals, who were spread between a fleet of Transit service vans, along with Sierra XR4x4s for chase and supervision purposes. The team, in

The RS200 was as short as possible, and naturally did not have a separate rear bumper. In the case of a collision, the entire rear section would presumably be damaged.

As laid out for rough road rallying at World Rally Championship level.

fact, had not merely turned up to prove they could be there – they wanted to win, and it showed.

Running in two legs from Karlstad, where the total length of the event was 1038 miles/1670km, there would be 30 special stages totalling 347 miles/558km, all of them on snow-covered gravel. Ford would have to face the full Group B might of Austin-Rover, Citroën, Lancia, Mazda and Peugeot, though Audi was no longer competing in Group B at the time.

The first few hours of the event, taking place under the wintry sunshine of a Swedish February, were exciting, intriguing, and puzzling, all at the same time. Although everyone expected the reigning world champion, Timo Salonen, to set the pace in his Peugeot 205 Turbo 16 – which he did by setting fastest times on each of the first six stages – no one, surely, could have expected Stig Blomqvist's RS200 to be quicker than almost everyone else in those hours. In those six stages he was second, third, second, third, fourth and fourth respectively, and was in third place overall, with the car looking neat and competitive; Grundel, the apprentice in the team, was close behind, and also looking serene.

Perhaps it could not last, and indeed it did not, for on the very next stage Salonen's Peugeot retired with a blown engine, and Blomqvist had to delay his RS200, for his car needed a change of engine water pump, which was leaking. Even so, his pace on the next five stages, which led up to the overnight halt back in Karlstad, was unrelenting, especially as at the same time he had seemed to make improvements to the RS200's handling by fitting narrower Pirelli tyres. Fastest time on one of the final stages cheered him up considerably.

Unhappily, the following morning saw most of Ford's fortunes flung into reverse, for although Grundel's RS200 set equal-fastest time of all on the opening stage (with Juha Kankkunen, the eventual winner of the event), everything went wrong for Blomqvist, whose RS200 'just stopped – no bang, no leaking oil, it just stopped', which made the sudden failure sound like an electrical problem.

Ford, therefore, was down to only one RS200 for the remaining 18 special stages; Grundel and his RS200 got on

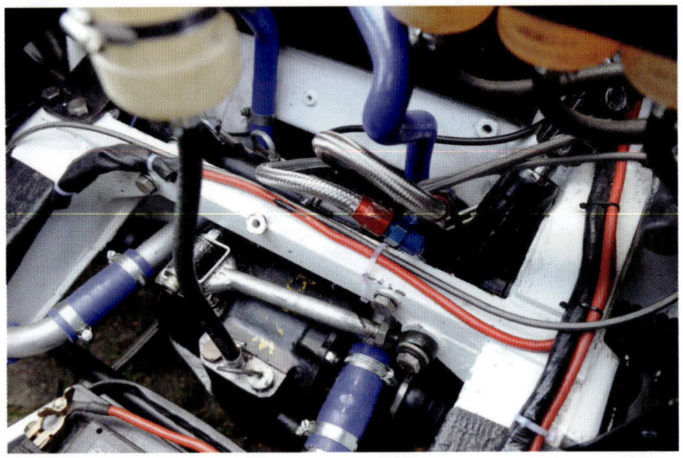

This page: When new in 1986, B200 YEV was one of the very small but exclusive fleet of works rally cars, which had a busy life at Boreham, and with private owners in the years that followed. It has been well and lovingly preserved , and is still in excellent original-type condition.

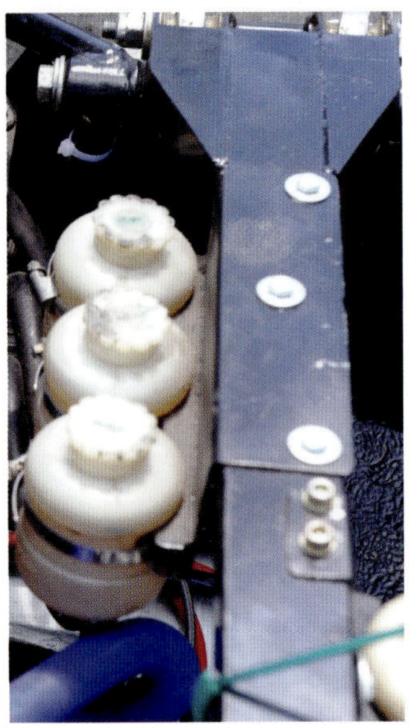

"No one, surely, could have expected Stig Blomqvist's RS200 to be quicker than almost everyone else in those hours. In those six stages he was second, third, second, third, fourth and fourth respectively, and was in third place overall, with the car looking neat and competitive"

Above: The front bodywork fitted as closely as possible around the wheels, and the moulding for the front 'bumper'.

Left: Short, stubby even, but very definitely functional in every inch, shape or emphasis – this shows, too, that the RS200 rally car was by no means near the ground, because efforts were always made to protect the underside from flying stones.

This page: Details of the well-preserved B200 YEV (Car No 14), completed and prepared at Boreham in autumn 1985. In 1986 it competed in Sweden, Portugal, the Circuit of Ireland, South Sweden and the Audi Sport. It also recorded world-record acceleration figures for Autocar *magazine when driving by Stig Blomqvist, sprinting from 0-to-60mph in 2.8 seconds and reaching 100mph in 7.3 seconds – quick even by modern supercar standards 30 years later.*

with the job. With Salonen and Monte-winner Henri Toivonen out of the running, Kalle aimed for third place at least (behind Juha Kankkunen and Markku Alén), though a two-minute visit into a snow bank on SS12 did not help matters.

After a few hours' rest back at Karlstad, the event settled down for its conclusion, with the three leading Group B cars – one Ford, one Lancia Delta S4 and one Peugeot 205 T16 – easily ahead of the rest of the field. Not only did Grundel set out to deliver a measured performance, and to get the RS200 home in its first-ever world championship event, he was still fast. By the end of the day, he had not only set five fastest stage times, one of them (at Häljebyn) was the longest of all in the event, measuring 29.2 miles/47km, which Grundel completed in a sparkling 25 minutes 57 seconds, which was a full 30 seconds faster than the leading Peugeot. Along the way he also finished second-fastest six times, and third-fastest on nine other occasions.

At the end of the day, therefore, Grundel celebrated Ford's return to world championship rallying by taking third place, standing on the podium. With the Rally of Portugal only three weeks ahead, would the same two cars be able to improve on that?

National Breakdown Rally (British Championship round 1) – 21 to 23 February 1986

Although Mark Lovell had already appeared in RS200s, driving as a course car or pilot car on lesser British events in recent weeks, it was the Shells Oils RAC Open Championship on which he was destined to concentrate during the 1986 season.

In January Lovell had turned up on the Bournemouth-based Citroen National Winter Rally in Car No 006 (B340 CAR) but ran uncompetitively as a course car. Its stage times, however, were all recorded, and proved it was not only faster than every other car on this event, but would indeed have won by around three minutes!

Two weeks later, on the same weekend that the RS200 was making its world championship debut in Sweden, Mark once again used B340 CAR. The event was the Skip Brown Rally – which was the first event in the second-division UK National Championship, based at Llandudno in North Wales – and this time he was an official competitor, starting first on the road.

Because B340 CAR was still virtually a road car running

The first British Championship event in Mark Lovell's 1986 programme was the National Breakdown Rally, but a blizzard in the Yorkshire forests played havoc with the stages. Lovell finished fifth.

with the standard 250bhp power unit, it was not expected to be competitive. Nor was it, for in a 14-stage event badly afflicted with snow and ice, it was always credible but not fighting (with David Llewellin's MG Metro 6R4) for the lead. A spin at one point pushed him back to fifth place, which was all that could really have been expected, until on SS10 he hit a large rock on a stage, which badly damaged the front suspension and he was obliged to retire.

Things were much more serious, however, on the National Breakdown Rally (humourists christened it the Nervous Breakdown), when Lovell turned up in a brand-new car – No 062, registered C200 KHJ – which had been prepared by Mike Little Preparations (MLP) of Carlisle before being rushed down to Boreham for a few days of final detail tweaking after the team got back from the Swedish Rally. This was the car Lovell would use throughout the 1986 season (except for the Circuit of Ireland), and would come to a fiery end on the Lombard RAC Rally at the end of the year, without harming either Mark or his co-driver Roger Freeman.

When it first appeared in Bradford, before the start of the National Breakdown, there were real fears that the car might not make it through all the scheduled 45 special stages, and with that in mind, along with Mark Lovell's acknowledged lack of competitive experience in the RS200, the new car reached the start line with little more than the road-car's 250bhp available. It was the team's intention to gradually improve output, by screwing up the turbo boost control, as the event progressed.

Before scrutineering took place, Mike Little's team carried out a precautionary side-of-the-road main gearbox change – 'to see how long it took' – and completed the job in a mere 18 minutes. Little did they know they were actually carrying out a rehearsal for something that would become quite frequent on Lovell's car during the rest of the season.

Visually there was one important change on C200 KHJ from that of the cars that recently appeared in Sweden. As well as the conventional headlamp/driving lamp arrangement (two headlamps in the upper moulding, two driving lamps mounted low down in the front spoiler), MLP had also mounted an extra four-driving-lamp display on the upper moulding, effectively adding to the headlamp alignment. With what amounted to eight full-blast lamps pointing up the road, this was a formidable frontal aspect, which caused some cynics to ask Lovell (sweetly, of course) if he would be wearing 'granny-glasses' throughout.

As it happened, all the preparation for this event, which would mainly be centred in the formidable high-speed forest stages of North Yorkshire, were thrown into confusion by the weather, where blizzard-like conditions had made many stages impassable. In the end, more than half of the original route had to be cancelled, and only 17 of the originally-planned 45 stages took place, reducing the planned 260 miles of stages to a highly-slippery 80. It was no wonder, therefore, that *Autosport*'s report was succinctly headlined *'The white stuff'*.

Although the new RS200 was demonstrably ready to get on the pace, everyone at Ford from Stuart Turner downwards made it clear to MLP, and to Mark Lovell himself, that they wanted to see the RS200 finish, and to get some rough-and-tumble experience.

In view of the awful weather and track conditions, the miracle was that four of the first 15 stages (all tackled overnight, usually with snow falling steadily) took place as planned. Although the RS200 never looked as if it might challenge for the lead, Lovell did a magnificent job of keeping it on track (almost, but not all, the time).

In the Ingleby test, where rally leader Hannu Mikkola had recorded just 4 minutes 49 seconds in his Audi Sport Quattro, Lovell was credited with taking 9 minutes 33 seconds – twice as long – to complete the 4.3 miles. The reason, it transpired, was hilarious, for the RS200 had spun on a narrow track, could not find anywhere to carry out a speedy turn, and was obliged to reverse for some distance down the track to find somewhere – anywhere – it could be accomplished. It was at this juncture that John Haugland's Skoda appeared, dived into a ditch to avoid the RS200, failed, and their joint efforts were required to get things moving again.

"The new car reached the start line with little more than the road-car's 250bhp... It was the team's intention to gradually improve output, by screwing up the turbo boost"

Almost all the second half of the event and its stages had to be cancelled, chaos ensured in and around the North Yorkshire area, and the stragglers finally returned to Bradford. Amazingly, apart from his nose-to-Skoda incident, Lovell managed to keep a virtually-undamaged RS200 going, and was finally rewarded with fifth overall, well behind Hannu Mikkola, who admitted that he had not enjoyed himself, as he had flown into this snowy hell from Florida, where the weather was more welcoming…

C200 KHJ therefore returned to Mike Little Preparations in Carlisle, and would not appear again until May, when Mark Lovell used it on the Welsh Rally.

Rally of Portugal – 5 to 8 March 1986 (World Rally Championship contender)

With only three weeks separating the Swedish Rally from the Rally of Portugal, Ford's works team had to move very swiftly to get back to Boreham and prepare two RS200s for Blomqvist and Grundel to drive in Portugal. They also had to cast an eye over the new Ford-Portugal car, which had originally been constructed at Boreham but was to be run by Diabolique Motorsport. This, Car No 072 (C440 BHV, a London, not Essex, registration number) was to be driven by Joaquim Santos.

The works cars chosen for use in Portugal were those that had already been used in Sweden – B200 YEV (Blomqvist) and B200 YOO (Grundel), and had received a thorough rebuild and freshen-up in an amazing eight days. This time, both cars were lighter than before (the saving was about 66lb/30kg), with the use of a Kevlar sump shield instead of the original Dural being a major factor; several other panels were now formed of carbon fibre or Kevlar, which all helped. As before, a 37/63 front/rear transmission torque split was chosen, and there had been a considerable amount of pre-event testing in Portugal (involving Car No 006, 'the old nail') to establish definitive tarmac and loose-surface spring and damper settings.

The Diabolique Motorsport car was prepared to a similar specification, though the engine was reportedly tuned only to 350bhp, and did not have a Kevlar undershield.

The entry facing the two RS200s was even more fierce than it had been in Sweden, for as usual Peugeot, Lancia and Austin-Rover were present, this time along with Walter Röhrl in an Audi Sport Quattro E2.

> "Stuart Turner made it known that he was uneasy about the way rally spectators were becoming foolhardy"

Based at Estoril, close to Lisbon, split into four distinctly different sectors, and scheduled to include 42 special stages, the rally was the first of the year in which snow and ice was not going to be a factor. On the other hand, because rallying in Portugal was very popular, huge crowds were expected to congregate on the Sintra loop, and so this transpired when the first cars started at 9.00am on a Wednesday morning in March.

Even before the start of the event, director of motorsport Stuart Turner made it known that he was uneasy about the way rally spectators were becoming foolhardy, and that he would have no hesitation in withdrawing works cars if the team judged that to continue was possibly dangerous.

And so it transpired. On the early stages, crowds several deep would gather at every tricky part of a stage (often those following a blind hump), were not controlled by organising officials – who were thin on the ground – and would often stray into the path of competing cars to take photographs, stepping back at the very last moment. Proof of this mad machismo habit exists in the detailed footage taken at the time – there was no exaggeration.

Unhappily and tragically, the forecast of a high-speed accident was confirmed on the first special stage of all, where Santos's RS200 (running at number 15, well after the even faster works cars had passed through) was involved. I am grateful for Martin Holmes's permission to quote from his World Rally 9 book: *'The former Portuguese champion, Joaquim Santos, lost control of his RS200 while driving flat-out over a crest and suddenly finding spectators across the road. A hundred metres further on he was still off-line for a left hander and the car spun off into the crowd on the right.*

'The organisers' lack of control in not immediately stopping the stage completely unnerved following drivers. Some completely lost heart for the fight and cruised through the first three stages…'

The result was horrifying, and the scene was captured by photographers who were clustered at the same point. The RS200 ploughed headlong into the vast crowd, where three people (two of them children) were killed and many more were injured. A fourth person later died in hospital.

The organisers' immediate reaction was to freeze the event, and to cancel the re-running of the Sintra loop. Ford, to its eternal credit, moved even faster, instructing team drivers Stig Blomqvist and Kalle Grundel to withdraw from the event there and then. Within hours, a tidal wave of world-class drivers' opinions led to every member of the works teams – every member, there being no dissenters – refusing to go any further on the event, no matter what their team bosses (and their contracts) might say. Their withdrawal was therefore abrupt, and complete. There is simply no point in trying to find and quote stage times for these first few stages they did contest, for none of them was driving at all fast after news of the accident became known.

As to the two works RS200s, neither was involved in the accident, or going flat-out in the three stages they did complete, so after only a few hours they had been withdrawn, loaded up onto trailers, and were already on their way back to Boreham. That, of course, was the bad news – the good news was they were immediately available for use in other events, and most conveniently that would be in the Circuit of Ireland, which would follow only three weeks later.

Rothmans Circuit of Ireland - 28 March to 1 April 1986

With the 1986 rally season now gathering momentum, and with Boreham committed to a World Rally Championship programme of its own, plus technical assistance to teams such as Mike Little Preparations (for Mark Lovell) and Ford-Belgium (Robert Droogmans), RS200 outings became more and more frequent.

For the Rothmans-sponsored Circuit of Ireland, therefore (an Easter-weekend event using many public roads, closed for the occasion, as the location of almost all 51 special stages), Ford entered two RS200s, one driven by Kalle Grundel.

Both cars were those that had started the Rally of Portugal in early March but (as noted above) had been withdrawn after completing virtually no high-speed motoring. This meant Mark Lovell was in B200 YEV (ex-Blomqvist), while Kalle Grundel used B200 YOO, as he had already done in Sweden, and briefly in Portugal.

Boreham, no doubt, had been delighted to send these two cars to Belfast, for it allowed the team to get on with building fresh recce cars (at least one of which would also appear in the Fram Filters Welsh Rally a few weeks hence), and to prepare entirely new rough-road machines for use in the forthcoming Acropolis event.

Except in minor detail, the two Circuit cars were running in their Portugal condition, though recent testing had resulted in the use of further changes to spring and damper settings. This meant Mark Lovell was to run in a car with the full-house 420bhp engine for the very first time.

Once again there was drama involving an RS200, all the fault of the spectator who dashed across the tarmac road of a stage ahead of the fast-moving car, in which Grundel tried to steer off the road to avoid him but could not do so; after a spell in hospital the spectator recovered, and the RS200 was only lightly damaged (though the windscreen was smashed), but for a time the Swedish driver was badly shaken. Even so, by this stage both RS200s were in gearbox trouble, and complete unit changes were necessary before they could get back on the pace, where – as became usual in a British event of 1986 – the main opposition came from a number of MG Metro 6R4s.

At the end of the first day, Grundel's RS200 was back up to sixth place, with Lovell not far behind, but for Grundel there was little time to relax, for his car needed a new rear axle unit, and a replacement rear driveshaft. As the rear axle was a separate casting, mounted below and behind the engine, it

Kalle Grundel was fast but unsuccessful on the Circuit of Ireland in 1986, for although he was always among the leaders, he was forced to retire.

Mark Lovell finished fourth on the 1986 Circuit of Ireland in spite of his RS200 breaking selector pins in the gearbox no fewer than six times.

was more of a nuisance than a major operation. Lovell, on the other hand, was rapidly coming to terms with 420bhp, but his main gearbox needed attention, which allowed the MLP team a chance to show off their expertise by making the change in a mere 12 minutes. Unhappily, there would be more such enforced changes to be made in the future. MLP admitted to replacing the RS200's 'box six times during the weekend, each time to replace a damaged selector pin.

In the next 24 hours, which led the rally all the way down through the Irish Republic to an overnight halt at Waterford, Lovell began to climb steadily up through the field, holding down eighth place (and more to come) at this point. Although fifth at the time, Grundel, on the other hand, disappeared briefly into a field at one point ("Thank goodness I have four-wheel-drive," he quipped), and suffered from a dislodged intercooler-to-turbocharger pipe on another occasion, which was easily remedied.

The traditional Easter Sunday run – ten stages from Waterford and back to Waterford – was eventful for Ford. On the one hand Grundel dropped out, and on the other Lovell, now on terms with the full-power RS200, muscled his way up to fifth overall. Grundel's demise was at once farcical, and terminal, for although his RS200 suffered a puncture (which would not normally have been more than a nuisance), the ruined rear tyre tread thrashed around, ripped its way through several internal pipes and wires in the engine bay, and brought the car to a stuttering halt.

Lovell, for his part, was always setting times in the top four, and even recorded fastest times of the day on more than one occasion. After the early months, when it had begun to look as if Boreham was mollycoddling him, he was showing just how rapid he was. Taking the loop as a separate rally, Lovell was fastest of all and would move up to fifth, just a minute behind Jimmy McRae's Rothmans MG Metro 6R4. Even so, the day was not without drama for his RS200, which suffered a faulty main gearbox yet again (another failing pin in the selector mechanism), the MLP mechanics getting more used to making roadside changes, as they would continue throughout the season.

The final day/night run back north through Ireland to the finish in Belfast was stirring and exciting, not only for the spectators but for the leading drivers too. With one of Lovell's leading rivals – Irishman Billy Coleman, of all people, driving a Porsche 911 – crashing out, Mark moved up to fourth overall, and would come within 22 seconds of getting onto the RS200's first podium. On the final night, although hampered by – guess what – a transmission problem, Lovell set fastest time after fastest time, but finally had to settle for

Stig Blomqvist took this brand-new works car – C200 LWC – on the 1986 Welsh Rally, set many fastest stage times, but was eliminated near the end of the event when his RS200 suffered a rear suspension breakage.

position four.

All in all, it was an encouraging time for the RS200. But the transmission problem would have to be sorted out – and rapidly too.

Fram Filters Welsh Rally - 3 to 4 May 1986

Only four weeks after the Circuit of Ireland had ended, the next event in the British championship – the Welsh – started from Cardiff. The two events could not be more different in character – the Circuit had mainly been contested on tarmac public roads that had been closed for the occasion, whereas the vast majority of the Welsh would be on forestry tracks. To Ford, this seemed like an ideal way of unleashing Stig Blomqvist in an RS200 (in Portugal, after all, he had completed only three stages, at low speeds, before the team's withdrawal).

Accordingly, a brand-new rally-prepared RS200 – C200 LWC – was sent down to Wales, the strategy being that it would then go off to be a recce car for the Acropolis Rally, which would follow at the end of May. Incidentally, this would be the first British rally that Stig had tackled since November 1983, when he had won the Lombard RAC event. Mark Lovell was reunited with the RS200 (C200 KHJ) in which he had finished a very tentative fifth in the snowbound National Breakdown event.

This, though, was not the only major change, for following the Circuit of Ireland, Mark Lovell had parted company with his original co-driver Peter Davis (the personal problems between them were never publicly spelt out), who had been replaced by Roger Freeman. Roger was very new to this project, for he had not even been in an RS200 before the start of the Welsh, and his colourful (and very chat-show-friendly) comments could often reduce an audience to tears of laughter in later interviews.

Ford, and Mike Little Preparations, had put every effort behind the preparation of the two RS200s that turned up at the start in Cardiff. Both were in full-house international specification, with one Ford source claiming 435bhp from the latest 1803cc engine, and both cars running with a newly-strengthened gearbox linkage.

This was an event where both RS200s were competitive and would battle for many hours with Hannu Mikkola's Audi Quattro and Jimmy McRae's MG Metro 6R4. It is no more than event shorthand to report that Blomqvist would set no fewer than ten fastest stage times, and Lovell two, but there was never an occasion (except for breakages and nudges with the scenery) when the cars were uncompetitive.

The cars' troubles were several, various, and irritatingly

trivial. First it was Lovell, whose engine shed an intercooler feed hose after a particularly heavy landing (he lost two whole minutes in one stage, struggling along with what was effectively a normally-aspirated 1.8-litre RS200), then Blomqvist's car suffered a gearbox problem that meant the lack of reverse gear (but who should need reverse on a rally?).

"Stig had a marvellously serene run in his native country, finally taking victory more than four minutes ahead"

Even so, when the cars later left a brief rest halt in Aberystwyth, both RS200s found themselves battling for the outright lead, sharing fastest stage times and looking impressive on the slippery surfaces of the Welsh forests.

Then the troubles set in again. First it was Lovell whose car suffered a rear wheel puncture in the Dyfi stage, and soon afterwards it was Blomqvist's turn to suffer a blowout, which led to him driving nearly ten miles on a flat. More punctures followed on the Hafren stage, when both cars suffered a great loss of time even though they did not stop to change wheels.

Although Blomqvist was sure he could have challenged Mikkola's Quattro for the lead, fate conspired against him. Just six stages from the end of the event, a rear suspension wishbone on Blomqvist's car broke catastrophically (seemingly caused by earlier damage due to flailing punctured tyres), which threw the car (which had, of course been brand-new before this event started) off the road in the Trawscoed stage, where it was left marooned and immobile.

For Mark Lovell, at least, there was better (if not perfect) news, for he kept his car going to the very end, always competitively, and thoroughly deserving the third place it eventually took. Most of the car's endemic transmission problems seemed to have been solved, Lovell's morale was rising steadily, and he was looking forward to the rest of a highly competitive season.

A brief halt in the heat of Greece, where the works team was practising before the 1986 Acropolis Rally. Left to right: Stig Blomqvist, Bruno Berglund, Kalle Grundel and Benny Melander.

South Sweden Rally – 16 to 18 May 1986

Some rally cars work hard for their living, and B200 YEV, which had been brand-new in February 1986 for Stig Blomqvist to drive in the Swedish Rally, was one of them. Only days after it had been involved in an accident on the Circuit of Ireland (see above), Boreham had refreshed the car and sent it to Sweden for Stig Blomqvist to contest the South Sweden event. Although this was not a world event, it attracted two RS200s (the other being Stig Andervang in the car he was already using in Holland and other European countries), where both faced up to Björn Waldegård in a full-works Toyota Celica Twin-Cam Turbo.

Stig had a marvellously serene run in his native country, finally taking victory more than four minutes ahead of Andervang in the other RS200 and – most importantly – six minutes ahead of the Toyota. This was not only encouraging for Ford, but for Stig, who was recording his first victory in an RS200.

Acropolis Rally, Greece – 2 to 4 June 1986 (World Rally Championship contender)

Because Ford had never intended to enter the Tour de Corse at the beginning of May, RS200s were not present on Corsica when the tragic accident that claimed the lives of Henri Toivonen and Sergio Cresto (in a Lancia Delta S4) took place, not only casting a gloom over the whole scene of world rallying but bringing the future of Group B rallying into doubt. Indeed, soon after this awful accident had been investigated, FISA decided to kill off Group B rallying for larger-capacity machines at the end of 1986 – and therefore signalled the premature end of the RS200 project almost as soon as it had begun.

Boreham, however, was well into the preparation of brand-new RS200s for the Acropolis Rally by this time. It was an event in which Ford, historically, had always shone with Escorts, for works cars had won several times in recent decades – three times on the run from 1979 to 1981, incidentally – and much was expected of the new cars.

Unhappily, things started to go wrong from the start, when Kalle Grundel's practice car (the ageing but still hard-working B55 CHK, which had made the RS200's debut in the Lindisfarne only months earlier) was consumed by fire in Greece and totally burnt-out. This was thought to be due to an experimentally relocated engine oil cooler being damaged by a flying stone, which let out hot engine oil close to the exhaust system – and the result was inevitable.

That was the bad news, whereas the good news was that practice showed just how effective the RS200's long-travel suspension was on rough tracks. It was at this point that, quite unofficially, John Wheeler went out on a stage with his old friend Hannu Mikkola driving an Audi Sport Quattro, finding that, because of its suspension difficulties, this ultra-powerful machine was quite uncontrollable by anyone except the Finnish world champion. This was different from the RS200, which could be driven flat-out using all of its well-controlled suspension travel and damping.

For this event, centred in Athens – always noted for the high ambient temperatures in which it was usually run, and for the rough and high-speed special stages incorporated – the team at Boreham had prepared two brand new cars: starting number 2 (B200 AYD), driven by Stig Blomqvist/Bruno Berglund; and starting number 6 (B200 XVX), by Kalle Grundel/Benny Melander.

Compared with the cars that had started in Portugal, these machines were fitted with larger cooling radiators, and the fresh air collected by the 'bunny ears' in the roof was rerouted towards cooling the engine and transmission oil coolers. Both cars had been thoroughly run-in, and tested, before the event, and team bosses were confident that this might yet be their best chance, so far, of gaining a world championship victory.

Right from the start, the RS200s seemed to relish the rough going. Grundel was fastest of all – beating the works Lancias and Peugeots on the first stage – while Blomqvist was never far behind, and was fastest on SS5. Unfortunately for Stig, B200 AYD broke a rear shock absorber, which sprayed oil towards a

The works RS200s had only just begun to show their pace when FIA culled the Group B category. This was Stig Blomqvist enjoying himself on the Acropolis Rally.

Stig Blomqvist pushing on a typically rough gravel stage of the 1986 Acropolis Rally, which he led briefly, before retiring after 17 stages, when he put the car off the road.

B200 XVX was a brand-new heavyweight works RS200 made ready for Kalle Grundel to drive in the 1986 Acropolis Rally. After setting two fastest stage times, and leading the event for a time on the second day, it was forced to retire when broken wheel studs caused the car to lose a wheel, and to plunge off the track.

hot exhaust pipe and started a fire (which he was able to douse during a brief emergency halt). Even so, after seven stages, at the first halt in Lagonissi, Grundel was handily placed, just 26 seconds off the lead. Blomqvist was fourth, only seven seconds behind his teammate.

Soon Grundel was back in the lead, which he would hold for the next five stages, which apparently caused the usually urbane Lancia team boss Cesare Fiorio to comment: "Now that we have got rid of the Peugeot for the moment, the bloody Fords are in the way!" And so they were, for Blomqvist had started to take time out of his teammate, and both were looking to secure the overall lead.

And so it was until stage 18, when Grundel had suffered the misfortune of having the wheel studs on his RS200 break off in the controlled frenzy of a service halt, which necessitated a hub change, and he ran out of time. Many minutes later, and driving through the very next stage on his way to regaining a public highway, Kalle then encountered Blomqvist's car off the track, nose down and tail in the air, and quite immovable. Right away, and having been first and second in the event, both the RS200s found themselves eliminated.

Lloyds Bowmaker Scottish Rally – 7 to 10 June 1986

Encouraged by the team's promising performance in the recent Welsh rally, MLP redoubled the efforts to make C200 KHJ as good as new once again, and sent Mark Lovell out to improve on his recent fifth, fourth and third places in British Championship rounds. By this time, though still a little heavier than the contemporary Boreham-maintained examples, this car was fully up to World Rally Championship specifications.

Although the bare statistics show Mark Lovell took second place, six minutes behind the winning Peugeot 205 T16, they do not demonstrate just how consistently fast he was (except for stage 41, Twiglees, as will be explained), or that he set fastest stage times on ten occasions.

For the oddest of seeding reasons, the RS200 started the event at number 9, which put it at a slight disadvantage because the stage surfaces were already being churned up when he arrived. But Mark had more on his mind, for he was having to compete with Mikael Sundström's Peugeot 205 T16, and also two works Toyota Celica Twin-Cam Turbos of Björn Waldegård and Lars-Erik Torph.

In an event where the fleet of MG Metro 6R4s, both works and private, gradually disappeared with a spate of engine failures, Mark eventually found himself behind Sundström's Peugeot, and although seemingly close, he saw no immediate chance of taking over the lead. Hampered by a gearbox failure on the very first stage (but it cost him only one minute), he then settled down to fight back towards the lead, with stage times usually only a handful of seconds behind those of the Peugeot. As the cars reached the night halt on their return to Glasgow, the RS200 was up to third place, with the leader

In the early stages of the 1986 Scottish Rally, Mark Lovell was always fighting for the lead until a massive rollover accident caused him to lose time – yet he still managed to take second place overall.

(Malcolm Wilson in an ailing MG Metro 6R4) about to retire.

On the next five stages Lovell then set fastest outright times on four occasions, taking a total of 11 seconds away from Sundström's lead. But on the very next stage, Twiglees, disaster overtook him. He overcooked a right-hander, closely followed by a left-hander, and there, in front of TV video crews (you can still see it on the internet), he rolled the RS200. As Mark later quoted, "I think we went off, landed on the roof or side, and bounced out. Spectators helped us back, and we did not lose too much time, but of course had to drive to the end of the stage with a crazed windscreen."

The bodywork was in something of a mess, which might explain the humorous aftermath of an exchange heard on the radios in the next few minutes. Co-driver Roger Freemen called the waiting Ford service crew, told them they'd had an accident and asked if they would 'please get the body sections out'. "Which ones?" was the response from Ford's technicians, to which Roger apparently replied, "All of them!"

Amazingly, the MLP team was able to rectify much of the obvious visual damage (the running gear not apparently being harmed), though the crew did not continue quite as fast as in the preceding hours. All in all, however, it had been a remarkable performance, and a remarkable recovery – for Mark was rewarded with second place.

It was at this time that Ford Motorsport had to make a series of big decisions, not only about the future of the RS200 as an ultra-powerful Group B rally car, and not only as far as future years were concerned, but even as pressing as to what to do about the rest of the current season. Whereas Peugeot and Lancia had monumentally higher budgets on which to draw, both had ambitions to win the 1986 championship, and were determined to compete in all the remaining events.

Not only that, but with the FIA insisting that world rallying would be for Group A cars in the future, Boreham could see it would have to spend a lot of a time working up the specifications of the Escort RS Turbo, Sierra XR4x4 and Sierra RS Cosworth.

Stuart Turner, ruthless, logical and fully cognisant of the public and political pressures that surrounded rally sport at this time, was quite open about speedily closing down the RS200 programme. Originally, works cars would have been entered for the 1000 Lakes in Finland, and possibly

One of Mark Lovell's finest drives in 1986 was on the all-tarmac Ulster Rally, where he finished second overall.

for San Remo, but once the impending end of Group B was confirmed, these entries were promptly annulled. For the obvious national, local and publicity reasons, works entries in the remainder of the British championship (for Mark Lovell, and even for Grundel and Blomqvist) were retained, and it seemed that a positive fleet of RS200s would contest the Lombard RAC Rally as their final fling in November.

Because FISA had also outlawed further development of evolution cars, such as Ford's intention to finalise a lighter and faster RS200 for works use in 1987 (the 100-100 model: 100bhp more and 100kg lighter), to John Wheeler's and Brian Hart's great sorrow, all work on evolving that car was immediately cancelled. Ford, however, was not about to miss a trick, even if this was a sad and rather short story. Only weeks after the truncation of the programme had been announced, the company held a press conference, revealing the phenomenally powerful Hart-developed BDT-E engine, which was to have powered the 100-100 Evolution car. This compact 2.1-litre unit was claimed to have 'only' 506bhp as shown, but could easily be boosted to 580bhp – and, as it transpired, was proven to be capable of at least 650bhp when later used in rallycross versions of the RS200.

Ford, as ever, was pragmatic about this fast-developing political situation, so not only did the team shrug their shoulders philosophically and get on with the development of Group A Sierra XR4x4s and RS Cosworths for 1987, they released Stig Blomqvist and Kalle Grundel from their contracts so that they could drive other cars for the remainder of the year, before returning to Boreham for one final fling with works RS200s on the Lombard RAC Rally.

British Midland Ulster Rally – 8 to 9 August 1986

Ford was determined to give Mark Lovell every possible chance to win the RAC British Open Rally Championship in the hard-working MLP-prepared RS200. Immediately after the Scottish Rally, the team had reprepared the battered car, then gone to carry out tarmac-surface testing in Southern Ireland. Not only was much work done on improving the engine bay cooling layout, but a mountain of development resulted in the use of new-type brakes, and what looked like racing-type external vanes on the outer surfaces of the road wheels themselves. As a result, Lovell was confident that the car was up to two seconds per mile faster than it had previously been when last it visited Ireland.

For the Ulster, however, much of the sting of a carefully-planned 29-stage event was negated by FIA's insistence on making changes to slow down some stages, and by requiring less demanding target times. This had been done as one of many knee-jerk reactions to the awful events of the Tour de Corse, and as it happened, meant no fewer than seven of the first ten stages could be cleaned by the top drivers, with six further cleanable sections later in the event.

As to the real rallying itself, Lovell immediately set about scrapping with the two leading MG Metro 6R4s of Jimmy McRae and David Llewellin, and Mikael Sundstrom's Peugeot 205 T16, but although his car (and theirs) was demonstrably quicker than ever before, it did not show up in the computer's brain, where car after car broke the target times, not just by seconds but occasionally by more than a minute. Ridiculous – but there was no getting around the new restrictions.

Not that the RS200 was able to cruise, and not that it was totally reliable. Even in the opening hours, Lovell's car needed a new main gearbox (but what was new?), and on stage nine there was a real scare when Lovell radioed in to say he had only front-wheel drive. As Mark later quoted to the media, "It wasn't too clever trying to drive with 420bhp going through the front wheels only. It was a bit like driving last year's Escort RS Turbo, except that I was getting wheelspin in all five gears!" Even so, because of FISA's diktat on target times, the RS200 lost only 28 seconds on that stage...

> "Trying to drive with 420bhp going through the front wheels only... was a bit like driving last year's Escort RS Turbo, except that I was getting wheelspin in all five gears"

According to the computer, after the overnight halt in Belfast, McRae's 6R4 was leading by – wait for it – just eight seconds. But soon Lovell, from third place, began to set fastest times that were not quite matching the targets, and battle appeared to be joined, especially as Llewellin (in the other competitive 6R4) reduced it to scrap in a high-speed accident. Lovell was now second, little more than one minute away from the lead. For a few heady hours it looked as if the deficit could be chipped away, but the easy-target syndrome proved too much to overcome, so the team opted to cruise home, still second, highly encouraged by what had transpired. In any case, and this was certainly a factor, Lovell was now leading the entire championship, with only one further qualifier (the all-tarmac Manx) to come.

Tudor Webasto Manx International Rally – 11 to 13 September 1986

In the run-up to the Manx, there was much pre-start speculation of the potential fate of the championship struggle. With just this one event to run, Mark Lovell's RS200 led the series, closely harassed by Russell Brookes (Opel Manta 400) and Jimmy McRae (MG Metro 6R4). On this all-tarmac event, any of them, it seemed, were good enough to win the event, and any of them were quite capable of lifting the championship crown at the last gasp.

Because the familiar RS200 (C200 KHJ) had performed so well in the Ulster Rally, Ford and MLP made very few changes to its specification for the 30 scheduled tarmac stages on the Isle of Man, where all the high-speed motoring was scheduled to take place in daylight, over three days. Regrettably, the

Mark Lovell enjoyed a meteoric rise to fame in 1986, for he took to the RS200 with real enthusiasm, started and finished every British Rally Championship round – and won the championship outright.

latest FISA edicts on special stage target times meant straw-bale-type chicanes were inserted in a number of those sections, the result being that no fewer than 12 were cleanable.

Tony Pond, having become a highly-paid member of the Austin-Rover world championship team, was at the time living on the Isle of Man as a tax exile so, having spent much spare time in unofficial practice on his new home roads was reckoned to be the firm favourite to win. He and Jimmy McRae were the fastest of no fewer than five drivers who had been provided with MG Metro 6R4s for this event.

With Lovell's RS200 setting fastest stage times right from the start, in the end he would record fastest, or equal fastest, on no fewer than 17 occasions (some of them when he and his rivals all beat the bogey times). This soon settled down to an RS200 versus Metro 6R4 battle, with Lovell, McRae, Pond and Llewellin all involved. By the end of the first day Pond's Metro was leading, and the RS200 had slipped to fifth place because – guess what – it had needed a main gearbox change.

On the second day, Lovell continued to be as fast, sometimes faster than the Metros, which soon began to wilt. The sensation of the day was that McRae's Metro engine suddenly expired, and the car coasted to a silent halt in front of several influential press representatives. By comparison, the third and final day's sport was less sensational. Pond and Llewellin continued their winning ways, and in spite of setting several fastest outright times, Lovell and the RS200 had to settle for third place.

Even so, it was enough to ensure championship victory, which left the ever-hopeful Brookes 12 points in arrears and no other Group B driver able to mount a consistent challenge.

Audi Sport Rally (Wales) – 11 October 1986

In mid October, and really as a warm-up to the forthcoming Lombard RAC Rally, Boreham decided all three of its leading UK-based RS200 drivers should get a chance to drive the cars once again on gravel stages. The event chosen – the Audi Sport – was the final qualifying round in the National Rally Championship, and though having its start and finish in the Midlands, had almost all of its competitive mileage in Wales.

The simple way to describe this event is that it was almost, if not quite, a clean sweep for the works RS200s, for each and every one of the special stages was won by an RS200 – six with Stig Blomqvist at the wheel, two of them Mark Lovell, and one by Kalle Grundel.

Although Lovell had his usual car – C200 KHJ – in which he was also intent on starting the Lombard RAC Rally, the two Boreham-based machines were those that had opened the team's world career in Sweden, Portugal, and the Circuit of Ireland. In the Audi Sport event, B200 YOO was to be driven by Blomqvist, and B200 YEV by Grundel.

Here, effectively, the men were to show the boys how to drive, for all the RS200s were demonstrably superior to the Metro 6R4s present (though, in fairness, there were no works 6R4s). As Keith Oswin of *Autosport* commented in his post-rally report: *'Stig Blomqvist calmly demolished the opposition to win at a canter… while teammate Kalle Grundel took third after a troubled day.'* The hero in second place, who also won the National Championship title, was Alistair Sutherland in his Metro 6R4.

The three RS200s led from the very start, and in the first two long gravel forestry stages Dyfnant and Gartheiniog (11 and 15 miles long respectively) it was Mark Lovell, not either of the Swedish superstars, who led the entire field by 25 seconds after just three stages. Unhappily for Mark, he then overdid it in the very next stage (Dyfi Main), putting the car well off the track where it could not be retrieved until every other competitor had gone through. As it happens, there appeared to be no damage ('except to the driver's morale' co-driver Roger Freeman later commented), and the car resumed during the afternoon session, untimed but testing tyres.

Except for Grundel's car suffering not only from a clutch problem, and then a puncture (why did it always seem to be Grundel's ill-fortune in 1986?) the two surviving RS200s clearly had the measure of every other car in this national-permit event, and ran out first and third. All the portents for the forthcoming Lombard RAC Rally looked promising…

Lombard RAC Rally – 16 to 19 November 1986

Having kept well clear of world rallying after the Acropolis Rally (and therefore not wasting money on a development programme that would be stymied by a change in regulations after the end of the year), Boreham got clearance to prepare and run three RS200s, and at the same time to offer support to multi-championship winner Stig Andervang in the Ford-of-Holland machine.

With several near-fresh cars on the works fleet, there was no need to build new machines, but merely to prepare what would doubtless be seen as the best of a dying breed. These, therefore, were the four RS200s that eventually took the start from Bath…

Right: Mark Lovell (left) and Roger Freeman were very successful in the 1986 British Rally Championship, finishing every round and winning the series outright.

B200 AYD (Stig Blomqvist/Bruno Berglund), new for the 1986 Acropolis and unused since then, would start at number 2; B200 XVX (Kalle Grundel/Benny Melander), also new for the Acropolis, and also unused since then, would start at number 6; C200 KHJ (Mark Lovell/Roger Freeman) was Lovell's familiar British Championship car, which had recently crashed out of the Audi Sport event, but had then been thoroughly reprepared by Mike Little Preparations. It would start at number 12; C200 JJN (Stig Andervang/Dave West), backed by Ford-of-Holland but maintained by Mike Taylor Preparations of Yorkshire, had already been rallied intensively in Europe, and had even made an unsuccessful dash to India to tackle the Rally of the Himalayas. Its exploits are described in full in Chapter 7. It would start at number 18.

Although it was good to see the cars seeded so high in the field, it brought a minor concern to Peter Ashcroft and the back-up team of mechanics that on some occasions all four cars looked likely to descend on a service point in a closely-packed group.

Although the works team had not entered full World Rally Championship events in recent months, John Wheeler and his team had still found time to carry out further development and improvement of the cars. Probably the most important change was that the 1.8-litre engines had been further improved, and were now officially rated at 450bhp (though unofficially they were thought to be even more powerful), this being due to a combination of increased turbo boost, different camshaft profiles, and more recent electronic control of the engines themselves. They were not, repeat not, running in 2.1-litre guise.

In addition, the oil cooling system had been simplified, and smaller fuel tanks had been fitted (not only to save weight but to provide extra and much-needed space close to the engine bay), the front/rear transmission torque split had been standardised at 46 per cent front/54 per cent rear, different spring and damper settings had been adopted, and the very latest in Pirelli forest tyres had been adopted. In the small theatre of world rallying, it was now acknowledged by all teams that at this time the RS200 handled better than all its rivals on rough and loose surfaces.

The early stages – from Bath to Harrogate on the first day – were mainly tarmac extravaganzas set to entertain the mass

B200 AYD seems to have been Stig Blomqvist's favourite RS200, though it let him down on the 1986 Lombard RAC Rally by blowing its engine after 26 stages.

World rallying is not always glamorous. This was Stig Blomqvist's car, in service in the dark, on the Lombard RAC Rally of 1986.

of spectators who were flocking to see this, the very last, of the major European Group B rallies. Blomqvist's RS200 led briefly, but the big battle was already with Juha Kankkunen's Peugeot 205 T16, and the other Peugeots and Lancia Delta S4s that surrounded him.

The second and third of four legs – Harrogate to Ingliston, an overnight halt, then Ingliston to a further overnight stop in Liverpool – were hard-fought, but no harder than what was happening to the fleet of RS200s. Blomqvist's engine struck trouble after leaving Ingliston, and although he continued gamely, retirement on stage 27 was inevitable. In the meantime, Andervang's car finally gave up the ghost of being probably the hardest-used of all RS200s, by suffering major chassis breakages and having to be withdrawn. Unfortunately for the hot-tempered Swedish driver, this was about the time that he had an argument with another competitor who had been reluctant to pull over on a special stage so that the RS200 could pass it, and blows were exchanged. The long-term result was that Andervang was thrown out of the Dutch team and took no further part in Ford's motorsport activities.

Mark Lovell's retirement, which came on stage 21, just before the Ingliston halt, was altogether more sudden and dramatic. Having suffered a serious delay in an earlier stage (Ogre Hill), he was trying hard to make up ground on the Cardrona stage, when the RS200 suddenly caught fire and was speedily consumed, in the middle of the stage, way beyond any hope of the fire being put out. The car was completely gutted, so in modern times if anyone ever tells you they own Mark Lovell's 'RAC championship-winning car', they should not be believed – the VIN number perhaps, but the car itself? Never!

The good news was that neither of the occupants – Mark Lovell and Roger Freeman – were even slightly injured in the fire. Because it now counts as a funny story, the author recalls talking to Freeman some time later, who said, "When the fire broke out, we both legged it to safety as soon as possible, and were of course on opposite sides of the car. There was a moment when we both feared that the other had been trapped in the flames, so the reunion was a great relief."

All of this left Kalle Grundel to keep going in the sole surviving RS200, but by then he was running ninth, and although competitive, was already 2 minutes 43seconds behind the leading Lancia Delta S4. For the rest of the event, and particularly after the second night halt in Liverpool, without suffering any major disasters in the arduous Welsh sections, Grundel gradually clawed his way up the field, along the way setting two second-fastest times, five thirds, five fourths and no fewer than seven fastest stage times. His reward was a fighting fifth overall, having defended a concerted attack by four Metro 6R4s, of which Tony Pond ended up less than a minute behind him. Ahead, partially benefiting from reliability, partly from long-term expertise, were three works Peugeot 205 T16s and a single Lancia Delta S4.

Memorial Bettega Rallysprint (Bologna, Italy) – 13 December 1986)

After the disappointment of the Lombard RAC Rally, there was just one more opportunity for works RS200s to compete in public and show just how good they were, this being the

Following the disastrous fire that consumed Mark Lovell's RS200 on the 1986 RAC Rally, not much remained for the mechanics to take back to the workshops.

Kalle Grundel drove B200 XVX (his ex-Acropolis car) into fifth place in the 1986 Lombard RAC Rally.

ULTIMATE PERFORMANCE – A WORKS RALLY CAR TESTED

Just before the end of the 1986 rally season, the works team decided it really should establish just how fast the latest RS200 machines were, and set aside one of the existing fleet for superstar driver Stig Blomqvist to drive while cooperating with *Autocar* magazine, which provided the latest timing gear to prove the point.

The car chosen was B200 YEV – Car No 14 – an already well-used machine that in a mere ten months had completed five international rallies, along with a great deal of testing, reconnaissance and general development, and was fresh from an impressive outing in the British Audi Sport Rally (held in Wales), with Kalle Grundel at the wheel.

Tested at Boreham on a cold October day, B200 YEV was running a full-works standard 1.8-litre engine, rated at 450bhp at 8000rpm, and with lowered gearing to suit its previous rally specification. Shod with Pirelli racing tyres, it proved to be quite astonishingly fast, as these acceleration figures confirm.

*On this car, the electronic engine rev limit was set at 8900rpm.
Because of the rally gearing chosen, this car ran out of revs at a mere 118mph when the limiter cut in, having recorded a set of figures that, as far as is known, were the most outstanding of any road machine at that point in history.

ACCELERATION	SECONDS
0-30mph	1.2
0-40mph	1.8
0-50mph	2.2
0-60mph	2.8
0-70mph	3.8
0-80mph	4.8
0-90mph	5.9
0-100mph	7.3
0-110mph	8.7

MAX SPEED IN GEARS	MPH	@ RPM*
1st	42	8900
2nd	63	8900
3rd	79	8900
4th	97	8900
5th	118	8900

GROUP B RALLY SUCCESSES 1985 - 86

1985	EVENT	DRIVER	RESULT
SEPTEMBER	Lindisfarne (UK)	M Wilson	1st

1986	EVENT	DRIVER	RESULT
JANUARY	Numedal (Norway)	S Blomqvist	2nd
FEBRUARY	Swedish	K Grundel	3rd
	National Breakdown (UK)	M Lovell	5th
MARCH	Ardennes (Belgium)	R Droogmans	1st
	Centro (Portugal)	J Santos	1st
	Circuit of Ireland	M Lovell	4th
APRIL	Tulip (Holland)	S Andervang	1st
	Swiss event	C Jacquillard	4th
	Hellendoorn (Holland)	S Andervang	1st
	Sierra Morena (Spain)	A Zanini	2nd
MAY	Welsh	M Lovell	3rd
	Rota do Sol (Portugal)	J Santos	1st
	Haspengouw (Belgium)	R Droogmans	1st
	South Sweden	S Blomqvist	1st
		S Andervang	2nd
	Llanes Asturias (Spain)	A Zanini	4th
	Wallonia (Belgium)	R Droogmans	1st
JUNE	Scottish	M Lovell	2nd
	Santa Cruz (Spain)	A Zanini	1st
	Ypres 24 Hr (Belgium)	R Droogmans	1st
JULY	El Corte Inglés (Spain)	A Zanini	2nd
	Hunsrück (German)	S Andervang	2nd
AUGUST	Ulster	M Lovell	2nd
	Limburg (Holland)	S Andervang	1st
	Bianchi (Belgium)	R Droogmans	1st
		S Andervang	4th
SEPTEMBER	Manx International	M Lovell	2nd
	Monroe (Denmark)	S Andervang	1st
	Loop van Flanders (Belgium)	R Droogmans	1st
	Asturias (Spain)	A Zanini	3rd
	Alto Tâmega (Portugal)	J Santos	1st
OCTOBER	Grensland (Belgium)	S Andervang	1st
		R Droogmans	2nd
	Audi National (UK)	S Blomqvist	1st
		K Grundel	3rd
	San Froilan (Spain)	A Zanini	2nd
	Rally du Valais (Switzerland)	R Droogmans	1st
NOVEMBER	Algarve (Portugal)	J Santos	1st
	RAC	K Grundel	5th
DECEMBER	Bettega Memorial (Italy)	S Blomqvist	4th
		M Schanche	6th

CHAMPIONSHIP VICTORIES IN 1986	
West Euro Cup	Stig Andervang
Dutch Open Rally Championship	Stig Andervang
British Open Rally Championship	Mark Lovell
Belgian Open Rally Championship	Robert Droogmans

widely-publicised Bettega Memorial Rallysprint, which was a media spectacular run in a converted car park alongside the Bologna Motor Show premises in Italy, the harum-scarum events being transmitted to millions of TV viewers in Italy.

Like many such events that followed, the Bettega was run on a tightly-cornered, straw-baled but tarmac-surfaced course, stadium-based and laid out so that each mano-a-mano duel between two superstars would eventually lead to eliminations – all in front of TV cameras. Tight? Indeed – for in the preliminary runs held on the day before TV transmission, Blomqvist's RS200 led the lists, at an average speed of only 38.8mph. With drizzle forecast for the final day, it looked as if there might be all manner of incidents.

Attracted by the favourable publicity that must surely follow (and even though they were preparing to dispose of the RS200 fleet to potential rallycross customers), the hard-working team at Boreham spent a few days preparing two cars. For the record, these were B200 AYD for Stig Blomqvist, the car in which he had recently competed in the Lombard RAC Rally, while the hard-working C200 LWC was allocated to no less than Norwegian rallycross champion Martin Schanche, and was fitted with an early example of the Hartpower-developed 2.1-litre BDT-E, which developed 550bhp on that occasion.

Eight drivers were lined up to contest the final day's high jinks – with four heats leading to semi-finals, a final, and a third-place run-off. In his heat, Blomqvist easily beat Saeed Al-Hajri's Rothmans-liveried Porsche 959, while Schanche was narrowly beaten by Miki Biasion in a works Lancia Delta S4. The semi-final race between Blomqvist and Biasion was as eventful as expected, with both drivers putting their cars briefly off the track, and carrying on. But it was Biasion who triumphed – just.

Blomqvist therefore had to take on another beaten semi-finalist – Marc Duez's MG Metro 6R4 in the third-place run-off. Although he could not beat Duez, to quote Keith Oswin of *Autosport* magazine: *'Blomqvist entertained with one of his all-singing, all-dancing crowd-pleasers, the Ford hammering round the track to rapturous applause'*.

And with this, the RS200 came to the end of its works rallying career. Within weeks the entire fleet had been sold off, to make space at Boreham for a brand-new programme involving Group A Sierras to be developed. In fact, and even before the end of the 1986 calendar year, when the British Rallycross GP was held at Brands Hatch in December (the week before the Bettega Memorial), no fewer than five RS200s turned up to compete. One was Mark Rennison's car, already familiar to British rallycross enthusiasts, while the other four were all ex-works machines with new owners, ready to start a new and fruitful rallycross career.....

What might have been

As early as March 1986, John Wheeler's design and development team were already looking ahead – both to making detail changes possible because of items already covered in the Variant Option sections of the homologation form, and also on what was originally (but never seriously) considered for an Evolution car, and which might even have been the basis of one of FISA's proposed Group S cars.

Because this design process was aimed at getting rid of a lot of weight and producing a much more powerful engine, it was informally known as the 100-100 car, which is to say that two targets – 100kg (221lb) of weight, and 100 extra bhp – were established. To make it clear, this was not proposed because it could possibly bring the car down to the minimum-limits of the class, and the team considered that to try this would have resulted in a rally machine that was no longer strong and fit enough.

One of the most important projects was to change and improve the existing 1.8-litre engine, while waiting for the formidable 500bhp (and more) Hart-designed 2.1-litre BDT-E power unit to be available. Although the works car engine outputs were outstanding – up to 450bhp was readily available, as the last outings in 1986 would prove – this now-venerable engine (the cylinder head, 16-valve, DOHC layout had originated in 1968, which was 18 years earlier) had reached the limits of reliability.

All this fell into the may/can/should/could category, because after FISA spelt out the imminent death of Group B, and proved to be incapable of setting the required layout of Group S, John Wheeler, Brian Hart and their colleagues had little idea of what engines – turbocharged or normally-aspirated, tiny or large – would be required. It was not until the autumn of 1986 that Group S was officially abandoned, and Boreham could then concentrate on the development of a new generation of Group A rally cars. That is where the RS200's rallying fate was finally sealed, and where the Sierra began to take over.

If the works competition programme had gone ahead in 1987, the cars would have been powered by the new 2.1-litre Hartpower BDT-E engine, which developed over 500bhp even in basic form.

THE MIGHTY 2.1-LITRE BDT-E ENGINE HARTPOWER UNIT

From the very earliest days of the B200 – later RS200 – project, Brian Hart's little company at Harlow was closely involved in the evolution, and improvement, of the car's engine. At first, this was limited to finalising the revised turbo and fuel injection installation in the existing RS1700T type of engine, and then by designing an outwardly similar, but actually very different, evolution of it.

It all started with a long meeting held at Brian Hart's premises, where Stuart Turner and Ford's currently-favoured race-car designer Tony Southgate were present. There, it became clear Ford wanted Brian to build the engines that would be based on the 13-year-old Hart BDA.

As Brian later commented, in his book *Hartpower*: *'This would keep us pretty occupied, as one can imagine. We were able to increase the capacity of the 1800cc engine, which meant we ended up with a 2.1-litre unit. So my brother, who was still working for us then, together with John Lievesley, did the RS200 Evolution engine during the course of 1985/86.*

'We had a three-year contract to supply those engines, so our future seemed to be secure. Or so we thought. Then Lancia rally star Henri Toivonen was killed when his Group B Lancia Delta crashed in flames on the Tour de Corse. The following Sunday morning I received a phone call from Stuart who simply told me, "The FIA has decided to cancel Group B rallying as from this moment. I'll call you." He put the phone down. I was shattered.

'The following day he talked to me at some length about this development. It looked as though we might end up with nothing. Then, in what was a very generous gesture from a major partner, he said, "Clearly Ford has got to pay you for what work has been done and what work is in progress." I think we were laying down around 100 engines – blocks, crankshafts, pistons, camshafts. Both Stuart and Ford were as good as their word. We finished off all the components, completed all the engines we were building, gave them to Ford, and they just put them all into storage.'

A BDT-E prototype engine was shown in public, admitted to be a 2.1-litre power unit because of FIA's ruling that it qualified it as the equivalent of a 3.0-litre normally-aspired engine, and could be rated at 500bhp. Ford never published any more about this engine.

BDT-E TECH SPEC

PUBLISHED IN HARTPOWER

- **Capacity** 2137cc
- **Bore x stroke** 90mm x 84mm
- **Maximum potential output** 580bhp @ 8000rpm (1.6 bar boost)
- **Peak torque** in excess of 400lb.ft @ 5000rpm
- **Maximum rpm** 9000rpm
- **Rally boost** 1.2/1.3 bar: 440/460bhp @ 8000rpm (provisional)
- **Weight** 110kg/242.5lb (fully-dressed but without clutch)

Chapter 7

Rallying in Europe (and India) The national programmes

Right from the start, in the early 1980s, Ford had been anxious to build on the long-lasting success record of its rear-wheel-drive Escorts, the original hope being that many of the various Ford national companies could be persuaded to offer support to at least one leading driver, who would compete in their national championship or (if well supported, technically and financially) in European Championship rounds.

Soon after Stuart Turner took over as director of European motorsports in 1983, he confirmed and reemphasised this strategy, not only for some carefully-chosen drivers to use the still-secret Escort RS Turbo as a Group A class car, but for several Ford territories' leading contracted drivers to use customer RS200s at the top European level.

"After setting a very slow time on the first special stage, he was then fastest of all on the rest of the day"

As has already been emphasised in an earlier chapter, during the late autumn and winter of 1985/1986, the impetus was to get a very limited number of suitable cars built up at the Shenstone factory before being moved to Boreham. It was there that the original prototypes were still based – though they were now to be housed in a different building, going through the detailed development work that Ford standards required – while the competitions workshops set about producing their own very limited fleet of works cars, along with a handful of hastily-prepared Ford-controlled customer cars to be shipped out to the territories, where Ford was looking forward to seeing them used in national motorsport programmes. With Group B homologation likely to be achieved on 1 February 1986, it was hoped that the first entries (and the first successes) would follow within days.

This is why, in January 1986, Stuart Turner was able to hold his annual press conference in which his season's strategy was laid bare. On this occasion, with Group B becoming the dominant factor in most events that held an international permit, he announced an ambitious line-up of RS200 rally cars, and their drivers, who were to compete with varied amounts of works (or a national company's) assistance (and to do it from their own premises), or use cars based at a very limited number of British preparation concerns.

As with all detailed programmes, what was planned almost immediately had to be changed to take account of national strategies, the signing or losing of sponsorship deals, and the available finance for a particular programme. This explains why the French programme was almost immediately cancelled because the French concern found it could not hire a leading driver (Didier Auriol, the prime target, was not yet available) and because suitable sponsorship was lacking, while there seemed to be little opportunity to make a German programme work, for the Cologne-based operation was heavily committed – functionally and financially – to its Eggenberger-based Sierra RS Cosworth race programme.

JANUARY

Even before homologation was achieved, the first RS200 rally car had appeared in European competition, for Stig Blomqvist and Boreham dearly wanted to get as much experience of the car's immediate abilities before it could start an event in international competition. Stig therefore took his Swedish rally practice car (B690 CEV) out on the one-day Numedal Rally in Norway. After setting a very slow time on the first special stage, he was then fastest of all on the rest of the day, and took second overall. This was a good, though not overwhelming, way to settle the new model into the rally scene, and it certainly caused rival team managers from Lancia and Peugeot to sit up and take notice.

Ford, of course, was not involved in the Monte Carlo Rally on this occasion, though team bosses turned up to see how their rivals were getting on. They must have been encouraged and discouraged on one and the same day, for although Henri Toivonen put up a remarkable performance to win in his Lancia Delta S4, the Peugeots and Audi Quattros were both well beaten. Not only that, but a much-hyped appearance by two works MG Metro 6R4s turned into a shambles (the first car was withdrawn after just one day's running, the other a day later), while the performance of the new Citroen BX4TCs was laughable, to say the least.

Robert Droogmans was almost invincible in Belgium and other European events during 1986.

JANUARY 1986 LINE-UP OF RS200 RALLY CARS AND DRIVERS

TERRITORY	DRIVER
BELGIUM	Robert Droogmans
FRANCE	Not specified – this planned programme was later abandoned
GERMANY	Stig Blomqvist (separate from his World Championship programme)
	Michael Werner
HOLLAND	Stig Andervang
PORTUGAL	Joaquim Santos
SPAIN	Antonio Zanini
SWITZERLAND	Marc Surer

Above: This became Droogmans's spare car for the balance of the 1986 season, but here it was, new and pristine, for the Ardennes event, early in the year.

Robert Droogmans, on his way to winning the Ardennes rally outright.

FEBRUARY

Two days after gaining homologation, a Group B RS200 should not have let the side down as rapidly as it did on the Portuguese Sopete rally. Joaquim Santos started the event, but after less than one kilometre there was a serious gearbox failure, and the car (the hard-working Car No 005, in which Malcolm Wilson had given the model its first victory in the Lindisfarne a few months earlier – still on loan while Santos's new car was being completed) was sidelined there and then.

Things, surely, could not get worse. But indeed they did, for on the Belgian Boucles de Spa event that followed a week later, Robert Droogmans's new car seized its braking system on the way from the start to the very first stage, and eventually crashed out later in the event. For Droogmans, however, this was just about the only letdown of the year, for his Belga-sponsored machine (C200 MNO) would later go on to win no fewer than seven Belgian Championship rounds outright, and win that nation's series at a canter.

Soon, however, things began to look up, for after Grundel's fine third place in the world championship round in Sweden (see Chapter 6), Antonio Zanini took his new car out on the Costa Brava Rally in Spain, and was handily placed in the top six of the event until two stages from the end, when fuel supply problems caused him to retire.

MARCH

Although Ford had to withstand, and suffer, the traumas of the horrific accident in the Rally of Portugal (see Chapter 6), the team was finally able to claim an important European victory when Robert Droogmans took his exuberantly-livered RS200 to a closely-contested victory in the Belgian Ardennes Rally, even though it suffered several gearbox problems along the way – this being something of an epidemic among all early full-spec RS200 rally cars of the period. The Belgians had already had to start using their second car (C200 MNO) as the first had been damaged in the Boucles accident. This was the start of what became a truly successful season for this particular car, in which Droogmans was virtually unbeatable.

In Switzerland, however, racing driver Marc Surer started his year with a disappointment, for although he was using what was incorrectly described in the press as 'Mark Lovell's spare car' (Mark never had a spare car; this was an ageing Boreham machine used by many individual drivers for practice, publicity occasions and much testing) and was setting fastest times on the first day of the Criterium Jurassien, he had to retire with an electrical problem that could not be solved at the side of the road. Surer's new car would be ready at the end of April, ready to make its debut in May.

In the same month, Zanini continued his efforts to win in Spain with a rapidly-developing MLP-prepared car, but found the usual RS200 transmission problem getting in his way.

APRIL

While factory and factory-supported teams were preparing for events like the Circuit of Ireland, and various European international events, news came of a privately-entered RS200's very first outing, and its very first victory, in a British Rallycross Championship round. Mark Rennison, a farmer from Darlington in the north-east of the UK, beat everyone at Lydden Hill on that occasion, and would soon go on to

Above: C200 JJN was driven throughout 1986 by the fiery young Swede Stig Andervang, and was probably the single most successful RS200 of the season. Here seen on the 1986 Lombard RAC Rally, this was its last outing of the year.

"Ford had to withstand, and suffer, the traumas of the horrific accident in the Rally of Portugal"

Andervang at speed and very close to brave spectators in the Rally Bianchi.

become one of the country's best and most successful RS200 privateers after Group B rallying was outlawed. By the end of the year, Rennison's car had become the star of the British rallycross scene, and for 1987 he had the use of a 2.1-litre Hartpower BDT-E engine and other Evolution pieces. Much more success was gained, and from that time on there was a rush of other drivers (who mainly bought examples of the Boreham works cars when they were pensioned-off at the end of the 1986 season) to emulate him. Rennison, incidentally, proved to be totally dominant in UK rallycross events in 1987 and 1988, where he won the British Rallycross Championship in both seasons.

It wasn't long, too, before the RS200's European-wide winning streak in rallies got under way, for from mid April a thrusting young Swede, Stig Andervang, began his campaign with a Ford-Holland-entered RS200, when he won

Works or non-World Championship? A bit of both really, for early in the year Boreham expanded its RS200 fleet and kept them busy on a variety of events. This was, indeed, a works car with Stig Blomqvist driving it – but it was competing in the Welsh Rally before being flown out to Greece to act as a training car for the Acropolis.

the International Tulip Rally; this was a car that had been prepared, and would be maintained throughout the season, by Mike Taylor Developments in Yorkshire.

Only two weeks later, he went on to win the Dutch Hellendoorn rally, and it began to look as if he could do no wrong with this fast-developing RS200. Even so, it was just the start of a controversial season for this driver and car (Andervang could be described as having a fiery temper), for although the combination would go on to win several events, and also the Dutch championship, the hard-driven car would end its season in the Lombard RAC Rally with a thoroughly broken chassis tub.

In the meantime, Antonio Zanini seemed to have solved his RS200's transmission problems by finishing second overall in the Spanish Sierra Morena Rally. In view of what we came to know only a year or so into the future, second was nearly as creditable as a victory, for on this occasion Zanini was beaten by no less than a young Carlos Sainz in a Renault 5 Maxi Turbo.

MAY

This was the month in which the RS200's rallying reputation in Europe began to rise, inexorably, for it signalled the start of an incredibly successful series of events, for instance in Belgium (Robert Droogmans), Holland (Stig Andervang) and Portugal (Joaquim Santos), where victory would follow victory.

On the Haspengouw, in Belgium, the first European Championship round in which the car figured strongly, it all started when Droogmans took his bright Belga-liveried car to outright victory – he set fastest times on 30 of the 36 stages, and won the rally by eight full minutes – and in the next months the same car (no clones, no need) would go on to win five more times. Indeed, only three weeks later, Droogmans repeated the trick by winning the Wallonia event.

Unhappily, at the very end of the month, F1 Arrows driver Marc Surer, driving the Ford-Switzerland RS200 (which had been prepared by MLP) on its very first event, crashed the car on an early stage; it hit a tree, burst into flames and was totally destroyed. Surer's life was saved by brave spectators who pulled him clear of the unstoppable inferno, but his gallant co-driver Michel Wyder could not be rescued.

JUNE

In June 1986 the highlight of the European rallying month was undoubtedly the running of the ever-popular and hotly-contested 24 Hours of Ypres event in Belgium. Although he was running second in the early stages of the event, when the opposition faltered, Robert Droogmans and C200 MNO cruised serenely into the lead, which they held to the end. This combination, exuberantly sponsored by a Belgian cigarette brand, was beginning to look unbeatable. During the same weekend, incidentally, Zanini notched up his first victory on

Top to bottom: Droogmans's first victory in C200 MNO came in the Haspengouw rally…

…which he soon followed in the Wallonia, another qualifying round for the Belgian rally championship…

…though it wasn't always plain sailing.

Above: Stig Andervang was always forceful – here seen getting the most out of his car on the Rally Bianchi of 1986, in which he finished fourth.

Right: C200 MNO won the Bianchi rally in fine style.

the Canary Islands (in the Spanish championship), though this was the only occasion on which this excellently-prepared team took a win in the MLP-prepared RS200.

JULY

As high summer approached, the European RS200s – based in various countries, though most of the cars were being prepared and maintained by British Ford satellite concerns – seemed to have shaken off their early transmission and lubricant-leaking problems, and were rapidly becoming seen as the class of the field in events that usually attracted fleets of Group B Lancias, Peugeots and MG Metro 6R4s to fight with them.

As an example, Stig Andervang's Ford-Holland machine (C200 JJN) had already not only won the Ardennes, Tulip and Hellendoorn events, it then battled away in a very high-class entry in the Hunsrück event, which was a leading European Championship round. Right from the start, the young Swede fought his corner against many other four-wheel-drive Group B cars (which on this occasion included Audi Quattros and works MG Metro 6R4s). In spite of suffering a gearbox malfunction (that particular RS200 'wrinkle' had not been totally eliminated), he held on to the end, and recorded second place overall. As a reward for his sparkling performances during the year, Stig and this particular RS200 would finally be invited to take part in the Himalayan Rally, which was to be held in India in October – and which would require last-minute tycoon-like cargo flights in the belly of Air India Boeing 747s. The author was fortunate enough to be involved in this expedition.

AUGUST

Though it was now well-and-truly the holiday season, RS200s found themselves as busy as ever in the international European events. Not only did Stig Andervang venture out to win the Limburg, but two weeks later Robert Droogmans won the Bianchi (held in Belgium, but still a qualifying round for the Dutch series). In the latter event, Droogmans narrowly defeated the Belga-sponsored MG Metro 6R4 of Marc Duez, also beating Patrick Snyers's Lancia Rally 037, and Stig Andervang in the Ford-Holland RS200 too. By this time, no question, the RS200 was fast becoming Europe's dominant Group B car, which is what Stuart Turner had hoped way back in 1983 when it was conceived.

SEPTEMBER

By this point of the season, there seemed to be no stopping the emphatic rise of the RS200, for Robert Droogmans took his familiar car to another convincing outright victory, in the Omloop van Vlaanderen. Stig Andervang won the Swedish Monroe Herning-Hallerne in his now well-used car, Joaquim Santos won the Rallye Alto Tâmega in Portugal, while Zanini took a very creditable third place in the Spanish-based European Championship Rally Asturias, finishing strongly behind a works-prepared Lancia Delta S4 and Carlos Sainz's Renault Maxi 5 Turbo.

OCTOBER

The season was by no means over, for in Europe and (amazingly) in India, RS200s continued to make headlines.

It was the Indian escapade, quite bizarre, which made all the rallying headlines, and totally defied rallying logic. Before the end of the summer, the organisers of the Himalayan Rally, a rough and tough event based in Delhi in India, and with hopes of breaking through into the world scene, approached Ford, waving financial support, to see if the factory team would send a spare RS200 to compete in their event, starting on 22

October. Much sponsorship would come from Air India, and even though Ford's marketing and manufacturing presence in India at the time was minimal, the publicity opportunities were not to be ignored.

Although Boreham, by this time, was totally taken up with preparations for the Lombard RAC Rally, and in developing Group A Sierras for the 1987 world championship season, the team found the proposal both intriguing and amusing, decided it was not for them, but approached their satellite teams to see if any were interested, and whether a car might be available.

Amazingly, they discovered that Ford-Holland's contender, complete with a hard-worked RS200, and with Stig Andervang newly crowned as the winner of the West Euro Cup, the Nordic Championship *and* the Dutch Rally Championship in just the one car (to emphasise, there was no spare car in any such programmes), was keen to make what was seen as a fun trip. Accordingly, once the last of its European commitments had ended (with victory in the Grensland event in Belgium, on 6 October), C200 JJN was speedily returned to the British business that had always maintained it (Mike Taylor Developments, of Northallerton in Yorkshire) for a refresh, a rebuild, and a speedy turn-around. It was one of the most unlikely projects ever undertaken by a works or works-backed Ford team, who had never previously been involved in an event that visited the foothills of the world's most famous range, and had usually been won by slow but rugged 4x4s of some type.

Less than two weeks after doing the deal, the car made the trip to India, travelling as cosseted freight cargo in the belly of an Air India Boeing 747 passenger flight from London Heathrow (the author was on the same flight, and saw the car being loaded at Heathrow). The entry was managed by Boreham's John Taylor (no relation to Mike, by the way), who had also arranged for a Boreham-registered Sierra XR4x4 to be sent to India for him to use as a chase car. It looked like a very professional entry.

C200 MNO had to be driven flat-out on tarmac, and also over loose surface stages, in its very busy international season.

Even though some of the roughest and most remote stages in the world would be used, and although the RS200 would start the event as an odds-on favourite to set all the fastest times, in almost every way it seemed to be a pointless entry, for the car was soon needed back in the UK for preparation for the Lombard RAC Rally, where Andervang and the British co-driver Dave West would drive it. In a matter of days, the car would have to go from conquering some of the highest and more remote roads in the Himalayas to Britain's wet, cold and often car-damaging special stages. There were no championship points at stake in India, and the only potential reward from a victory was glory – and rather quirky local glory at that.

"From conquering some of the highest and more remote roads in the Himalayas to Britain's wet, cold and often car-damaging special stages."

As it happened, Andervang's RS200 was the only modern four-wheel-drive Group B car to start the event, for the only other competitive European-type cars with rallying pedigree included Opel Ascona 400s, Group N Toyota Corollas, a couple of home-built UK-prepared Ladas, and an ex-works Rover SD1 driven by Himalayas enthusiast Philip Young. Each had to face up to a four-leg event of 2840km/1765 miles, which included 40 competitive sections, for which there was to be no pre-event reconnaissance. The rally was to cover five days, and would start and finish in Delhi, by way of night halts at Nainital, Mussoorie and Chail Palace (close to Simla), with the rough-and-ready route touching on Kashmir, approaching the foothills of the Himalayan mountain range itself, and occasionally getting a (very distant) view of Mount Everest itself.

If all had gone well with the RS200, it should have won the

Droogmans notched up another fine win in the Omloop (circuit) of Flanders, faced with what looks like very sparse spectator control.

"Group B had summarily been sentenced to death by the sporting authorities, a move that would ban ultra-powerful Group B cars from rallying"

Joaquim Santos's RS200 was always competitive, and often successful in Portugal in 1986.

event – and won easily – but it was not to be. Having been seeded number one, and after heading the entire 68 starters towards Corbett Park (where tigers were rumoured to be roaming), it led at first but was then delayed by an oil loss due to a loosened oil filter bowl, before sprinting back into a convincing lead. On the second day of the event, the RS200 let the side down by breaking its throttle cable (Andervang had to drive 'on the key' for some distance before he could get together with his service crew, for this was in a part of India where roads of any sort were spread far, wide and few), after which a cooling fan support broke away, puncturing the cooling radiator, which allowed all the water to leak, and destroyed the engine very quickly indeed.

After this there was no solution, except to drag the RS200 back to Delhi, load it into the belly of another 747, then rush it back to North Yorkshire for a major rebuild before it started the Lombard RAC Rally.

In the meantime, Joaquim Santos won the Portuguese Algarve event, which brought that car's 1986 record to five outright wins, while Antonio Zanini took a second place on the Spanish Rallye de San Froilan.

NOVEMBER

This, effectively, was the enforced end of the road for the RS200 as an international rally car, not because it was not winning (on the contrary, it was beginning to dominate most events it started) but because Group B had summarily been sentenced to death by the sporting authorities, a move that would ban ultra-powerful Group B cars from rallying, finally and completely at the end of 1986.

With the 1986 calendar, therefore, closing down rapidly, all the competitive RS200s that had become an increasingly important part of the scene had to find new homes or new careers. Most were sold to well-heeled members of the rallycross fraternity (no banning of Group B cars affected that branch of the sport) where they soon became winning machines, while others went into private collections or museums.

Ford Motorsport was really too tied up with developing plans (Sierra RS Cosworths, Group A racing and all such related activities were of vital importance in 1987) that it could no more than let such matters take their course. On the other hand, as the next chapter will make clear, there was a large stock of new RS200s ready to be sold as soon as possible.

It was in 1986 that Stuart Turner first met and befriended the Spanish champion Carlo Sainz, who would later drive RS200s, but not in the Spanish championship. Carlos went on to join Ford works teams on no fewer than three occasions.

Chapter 8

Rebuilding, marketing and living with the RS200

Once the rush to complete – no, let's be brutally honest, throw together at high speed – the production run of RS200s at Shenstone, the pressure on the team was somewhat reduced. Starting the following week, the same dedicated workforce started to complete every nearly-finished car that was still on site. This meant shortages that existed on 31 January 1986 could gradually be eliminated, and there was always pressure for this to be done as the available floor-space was at a premium.

Once any of the cars was ready for dispatch it was then transported, sometimes to a holding warehouse at what had once been the AVO production area of the ageing Ford factory at Aveley in Essex, although a growing number (already destined for rally use, and therefore for eventual delivery to customers overseas) were immediately diverted to one of the yawningly empty hangars at Boreham. From time to time RS200s found themselves parked up inside the gates of the Reliant factory in Tamworth itself, but this was strictly a temporary arrangement until suitable transport to Essex could be arranged.

"Someone painted up an actual Reliant Robin with authentic Boreham-style diagonal paint stripes and all the sponsors' decals"

Such was the relief that this major project had become successful that some hilarity finally broke in. With the arm's-length three-wheeler Reliant story always in the background, one wag based at Shenstone produced an excellent cartoon of a three-wheeler RS200 leaving the factory gates, and at a later date someone painted up an actual Reliant Robin with authentic Boreham-style diagonal paint stripes and all the sponsors' decals in evidence.

Even so, it was not yet time for deliveries of road cars to begin, simply because it was agreed that, at first, the marketing emphasis would fall on getting rally cars out into the world – either those for the factory or for its satellite teams – and to get a small number ready for preparation or tune-up purposes for private owners who, Ford hoped, were bound to approach the company. Even so, the fact was that the company still did not know how easily the cars could be sold, nor what the eventual split between road and competition machines would be.

There was nothing unique about this situation, as all the other Group B manufacturers had already, or would, find out. Way back in history, for example, Jaguar had set out to build 100 of the famous D-type racing sports cars, found itself struggling to sell them, and was then only partially rescued by turning some into XKSSs, and a factory fire that devastated some surviving machines and wrote off every remaining chance of making the numbers. Ten years later, Ford's totally separate FAVO operation (Ford Advanced Vehicles Operation – not the AVO operation that later built hot Escorts) had set out with similar ambitions, ending up by sending many cars out to be museum pieces all over the world.

As far as is known, paperwork forecasting the likely sale of how many RS200s would probably go to various countries has not survived (were such forecasts ever made?) but in early 1986 it was supposed that at least 50 cars would eventually be prepared for serious rallying use. This, of course, was before FISA immediately cracked down on Group B motorsport in mid 1986, and threw the world of motorsport into shocked confusion.

Mike Moreton, as ever, was disarmingly honest, and analytical about the fate of all these new cars, and had this to say about the situation in his book: *'In May 1986 the decision was taken to clear the Shenstone plant. We had already dismantled 46 cars, ready for rebuilding to a fully saleable quality, and this left 148 still on wheels but needing a lot of work. We moved them all to storage in a hangar at Boreham airfield, and handed over the 46 sets of parts to Charlie Mead for his Performance Parts [sales] depot. This was almost the end of the Shenstone project, and the premises were sold to another company'.*

Even before the factory was finally cleared, but after the lease had been sold on to another company, there was one outstanding, later hilarious, incident that combined a small number of RS200s, a fire, Mike Moreton himself, and Stuart Turner's mordant wit. The timing of all this is important, for it occurred after the awful events of Corsica at the beginning

RS 200

Not content with sharing much of the heavy lifting in the RS200 project, Mike Moreton and John Wheeler got together again in 1988 to conceive what became the Escort RS Cosworth. The car they are leaning on is the mule that was built to prove their theories.

of May, and almost immediately after the authorities had suddenly dealt a blow to Ford's chances of selling all its RS200s by killing off any future that Group B might have had. Stuart Turner had already concluded that without a viable motorsport programme to fall back on, the prospect of selling all the RS200s – even 148 of the original 200 – was suddenly looking doubtful.

Two written versions of what happened have survived – Mike Moreton's and Stuart Turner's autobiographies – and though their stories differ in detail, it is well worth quoting (with their generous permission) from those books.

"He would sometimes be able to borrow one of the superstar drivers to show just how quickly an RS200 could be driven"

As Mike told it, *'One evening, quite late, some mechanics from Boreham were preparing cars prior to shipment, and I was in my office writing the final status.... Suddenly there was a commotion, with shouts of "Fire, fire!" A contractor, removing a paint extraction chimney with his welding torch had set fire to 25 years worth of old paint. Rally mechanics are used to handling disasters, and quickly pushed about ten RS200s away from the fire... I phoned Stuart to give him the news.'*

To which Stuart Turner recalled, *'Mike called me to say that fire had broken out....and that although there was no threat to the staff, he had feared for our own stocks. He said: "I wasn't quite sure whether to have the RS200s pushed away from the wall to save them, or to have pushed them the other way, so that we could claim the insurance money. I think I might have made a mistake."*

'At which point I guessed, "You've saved the damned things, haven't you?"

'To which point Mike replied: "Yes Stuart, sorry but I have".'

In all other respects, however, the withdrawal from Shenstone went smoothly. Car No 200 (which is still a part of Ford's Heritage Collection) was liveried up with 'Car 200' emblazoned on the nose, posed against one end of the hall, and a poignant image exists of Mike Moreton wielding a broom to clean up the floor before handing over to the new tenants.

With the motorsport programme about to begin in February 1986, Ford had always hoped the RS200 would generate a lot of favourable publicity, and preparations had already been made to intensify the effort (we now know that for 1986 alone the operating Boreham budget had been set at $14.4 million). But from late May 1986 the situation had changed completely, with Group B about to disappear and no likelihood of preparing, rallying and selling 50 competition cars, which meant that perhaps the balance of about 125 would eventually have to be made into complete, as refined-as-possible, road cars.

Fortunately, Bob Howe's efforts had ensured the car already had national type approval, and had scaled a mountain of other related legal obstacles to qualification, which meant individual examples could be sold in most countries of the world. Stuart Turner soon demolished another obstacle by persuading Bob Howe once again to postpone his well-deserved retirement, and to become the company's one-man RS200 sales force. Earlier in the year, much of the Boreham-based (as opposed to Aston Martin Tickford-based) road car development and refinement had been carried out by Bill Meade and Terry Bradley, so they carried on with their sometimes onerous, and always overworked, tasks.

However, even before any framework for selling these precious cars had been finalised, there was the question of pricing to be settled. Way back in November 1985, when type approval and all such legislative hurdles had been cleared, Ford decided to put a UK retail price of £49,950 on each car, and at the same time to offer a tune-up kit (to 300bhp, from 250bhp). Having gone through the earlier horrors of originally hoping to sell Escort RS1700Ts at a knock-down price, and having to keep jacking up that suggested price even before it went on the market, Stuart Turner's colleagues were nervous of how such a headline price for the RS200 would be greeted.

In this consideration, at that time Ford-UK's price list began at £4097 for the entry-level Fiesta, went through £11,914 for the excellent Sierra XR4x4, and topped out at £13,164 for the Granada 2.8i Ghia. In other words, the new RS200 was all set to be priced at 380 per cent of that of the most expensive Ford car of the day! Austin-Rover, by comparison was proposing to sell the new Group B MG Metro 6R4 for a mere £35,000, even though its lack of type approval meant that further paperwork would be needed by a new owner before it was technically legal to drive on the roads. In any case, Austin-Rover, it is said, was never sanguine about selling all the cars.

Ford – and Motorsport in particular – was stubborn about the recommended £49,950 price for the RS200, as the general sales/buying atmosphere in Europe was booming. Interest in all such cars that were already classics, or even forecast to become classics, was blossoming as never before (the Porsche 959, for instance, had recently gone on sale), and even at an early point Ford received several approaches from rich petrolheads on the basis of 'well, I might as well have one, to add to my Ferrari and my Porsche, because their value is sure to go through the roof soon'.

Ford, however, was still uneasy, but received a boost when cooperating with a supercar specialist, Stratton's of Wilmslow in Cheshire, regarding the production of a luxury-trim version of the car, complete with Stratton's own interpretation of the best leather and carpeting. To Ford's delight, not only was Stratton's willing to produce a small number of such bespoke conversions, the specialist thought the suggested Ford retail price was wrong.

As Stuart Turner later noted: '*When they said that £49,950 was wrong as a British retail price, I assumed that they meant it was too high, and I stressed that it was as low as we could go. In fact, they meant that it was too low, and that in that area of the market a £50,000 car sounded far more appealing than a £40,000 one…*'

Ford took note, and at the end of 1987, to counter various snide and quite unjustified comments about the demand for the car, announced a changed price – not a reduction (as Austin-Rover had been forced to shift unwanted stock of MG Metro 6R4s) but a rise to £52,950.

By this time, too, the decision had been made that the cars were to be sold outside of Ford's normal marketing machine. Usually, supplies of a production Ford models would be channelled through the company's prestigious system, efforts would be made to locate demonstration models with key dealerships, cars to make a blitz of road tests possible would be fettled, and allocated, and it needed a team of highly experienced people to make it all possible.

This, of course, was an appropriate strategy where cars could be made available in considerable quantities (even the AVO production plant of the 1970s, while making up to 5000 cars a year, had been considered a marginal case). With so few cars to be sold – and at a colossal price by any previous Ford standards – with the RS200 it was not even considered. Instead it was agreed that there should be a one-man selling operation, that this would be based at Boreham, and that Bob Howe should do that job.

With only a tiny budget made available for Bob to set up an office, and to arrange for cars to be displayed, it was always going to be a difficult task. But at least Bob had several advantages – one being that his office was situated alongside the various test tracks on the airfield so that he could demonstrate the RS200's virtues to a possible customer; another being that he could often sweeten up the selling spiel by taking a customer around the hallowed works rally preparation shop, and he would sometimes be able to borrow one of the superstar drivers to show just how quickly an RS200 could be driven.

In that regard, he would often find Stig Blomqvist, John Taylor, Mark Lovell and Malcolm Wilson on site – and the author still treasures the memory of lining up in the queue for lunch in the Boreham canteen immediately behind the handsome and charismatic Carlos Sainz, who was new to the team, when Carlos caused every girl in the building to immediately rush to serve him! Let us not forget, too, that Bob Howe himself was a talented RS200 driver.

The selling operation began in earnest at the end of 1986, by which time the 'stud' of available cars had developed into four basic fleets – left-hand drive or right-hand drive, and road or rally specification. Surviving written notes suggest that of the 57 road-specification cars eventually sold in the UK, just 14 were to rally specification.

In fairness, there was perhaps less to rally specification than met the eye, for it did not include any engine and transmission tune-up kit. In summary, 'rally' meant the cars were available without carpets or any sound-deadening NVH (noise, vibration, harshness) suppression, but featuring firmed-up

Soon after RS200 assembly was complete, Stratton's (of Wilmslow in Cheshire) offered a dress-up interior kit, which included these smart leather-trimmed seats.

springs and dampers allied to harder and more robust bushes supporting the engine, transaxle and the rear axle casing, plus an extra moulding to be mounted on the front bodywork to accept four extra driving lamps, hard and narrow rally seats, and the two-tone blue works team striping job.

Even so, by this time, Howe and the RS200 programme had begun to feel like orphans at Boreham, because the resident works rally team had turned its attention to the new Sierra RS Cosworth and the Group A competition in which that car would soon have to give battle. Yet Mike Moreton and Bob Howe concluded that the rush to complete the cars at Shenstone, and the fact that some of them were by no means complete when inspected by FISA officials, meant every RS200 needed to undergo a detailed inspection, update rectification and – in some cases – repaint before it could be ready for delivery.

At first it was thought that JQF Engineering (which had already provided the invaluable service of rebuilding 200 BDT engines from Escort RS1700T to RS200 specification) could tackle this job, but Bob Howe's early success in converting a number of enquiries into definite orders meant demand threatened to overwhelm the rather limited staff and premises.

It was at this point that Aston Martin Tickford came into the picture once more. In recent years, as has already been noted in an earlier chapter, AMT had acquired a rather ancient

Work proceeding at the Aston Martin Tickford premises in Bedworth, on preparing a new batch of RS200s for delivery to customers.

At Bedworth in 1987, 1988 and 1989, the workshop floor of the Aston Martin Tickford factory was always packed with new RS200s, which were being refurbished and freshened up before delivery to their purchasers. Only months earlier, this shop would have been full of Sierra RS Cosworths being converted into RS500 Cosworths.

factory building close to the town centre of Bedworth, north of Coventry, where it was building a series of special Ford Capri Tickfords, complete with turbocharged engines and many styling changes. AMT had also just astonished everyone at Ford by taking on the production of 500 very special Sierra RS500 Cosworths – a process that started by taking over a stock of already-built Sierra RS Cosworths, stripping them as necessary, and reinstalling all the new parts, including potentially much more powerful engines. In a rather cramped assembly hall (whose floor area was only about 20,000 sq feet) containing a line-up of workshop ramps, a very willing workforce, and a ready supply of RS500 engines but very little else, AMT had completed the task with great aplomb in a mere six weeks, achieving a peak output of 25 cars per day at one time.

With Mike Moreton pulling all the strings as usual, and Tickford's David Orchard as engineering project manager, it seemed to make a great deal of sense to slot the RS200 refurbishment programme into place at Bedworth as soon as the Sierra RS500 Cosworth stock had cleared the building. Well before the end of 1987, therefore, ex-Shenstone RS200s began to flood into this building (they were trucked up from storage at Boreham), and by 1988 it was usual for a privileged visitor to be led into the hall, to see not one, not two, but probably between ten and 20 RS200s in one state of dress or another.

Except that Tickford did not tackle engine or transmission rebuilds, it seemed able to deal with all requests, special modifications or completions with ease, in a good-humoured way. For the author, as a regular visitor, it was quite normal to go into the hall and find cars clearly in the middle of having paint rectification carried out, of suspension changes being made, or having complete engine and transmissions being craned in and out. This was all being done on new, yet-to-be-delivered, machines, of which – in 1987, 1988 and 1989 – there appeared to be a good supply.

By this time, Ford had settled on a more organised programme of ongoing development, and of gaining experience with the road cars. Two 'endurance' cars were always in daily use, not only for commuting duties but for long-distance dashes to motoring events, club gatherings, publicity appearances (for the cars) or Ford RS dealerships all around Great Britain. Both were intended to be driven regularly for up to a year at a time, then replaced by other new cars, after which they could (and always were) sold off to customers as genuine used vehicles, usually at satisfyingly high prices. One such car was always being used by Bob Howe, and – as the registrar of the newly formed RS200 Club – the other would be used by the author. In just over four years I would have the regular use of four different cars (073, 127, 183 and finally 192), whereas Bob Howe had more than that.

In 1987 and 1988, the two daily-use RS200s had busy lives. Bob not only made many trips to show his current machine

Once the 200-off production had ended at Shenstone – where all the hastily-built cars were painted in Diamond White – one or two cars were resprayed to special effect, this being a left-hand-drive machine in a rather fetching shade of blue. Its destination was unknown.

Business as usual, with two factory-owned development cars, and three more brand-new RS200s, parked outside Peter Ashcroft's office at Boreham in 1987.

to prospective buyers (and clinched several deals, he was always convinced, because he actually turned up in a real car instead of merely waving a glossy brochure) but visited many motor clubs, business groups, and almost any organisation that seemed to have a genuine interest in RS200s, Boreham, and the Ford RS set-up. The author's car provided transport for his many visits to report on rallies around the British Isles (spectators were often astonished to see a non-competing RS200 turn up at a service point or time control) and was also used for day-to-day business trips to all corners of the country. These activities, Stuart Turner thought, were excellent publicity for the cars, for it proved that they existed, rather than just appearing in adverts.

If a prospective RS200 purchaser took what he thought was the obvious route, of contacting his nearest RS dealer, or concessionaire, he would be politely redirected to contact Bob Howe at Boreham. Bob, in turn, would either invite him or her to visit Boreham, or would arrange to visit the prospective buyer in one or other of the demonstration cars he was running at the time. The author vividly recalls standing in for Bob on one occasion where he was double-booked, turning up at a house in the Home Counties, to be greeted by a man who said he already had a Metro 6R4, a Lancia Rally 037 and a short-wheelbase Audi Quattro, so he thought he 'might' buy an RS200 to fill a corner of his garage; in the end he did not do a deal that day.

Selling the cars was a procedure that Bob Howe had to learn from scratch, for his earlier Ford career had embraced product planning, quality measures and gaining a thorough

Above: As fitted into John Wheeler's own post-retirement RS200, this shows how the more modern Cosworth-engineered YB engine might have been installed in the later evolution of RS200s.

Right: This was the front of John Wheeler's post-production car, with a stiffened-up front end, and in this case only single coil-over-shock front suspension.

Left: John Wheeler redesigned the rear end of the RS200 considerably when he came to build his own car, not only with a different tubular arrangement of the rear chassis, but with the engine intercooler repositioned from the roof to be placed above and behind the engine.

John Wheeler continues to develop his own RS200, which is here seen on an Eifel rally of the 2010s.

Mark Rennison was an early private buyer of an RS200. This car was delivered in 1986, and rapidly came to dominate the British rallycross scene…

…as can be seen at the start of the end-of-season race at Brands Hatch in December 1986. The RS200 immediately behind Mark is thought to be Martin Schanche in his recently-purchased ex-works rally car, which used the Hartpower 2.1-litre engine.

knowledge of all matters legislative – but not persuading individuals that they really, truly, felt like investing £50,000 in a car that did some functional things incredibly well but lacked refinement and reliability in others.

The sales set-up, at Boreham, was simple and modest, to say the least. In an office remote from the famous works rally team's workshops, but separated from the stock of RS200s only by a door and a hangar access, the unprepared visitor might have found it on a suitable scale for a small, independent concern that built and sold only dozens of cars in a year, rather than being an off-shoot of a global business geared up to delivering hundreds of thousands of cars to British customers every year.

"Every possible spare part was still available... including complete aluminium honeycomb tubs, engines and four-wheel-drive transmissions"

In mid 1988, when Shaun Campbell of *Autocar* reacted to the news that about 50 RS200s were still looking for good homes (more than half had left-hand drive and were destined for export) he made haste to visit this 'corner-shop' operation, and submitted himself to the Howe treatment. It was then that he discovered that more deposits had recently been taken, and that perhaps only 30 cars remained.

Not that it had all been easy. As Bob Howe told Shaun: '*When the rally regulations changed we recognised that we weren't going to sell them as rally cars. I had 140 orders, and they disappeared overnight. Immediately we took 46 to pieces for spares and the debate started with management as to whether we should sell the rest or scrap them all. After two or three months we agreed to sell them.*'

By this time, the list of options had grown significantly, and it was already possible to order a car with a 300bhp engine for just £685 extra. Plus '*we're also working on a 350bhp version which will add £1000 to the price. There's almost no limit – one rallycross competitor is claiming 750bhp.*'

To Bob's relief, everyone from the chairman downwards retained their faith in this operation, and after individual machines had been refurbished they gradually began to find homes. Although news came that cars were to be sold, individually, in the autumn of 1986, only six found customers before the end of that year. However, a further 41 followed in 1987, and another 50-or-so seemed to be on the brink of sale in the first half of 1988.

This estimate was buoyed up by what proved to be an over-confident approach from an entrepreneur in the North American continent, who originally ordered not one but 20 cars, asking for them to have certain special trim and furnishing features, and for them to be labelled RS200S. At the time, no doubt, he was convinced he could sell them, but eventually only two such cars were delivered, and a rather messy stand-off developed before the rest of the cars (which were never delivered across the Atlantic) could be redirected to customers whose money was real.

By the summer of 1988, therefore, it was clear than 53 cars remained unsold, and Stuart Turner duly reported this to his bosses. To their eternal credit, it was decided to keep lugging on, and after certain semi-official comments were published in the specialist press – that 'the RS200 is nearly sold out' – this clever ploy saw several wavering enthusiasts put in firm orders, such that in the first days of 1989, Turner was able to circulate this convincing internal document stating that, '*With some relief, I am able to advise that orders, with deposits, were taken for the last cars in the dying days of 1988... The "prepare for sale and delivery" programme will continue at Aston Martin Tickford until July 1989... I sincerely hope the motorsport authorities never again cancel a rally category at six months' notice, but this particular project is now completed. RIP!*'

Among the many replies Stuart received was one from the company's finance director, who noted: '*Well done, we never thought you'd shift the damned things.*'

In the end it appeared that 52 cars had been delivered to British customers, 27 had gone to the USA, 20 went to Canada, 14 to Japan, and small numbers went to other European locations, including one car to the Schlumpf museum in France, and one to Ford-of-Germany.

This, of course, was not the absolute end to a project that had captured the hearts of several people. Because almost every possible spare part was still available – at the time including complete aluminium honeycomb tubs, complete engines and complete four-wheel-drive transmissions – a small number of continuation cars took shape, including one that designer John Wheeler eventually turned into what his idea of a Group S RS200 might have become (complete with a Sierra RS500 Cosworth type of YBD engine); several more were built up as rallycross cars. There was also a car that began to take shape in the department where Ford apprentices were being trained, and although it was never completed, it is thought still to exist somewhere within the Ford organisation.

In the meantime, Motorsport let it be known that in 1989 all traces of the RS200 programme were to be put aside, though never forgotten, and that three cars would be retained – No 200 (which eventually joined the Heritage fleet), a regular usage car for Bob Howe to continue driving, and the already-famous Ferrari Rosso Red Car No 192, which would be run by the author until the early days of 1991.

This, therefore, seems to be the appropriate moment to recall some of the highlights of the four years in which I lived with (and loved – most of the time) RS200 road cars.

1986 to 1990: a never-ending love story

Unless there are any anonymous heroes out there, I think I can state, quite categorically, that when the RS200 was a current model in the 1980s, only two people used the cars regularly, and consistently, as road cars. One was Bob Howe, and the

RS 200

other was me. Although Bob, as the hero who directly sold each and every one of the road cars to customers from his cramped but tastefully-equipped office and store at Boreham, probably completed more miles than the author, in four years (1986 to 1990) I was privileged to use four different road cars, and completed more than 80,000 miles in that period.

Both of us used Boreham as our 'dealership', rather than having to burden a Ford RS dealer to whom such models were still unknown. This was very easy for Bob, as his office was on the site, but potentially more difficult for me because I lived 200 miles away from Boreham, and visited the site perhaps only twice a month. Here and now, I should pay tribute to my principal long-range contacts at Boreham, who were Bill Meade and Terry Bradley (they had already spent much time working on everything from British Touring Car Capri projects, the Escort Turbo rally championship, and a lot of initial Sierra RS Cosworth development, while Terry would later go on to run the engineering design office that developed the Escort World Rally Car, the Puma Racing, and other related machinery), for it was they who usually had a solution to the minor problems my cars picked up in four years of regular use.

Even so, right from the start I realised that regular use of an RS200 was not likely to be an easy ego-trip. Purely as an example, early in 1987, in the very first week following my collection of the first of four RS200 cars that I would be using for normal, conventional, road-car transport, I had to drive it through the outskirts of London to a scheduled magazine interview that I was due to hold with the CEO of Rolls-Royce Motor Cars, Sir David Plastow.

It was to be an important interview with a very busy man, and I was anxious to arrive unflustered, and on time, but I was not prepared for the immediate aggravation I had in trying to insert a still-unfamiliar RS200 (C142 JJN was a left-hand-drive machine, by the way) into the multi-storey car park behind the Millbank Tower, just south of the Houses of Parliament. The RS200 had no power-assisted steering, of course, had a dramatically fierce in-out clutch, and zero rear visibility except via the door mirrors; I realised, there and then, this was going to be a different type of motoring. For sure, I should fall in love very quickly, or I might just begin to hate the experience.

It had all come about by accident, really. By 1986, although I was already heavily involved at Boreham in the motorsport

'OPEN SESAME' AT BOREHAM

While I was running RS200s as road cars, I tended to make frequent visits to Boreham, often more than once a week. Those who know the layout of the now-closed Motorsport site near Chelmsford will recall that the approach was made up of a narrow, but surfaced, farm road, past a high fence protecting the famous Motorsport workshops on the right, before finally arriving at a lift-up barrier.

Access was diligently supervised by Ford security men, to ensure time-wasters and interlopers did not gain access to the site, and the airfield itself. Oh, and I nearly forgot, there was also another resident gate-keeper – a rather stern cat, who had his own little bed inside the hut, who was very definitely in charge, and who was universally known as Cosworth!

Usually, a visitor would have to come to a halt in front of the barrier, and be quizzed as to his purpose by a security man, before being allowed to drive further in and park close to the workshops or offices. That applied even to regulars like me, so the fact that previously I would have approached the barrier in a Capri 2.8 Injection, an Escort RS Turbo, or a Sierra XR4x4 did not make it any easier.

Until I started turning up in an RS200, and found to my amazement that as I approached the barrier, it would seem automatically to rise up and allow me to sweep through, to find a parking place outside Peter Ashcroft's office. So, one day, wondering if some device had been fitted to my RS200 to trigger some electronic signal in the barrier, I asked the question.

"Oh no," said the gate-keeper, "whenever we see an RS200 coming up the drive, we know it can only be one of two people – Bob Howe or you. You two are the only ones who use RS200 road cars every day."

Following his success in nursing the RS200 into health, and success, John Wheeler went on to direct the efforts of several high-performance Ford model teams, including the birth of the original Focus RS MkI of the early 2000s.

departments, in the compilation of the RS200 owners' handbook, in the compilation an RS200 repair operations manual, and in setting up the Boreham-controlled RS200 Club, I never thought I would have the pleasure of driving one of these cars on a regular basis. My experience, so far, with the cabin, had been quite limited. At first, in 1985 and 1986, there had already been a succession of quick bursts around Boreham test tracks – never as a driver, but invariably as a passenger, sitting in prototypes alongside superstar rally drivers like Stig Blomqvist, Malcolm Wilson, Mark Lovell and John Taylor – which was one thing, but merely confirmed I could never drive at their pace or control such a sensitive chassis anywhere near its roadholding limits. Even so, I knew for sure that the RS200 was going to be an exciting machine to drive. Later I would be allowed to drive one or other of the road-car prototypes, but would always be slightly in awe about my responsibilities.

On one occasion in 1985, I was still heavily involved in writing the repair operations manual, and found myself visiting the British motor industry's proving ground at MIRA, near Nuneaton in Warwickshire, to observe an RS200 test session of one of the left-hand-drive road-car prototypes. Using the twisty figure-of-eight tarmac testing circuit that is squeezed into the infield at MIRA, Ford seemed to have secured its exclusive use for the day. The object was to assess, and trim, the handling, to finally decide whether single or twin dampers at each corner of the car would be right for the suspension (dampers for high-performance cars were costly, their arduous use on rough-surface special stages would work their hydraulic fluid to its limits, and – as ever – a search for financial savings was well under way). On this occasion, no less than three-times F1 world champion Jackie Stewart (the knighthood would follow later) was doing all the driving, with top designer John Wheeler running the day.

For much of the morning I was merely an observer, until suddenly Jackie (with whom I had already worked at Ford on several publicity occasions) said, "I'd like to be a passenger to see what it feels like now," and asked me to drive him around for several laps. Although the thought of making a fool of myself worried me, I somehow managed for a few laps, after which Jackie said he would like to drive again, using me as living and breathing ballast.

That was exciting enough – later he suggested he personally had only been driving at about seven tenths – until he then said, "Well, it's nearly time for lunch – before then, let's just go quite fast for a few minutes…" The few minutes of 'quite fast' that followed were an outstanding reminder that superstars like Jackie worked within unfamiliar parameters, driving standards and reactions that I did not even begin to understand. When it was all over, and we coasted serenely back into the Ford pit at the crossing of this track, he had barely broken sweat, while my colleagues said I seemed to have looked death in the face, and somehow survived.

Country life, RS200-style, in 1987, with the author's left-hand-drive 'endurance' RS200 lined up next to an enthusiast's Escort RS1600i (he took the picture). The rest of the residents of this village rapidly got used to seeing such machinery parked outside.

As to Jackie, and his summing up of the morning: "Och yes, we're improving it, but I'd still like to do some more work later." We did, but not until several weeks later.

As is now clear from what has been stated in previous chapters, by the end of 1986 the RS200 was already becoming 'yesterday's model' as far as motorsport (and Boreham) was concerned, for Boreham's workshops were already filling up with works Sierra XR4x4s and Sierra RS Cosworths, ready to contest the 1987 rally season. Mike Moreton, for sure, had other things on his mind, for he was already masterminding the speedy development of the Sierra RS500 Cosworth, which from mid 1987 would become Ford's phenomenally successful touring car racer.

Elsewhere at Boreham, however, the RS200 had not been forgotten. Apart from one of the airfield's hangars being used as secure storage for the stock of unsold road cars, Bob Howe had already set up an office in which he could entertain potential customers and encourage them to sign up for one of the cars. Not only that, but at least two of the production cars, No 073 (C142 JJN) and No 122 (C829 FHK) were in regular, if not tightly scheduled, use in and around Boreham, with Bob Howe, Bill Meade and Terry Bradley driving.

At the time, my personal car was a Sierra XR4x4, which was building up a considerable mileage, including making long trips to follow, and report on, the British Rally Championship, and it was on an early visit to Boreham in January 1987 that the suggestion was made that the person in charge of the RS200 Club really ought to be running one of those RS200s as a road car. Would I like to take a car on permanent loan, my part of the deal being that I should keep a careful note on the mileage covered, the operating economy, and report on any problems that might develop as time passed..?

BEWARE KNOW-ALLS

Soon after I became a regular RS200 user, it did not take me long to become cautious of parking up the car, especially at petrol stations. It was one thing to be greeted by admiring enthusiasts, most being genuinely amazed that they were seeing an RS200 in normal road use, but it was quite another to be accosted, cornered or lectured by people who seemed to be intent on ruining my day. There were several categories…

KNOW-ALLS. These people, usually young men in their boy-racer period, would say things like, "Nice-looking special, mate. Cortina-based, I suppose. My mate has a Lamborghini Countach replica with a Rover engine – it would see you off, without any trouble at all."

Usually I allowed this sort of barb to float over my head without responding. Would his 'Lamborghini replica' see me off ? Maybe – but only in a straight line, for the moment we came to the first bit of twisty road, preferably in the wet, he would soon have discovered what his rival's four-wheel drive and handling was all about.

"YOU'RE A SHOW-OFF." Refuelling the RS200 (which was a regular business, as 18-to-20mpg seemed normal on my cars) meant lifting up the entire rear body section, as the fuel filler cap was under that cover, immediately behind the passenger bulkhead. More than one person (who was presumably not watching the procedure very closely) suggested that I lifted the lid to make sure people would come across to inspect what was going on, said it was a stupid system or that I was doing it to attract attention.

"WHY ARE YOU NOT USING UNLEADED FUEL?" This was in the late 1980s, the days when there was still a free choice of fuels at every pump, and naturally my RS200s used 98-octane fuel. Unhappily, the environmentalist movement was already on the rise, and I would occasionally receive verbal broadsides from followers.

A classic case, which one day unfolded at a Shell station in Somerset was when I drew up, lifted the RS200's rear section and began to refuel it with super-leaded fuel. At this point a rather fierce-looking tweed-clad woman with a rather amiable Labrador got out of a very scruffy Citroen 2CV stalked across to my car, snuffed disapprovingly, and demanded to know why I was not using lead-free fuel. When I politely suggested this car had an engine that needed high-octane fuel, she told me quite firmly that I was anti-social, and that if she had her way, all such cars would be banned from the roads.

THE ROUNDABOUT CHALLENGE…

In regular day-to-day journeys all around the country (20,000 miles in a typical year) I tried very hard – I was almost paranoid about this – not to get drawn into any sort of public road race. There would always be the opportunity to be beaten up, not just by fast Ferraris, Mercedes-Benz types or whatever, but quite regularly by the fast Ford brigade, who were often driving Capri 2.8 Injection or Sierra RS Cosworth types. Most of them realised they could not beat the RS200 on straight-line performance, but they seemed to delight in muscling ahead of me on busy dual carriageways or heavy traffic.

In the end I developed a response for the 'I can beat an RS200' brigade. In most cases, the attackers would have caught up with the RS200 under braking, but found themselves in all sorts of trouble when trying to negotiate these roundabouts at speeds that I came to consider quite normal. In the case of the four-wheel-drive RS200, whose steering and handling was unworldly compared with any car I had previously driven, it was a matter of only 'dab the brakes, down two gears, left, right, left', then away up the next stretch, having experienced no body roll and no wheelspin. But as for the attackers… Let's just say I never saw accidents but saw a lot of tyre smoke at times – and it was quite often at this stage that the pursuit was abandoned.

I think I hesitated for just one nanosecond before accepting the deal – even though I felt a little uneasy about using a left-hand-drive car for my day-to-day motoring – and it was not long before I was suitably installed, and waved off on my first long trip, by people who were used to this sort of thing.

At the time, I had no say in what and how the car was to be equipped, for it was already nearly a year old, had been used ruthlessly as a test and development car, including being taken to the Nardo high-speed circuit in the south of Italy to see how long the engine would last in flat-out use. Except that it had left-hand drive, and (at my request) was eventually fitted with leather-trimmed Recaro seats instead of the figure-hugging rally seats that were otherwise supplied, the only non-standard feature was an early-type mobile phone (courtesy of Securicor, a Ford Motorsport sponsor of the period). Because it was a left-hand-drive car, it also had a KPH speedometer, which registered 24,833km (15,433 miles) when I took over.

At first, to be honest, I wasn't too ecstatic about the car, for I found it noisy inside the cabin, with an awful turning circle, and a fierce clutch that I took ages to conquer. Then, after a few weeks, I began to get the point, and can do no better than to quote from the big feature article I wrote about this car for *Autocar* in October 1987: *'On the open road, traffic permitting, it soon showed that it is one of the fastest and most nimble cars in the business… I'm utterly convinced that no other road car (OK, perhaps a Porsche 959) can match it on a twisty road.*

> "I found it noisy inside the cabin, with an awful turning circle, and a fierce clutch that I took ages to conquer"

'From the outset, the four-wheel-drive chassis, coupled with amazingly supple suspension, didn't seem to have any vices, and I for one wasn't brave enough to discover the limits. When Autocar's technical editor Jeff Daniels sampled another RS200 last year he wrote: "In a sense there is no handling – not in terms of the usual analysis of under- or oversteer. The RS200 simply goes where it is pointed, up to very high limits. And those limits really are high".'

I also recalled that quite soon the car was returned to JQF, which not only replaced the transmission with a new unit that had not already had a hard life, but fitted the Stratton-trimmed £1000-worth of seats, a tighter-turning-circle steering rack, a less-fierce clutch and a radio-cassette unit. Suddenly this was a car I was not only privileged to drive, but also to enjoy using on a very regular basis.

To answer the usual boys' queries, it was, and felt, extremely quick by the standards of the 1980s, with 0-to-60mph in 6.6 seconds, a top speed of about 140mph, and an average open-road fuel consumption of 20.5mpg. It also seemed to start at

Ford

RS200

Ford

Country life for the author in 1988, with an RS200 available for business travel, and an Escort XR3i for normal private mileage.

Soon after taking over C142 JJN as a road car, the author used it as a chase car in observing, and reporting on, British events.

Before the author's fourth 'endurance' RS200 was delivered, it was repainted in that wonderful Ferrari Rosso Red shade. Further pre-delivery preparation then took place, including the changeover of seats, installation of a mobile telephone, a radio/cassette player and electric window lifts. It would complete 48,000 miles in the author's hands until early 1991.

the first twist of the key, every time, even on wintry mornings (and I mean every time), and there were no signs of engine overheating even in heavy traffic. This, though, was in the days when traffic densities were much less severe than they would become in later years, and both Bob Howe and I were quick to dive off any main road when a standing-traffic hold-up looked as if it might last.

In a year there were several minor problems and breakages, which could usually be traced back to this car's earlier life as a high-speed test machine – except for one, and once again I must repeat the words used in my *Autocar* tribute: *'At 25,270 miles, as I was accelerating down a ramp from the M25 onto the A12 at Brentwood, on the way to Boreham, there was a loud 'pop' and the engine lost all turbo boost. The lack of oil smoke – and other dramas – meant that the turbo itself had not failed. The large-diameter flexible pipe linking the turbo to the intercooler had slipped off, too contaminated by oil mist to keep its grip. Boreham's mechanics fell about at the thought of a normally-aspirated RS200 being slower than every XR3i and Golf GTI on the A12 (it was highly embarrassing), but the cure was quick and straightforward.'*

By the end of 1987, however, Boreham decided that C142 JJN should be sold off, so it was returned – this time to Aston Martin Tickford in Bedworth, where it was replaced by Car No 127, registered E946 BNO. The rationale was that I, along with Bob Howe who also benefited from a car swap at this stage, should start using a brand-new car, which had undergone the complete refreshment treatment being given to all the cars still in store. For me, the good news was this was a right-hand-drive car, to which my Stratton seats, the mobile telephone and the radio/cassette feature were all transferred.

Unhappily, this car only stayed with me for two months, for in February 1988, on a bitterly cold and icy morning, I had started out on an early dash from home to Boreham, when the car struck a lethal patch of ice on the main road between Dorchester and Blandford, spun viciously and – bang – ended up across the road looking very sorry for itself. The car was still driveable, just, but soon after I started creeping back to my nearest RS dealer, I realised that the main transmission casing had cracked open, released all its oil, and was about to seize – which it duly did.

The good news was that Ford was very nice about it, soon made sure it was returned Boreham, and the even better news was that the main chassis and most of the bodywork were found to be unscathed, so they were repaired later in the spring. Although I was still ashamed of myself, I was bucked up by the news that the engineers had found the crash valuable, for it confirmed that the design that they had originally laid

Right: This group of shots shows the condition in which a standard-specification car would be handed over for road use. Many owners would immediately begin to modify or upgrade their new machines for personal use.

RS200S ATTRACTED POLICE CARS LIKE BEES TO A HONEYPOT

I was always very careful not to drive at unseemly speeds on public roads (I needed my licence more than I needed the adrenaline rush), and because the RS200 had no cruise control I tended to sit with the rev counter reading about 3500rpm (70mph) in fifth gear wherever possible, and police cars (which seemed to be much more frequent on the roads in the 1980s than they are now) used to ignore me.

> **"It didn't take me long to realise that I was being tailed by a police car, but it was at least ten miles before it closed up behind me"**

There was, however, one memorable occasion when this did not happen. It was a Friday afternoon, on a sunny summer's day, when I was cruising home down the A433 north of Bath. It didn't take me long to realise that I was being tailed by a police car, but it was at least ten miles before it closed up behind me, flashed its blue lights imperiously, and pulled me over.

The usual police pantomime was then enacted – the leisurely dismount by both police driver and passenger, the placing of hats on heads, the careful manoeuvre of their car so that I could not swoop off before they could arrest me, the 'please get out of your car, sir', and the ostentatious sniff to see if there was any evidence of alcohol or drugs.

This was then followed by, "Is this your car, sir?"

"No, it is not."

"So who owns it, then?"

"Ford Motor Co, but you knew that already..."

"But it is registered in Essex, so why are you here?"

"Because I live in Dorset."

Before long, they mellowed, became positively amiable, and asked if they might have a look around the car. There was clearly no hurry, and their radio system was reassuringly silent. After a few minutes, therefore, I felt bold enough to suggest that it didn't look as if they were at all busy, and got a wry smile, and a response I have never forgotten...

Waving an arm across the vista of the sky line, which include the outline of a house I knew to be Highgrove, Prince Charles's country residence, he said: "Quite right, sir. We are on personal protection duties of the royal family – and they are all away for the weekend."

down, with rough handling in mind, actually did its job.

My third RS200 followed very soon after, and had a longer and altogether more peaceful time with me. Car No 183, registered E994 BNO, and in the same specification as the previous machine, had been thrown together in the last two or three days of that frantic pre-homologation period at Shenstone, but proved to be remarkably trouble-free throughout 1988.

For the two of us, the highlight of the year was that I acted as a steward on the Pirelli Classic Marathon rally, which not only linked London with Cortina (in the Italian Dolomites), but the cars drove all the way back to the end in London too. Naturally I took my RS200 as personal transport – all the way there, and all the way back – and as a steward with all the rally authority I needed, I also drove around the famous F1 circuits at Spa and Monza, and climbed most of the famous passes in Italy that had been slotted into the route.

All this was a gentle preview to the arrival of the fourth and last of the RS200s I used on behalf of Ford, all of them really as 'endurance' machines. This car – No 192, registered F938 MJN – was scheduled to arrive early in December 1988 but delayed until Christmastime, and was one of the most gratifying Christmas presents I ever had. Not only was this a car that had originally been built on the day before the FIA homologation inspection took place on 31 January 1986, it was the only RS200 of the period that had electric window lifts (modified Sierra installations), and it was painted in that most lustrous colour: Ferrari Rosso Red.

> "With all the rally authority I needed, I also drove around the famous F1 circuits at Spa and Monza, and climbed most of the famous passes in Italy"

The use of this colour came as a real surprise. Just a few days before I was due to travel to Bedworth to swap cars, I got a phone call that more or less said:

"Sorry, your new RS200 is going to be a few days late."

"Why?"

"The paintwork was in rather poor condition, so it will need a respray."

"But you're used to doing that, right?"

"Yes, but would you like a different colour than white?"

"What choice have I got?"

"We thought you might like Ferrari Rosso Red."

"Great – but why, and how?"

"Oh, we've just finished a restoration of a classic Ferrari, and we have paint left over!"

To which there was no need to answer, and I was utterly delighted to have the use of an RS200, for two whole years, in that most charismatic of all colours.

Simply, that RS200 became a totally integral part of my life – for in two years, until January 1991, it completed 48,000 miles, and I loved almost every minute. By that time, of course, RS200 quality had improved considerably, the clutch was almost bearable, and I had become accustomed to the abysmal

Right: Many contemporary RS200s look as good today as they did when originally built at Shenstone in 1985/1986. However, as these detail studies show, there is so much for a diligent owner to keep clean if his car is used regularly.

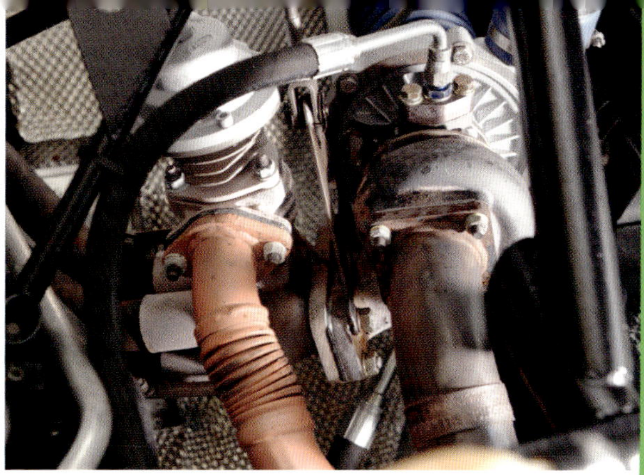

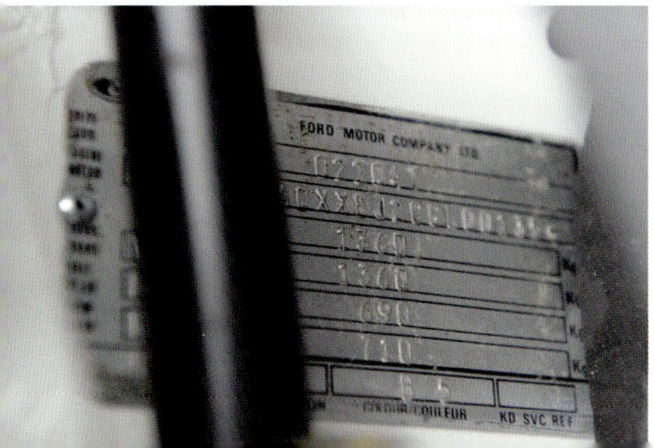
FORD MOTOR COMPANY LTD

performance of the heating system. In addition, there was the sheer joy of being able to push a switch to have the door windows retract, when everyone was expecting me to have a poor-quality car where such things were simply not available.

Along the way, I got used to fending off frivolous questions like 'when are you going to get the Evolution engine?' or even 'Rick Lee has developed power steering. Has your car got it yet?'

"Unhappily – and it would be quite wrong to hide this from future generations – there were two engine failures"

Although I never succumbed to a boiling engine when the traffic jam was unexpected (I believe this happened once to Bob Howe) it was a relief, as a blown cylinder head gasket was sure to follow shortly afterwards. Unhappily – and it would be quite wrong to hide this from future generations – there were two engine failures, both due to broken camshaft drive belts. The first occurred one morning when I was pottering slowly in to Boreham from my hotel in Maldon, so it only involved a short tow to the workshops, where a repair was completed in a couple of hours. The second – at about 40,000 miles – came as I was cruising along the A38 dual carriageway towards the RS dealership in Plymouth when the engine suddenly stopped, and it was only after the car had been retrieved to Vospers, then taken back to Boreham, that another broken camshaft belt breakage was diagnosed.

Even so, I enjoyed more than two years of almost non-stop pleasure with The Red Car, which attracted attention wherever it went. However, by January 1991 it was time to wind down the entire RS200 programme, for all except the three cars, as already noted, had been sold off and delivered, Bob Howe had closed his office, and it was time to hand over the administration of the RS200 Club to an existing owner (who, at the time, was Allan Fenwick).

When the car finally returned to Boreham it had completed 48,000 miles, and although I offered to buy it, the suggested price was out of my reach. On that day I gave a sad farewell to the car, and left Boreham in something entirely different – a Sierra Cosworth 4x4.

That was almost the end of my close links with the RS200 programme, but my joy is in occasionally seeing examples at major events, and occasionally – very occasionally – being allowed to drive one again. This, incidentally, was not the end of my links with Ford homologation specials, for almost as soon as the beloved red car left my possession, I was swept up into the pre-delivery demonstrations of yet another special – the Escort RS Cosworth – and eventually I went on to use two such cars in future years.

Driving, and loving, ultra-rare Fords like these is a certifiable disease – and I freely admit that I caught it in 1983.

When the RS200 sale campaign was at its height between 1988 and 1990, the author ran this uniquely-liveried RS200 (chassis number 192) as a normal road car, completing 48,000 miles during that time. Naturally there was another Ford – in this case a white Escort RS Turbo – in the garage too.

RS200
Ford

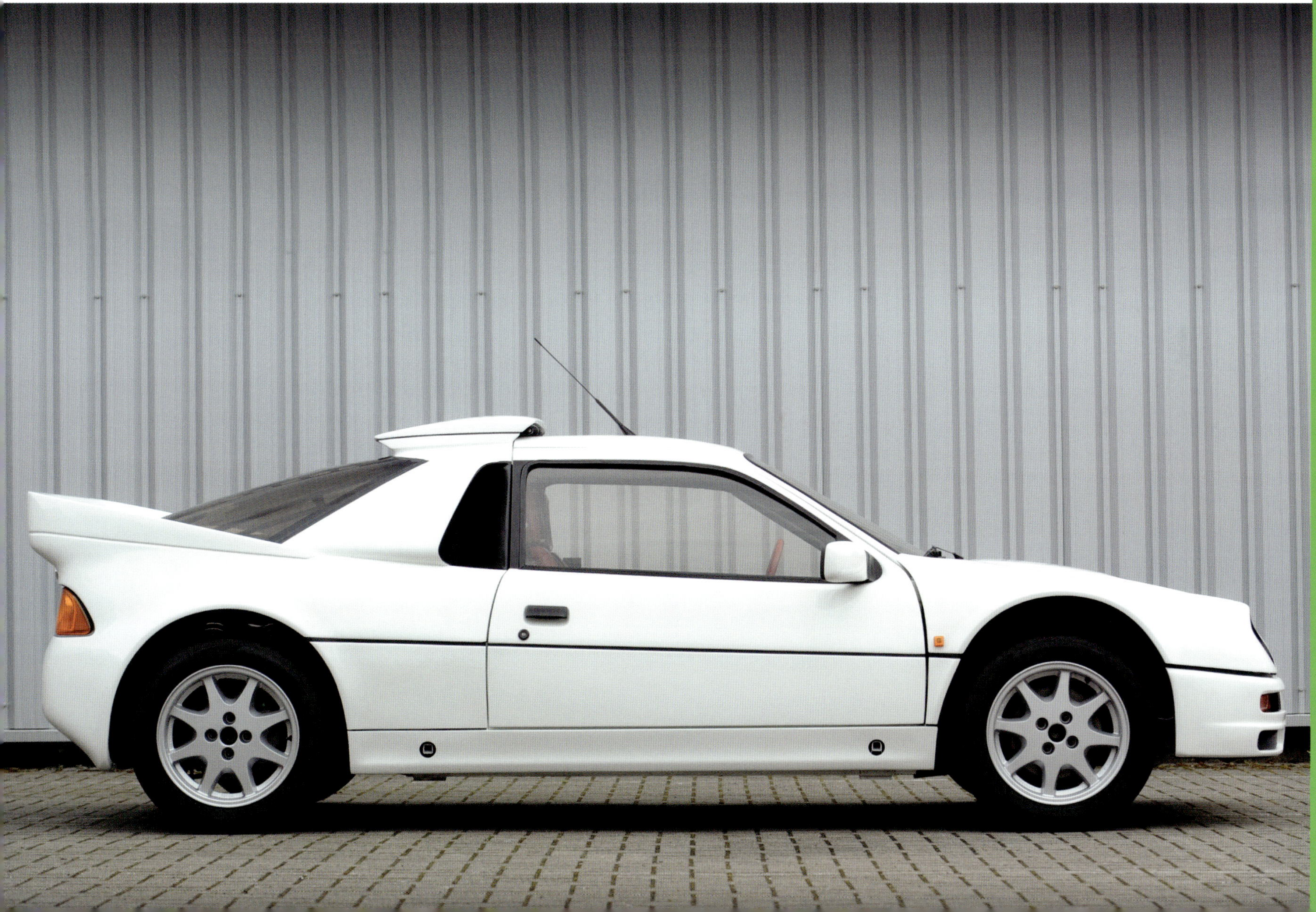

Significant production cars

This is a detailed selection, listed by VIN (vehicle identity number) of some of the most significant RS200s that Ford built, scheduled for production (but sometimes did not quite complete) and completed between March 1984 and the spring of 1986.

A significant number of cars, though built (perhaps one ought to say 'almost completely assembled') in time for FIA inspection in January 1986, were never completed, nor sold. They are not listed here. Such cars, as entities, certainly existed, and Ford insists that it acquired 200 chassis tubs from Arch, and more than 200 sets of every component or sub-assembly – including complete engines and transmissions – which would have made delivery possible, but in the fullness of time (and in particular due to the aftermath of the cancellation of Group B motorsport, and the drop in demand for competition machines), a quantity of such incomplete cars were then dismantled. In later years, a number of privately-financed Evolution and privately-assembled RS200s seem to have been created using many such VINs, and many of the otherwise spare parts.

This list does not include any of those so-called Evolution cars, because no such production car was ever completely designed, nor built, by Ford, at Boreham or at Shenstone. So-called Evolution cars were never factory products (though for Group S homologation purposes 20 such machines might have been built in 1986/1987 if the RS200 project had not been curtailed), and all later came into existence by courtesy only of private owners, and were invariably built around the 2.1-litre BDT-E engine designed by Brian Hart in 1984/1986. The majority of such cars came into existence through a renowned company called Gordon Spooner Engineering, of Witham in Essex, which carried out conversions on already-existing 1.8-litre cars.

What follows is a list of the most significant, and interesting, cars built by Ford, either at Boreham or at Shenstone, along with a brief history (where appropriate) of their immediate usage. Although each car had the usual DVLA chassis/VIN number of 17 digits, as the project evolved each car was always affectionately known by everyone at Ford, or connected with the project, by the final three numbers. The author's much-loved red example, for instance, was always known as 192.

Purely as an example, these are the details of the third prototype to be built:

OFFICIAL NUMBER	SFACXXBJ2CED00003
ALWAYS KNOWN AS	003

VERY IMPORTANT PRODUCTION CARS

VIN - 001 B200 FMC

Although B200 FMC is thought to be a false publicity plate, this was the very first prototype car, built at TC Prototypes and Boreham in autumn/winter 1983/1984, and completed in March 1984, when it was immediately taken to a Ford retail premises in Balderton Street, London, to be shown off to Bob Lutz of Ford, HRH Prince Michael of Kent and the author – separately, of course – on the same evening. Therefore, and following a wider (secret) showing to senior members of Ford management, it was returned to Boreham and set to work.

In 1984 and 1985 it mainly functioned as a prototype test car, helping to finalise and prove the specification of the forthcoming 194-car production run. In September 1984 it first visited MIRA, where Jackie Stewart spent much of the day exploring roadholding settings with John Wheeler and his team.

As is now clear (and detailed in the text), it was different in many significant ways from the production car that was to follow – the lack of a roof-mounted engine intercooler, the front bodystyle, the way the front body moulding was attached to the main body/chassis section, and the plain Perspex cover over the rear/mid-mounted engine, for instance.

As far as is known, when the production run had been completed, 001 effectively became surplus to all requirements and was stored at Boreham. As is now clear from the many comments in this book, the author ran the Ford-financed RS200 Club until the end of the 1980s, and in one of the final newsletters, it was reported that 001 was shortly to be destroyed by Ford. One is confident this was done, for no trace of 001 existed thereafter.

VIN - 002 NOT REGISTERED

Construction of this, the second RS200 to be built by TC Prototypes, and refined at Boreham, began early in 1984 even before Bob Lutz gave his approval for Cars No 002 to 006 to be produced. Completed in the first half of 1984, it was never road registered but was used in many ways as the car on which many of the ready-for-production changes were made to the structure. Originally, for instance, it was not equipped with the roof-positioned intercooler housing, and had a front body moulding that was hinged at the passenger box bulkhead rather than in the nose. Certainly it then spent some time with Aston Martin Tickford, as the firm proceeded with productionisation and legislation procedures.

Although we know it was used for testing at MIRA in September 1984, photographic evidence confirms that in October 1984 it was subject to the 30mph barrier-crash test that was essential for the RS200 to gain road-going type approval. It was totally successful in this test, after which it was rebuilt and eventually used for some static exhibition work, though it never became a normal road car.

Ford later had the car destroyed.

VIN - 003 B888 CHK

Completed in mid 1984, the third of the six cars originally constructed at TC Prototypes and at Boreham, the left-hand-drive 003 was always meant to be a hard-working prototype of what would become the standard road-car specification. In and out of Boreham, in and out of AMT in Milton Keynes, and often espied on the road, it covered a considerable test mileage.

As a change, and towards the end of its official working career, it was also used as one of the two RS200 prototypes demonstrated to the specialist press at a high-speed ride-drive occasion in Sardinia in September 1985, where John Taylor was in charge of that expedition.

Once 200-off production of all the cars had been completed, 003's task was over, and shortly after that it was handed over to Ford's Heritage fleet in Dagenham, and became a permanent member of that operation. Although apparently still in residence, it gets very little use these days.

VIN - 004 B690 CEV

This was the car revealed at the Turin Motor Show in November 1984 as a fully-equipped left-hand-drive road car, though it did not carry a registration number at that time. It had been flown there from Essex, not driven. Once the show closed, it was returned to Boreham and joined the other prototypes (three – 001, 002 and 003 – already existed, while 005 and 006 were about to join them) on the pre-production testing fleet.

In the next year or so, it carried out many testing duties as a working prototype, not only with the Boreham team themselves, but by making visits to Aston Martin Tickford at Newport Pagnell, where much of the productionisation work was being carried out.

Although there is no absolutely conclusive proof of what follows, 004 was almost certainly the car completely stripped out at Boreham, so that many photographs could be taken (a number being reproduced on these pages) in connection with the preparation of the repair operation manual and the owners' handbook – both of which were initially written by the author.

However, to confuse matters still further (it happened frequently in works teams of the period) the B690 CEV identity appeared on Stig Blomqvist's recce car at the beginning of the 1986 rally season, though John Wheeler tells us that 005 and 007 were the works team's early recce cars of that period. Make of that what you will.

The real 004 was apparently later destroyed by Ford.

VIN - 005 B55 CHK

Completed early in 1985 at Boreham, this was the very first rally-specification car, and the one most often shown (with no number plates attached) in pictures to the public during 1985.

Famous as being the very first RS200 to take part in a rally – the Lindisfarne of September 1985 – and as a crowd-pleaser (but not a competitor) before the start of the RAC Rally, it then started its serious works career as a test and practice car for the 1986 World Championship season.

As stated, it started 1986 as one of two cars that Boreham allocated as World Championship practice/recce cars (005 and 007). Used before the Swedish (February 1986) and Portugal (March 1986) events, it was then returned to Boreham, re-engineered and reprepared for use before the Acropolis rally of Greece (May). On practice, a mishap led to the car catching fire in the engine bay, which subsequently resulted in it being totally consumed.

Although the wreckage was returned to Boreham (for legal reasons, the Greek authorities always insisted that foreign cars that entered their country must be re-exported in due course) it was then ceremonially written off.

VIN - 006 B340 CAR

This RS200, the last of the Boreham-located prototypes and originally a right-hand-drive machine, was first registered in March 1985 and soon put to work as the final production-specification prototype. It was not only to become involved in all manner of testing, but as a demonstration/show car at several Ford-organised events throughout Europe. It was, for instance, used in the famous Beaujolais Run of 1985, when one of its drivers was the multi-British Touring Car Championship winner Andy Rouse.

Early in 1986, with production of the Shenstone batch of cars almost complete, and with sporting homologation about to be achieved – but with true competition versions still extremely rare – B340 CAR was briefly pressed into service as a works competition car. As detailed in Chapter 6, in January and February it was driven by Mark Lovell, in near-to-standard mechanical condition, on two minor British loose-surface events, the Citroën National and Skip Brown rallies.

Although details are sparse, Boreham then seems to have sent it off to Portugal, as one of two RS200s being acquired for rallying by Diabolique Motorsport. Badly damaged in a crash in Portugal, 006 was eventually used as a donor to Diaboloque's other car, No 072.

VIN - 007 C98 FHK

This car is notable for being the first RS200 to be completed by the original Shenstone workforce during the summer of 1985 (a left-hand-drive machine) before being shipped to Boreham, where it was immediately stripped out and reprepared before beginning its career as one of the rare works competition cars. Although it was not seen on the start line of World Championship rallies, it was used as a hard-working development rally car, test car and recce machine. Along with Car 005, it became a practice/recce car behind the scenes on the Swedish, Portuguese and Acropolis rallies before Boreham's programme was truncated.

Details of its later life are scarce, but it seems certain that it was written off/destroyed by Ford in 1989 after the RS200 programme was run down.

VIN - 008 B200 COO

Except that it was one of the first two cars to be built at Shenstone, that it was a right-hand-drive machine first registered late in 1985, very little indeed is known about this car.

However, the registration number included what became one of the familiar '200' sequences, which suggests it was originally meant for use as a competition car by the works competitions department at Boreham, which took control of it in 1986.

VIN - 012 C200 LWC

This was one of the original dedicated fleet of works cars that were centred at Boreham in 1986. Partly built at Shenstone in the autumn of 1985, it was then shipped to Boreham where it was completed, prepared and continuously developed as a 1.8-litre works car. Driven by Stig Blomqvist on the Welsh Rally of 1986, it led convincingly for much of the event until pitched off a stage by a broken rear wishbone, this having been caused by a catastrophic puncture/tyre/wheel blowout at an earlier point.

Shortly after this it was used as a practice car for the Greek Acropolis Rally, then returned to Boreham to be used for some testing, development and rebuilds in connection with what might have been a Group B/Group S project – which included becoming the very first RS200 to be fitted with the Hartpower 2.1-litre BDT-E engine.

In this guise it was loaned to Martin Schanche for use in the Bettega Memorial Rallysprint in Italy in December 1986 before the entire Boreham programme was finally wound down.

VIN - 014 B200YEV

This was one of the front-line Boreham works rally cars, which competed extensively in 1986, and whose career is described in detail in Chapter 6

In much modified and modernised form it survives to this day, and many colour images of its 2010 state are within these pages.

VIN - 015 B200 YOO

This sister car of Car 014 (above, B200 YEV) was built/prepared for world-level rallying in 1986. Its career is described in detail in Chapter 6.

VIN - 020 NOT KNOWN

This car was originally ordered by representatives of King Hussein of Jordan. Delivered in 1987, it was driven in off-road events by the king, but was eventually returned to Boreham in 1989/1990.

VIN - 034 C829 KWC

Built at Shenstone in the autumn of 1985, and retained at Boreham for some time, this RS200 then became a development car for road use. Not only that, but it was also used for some flat-out endurance test-driving at the massive circular oval at Nardo in the very south of Italy (in the heel, close to Taranto) in April 1986.

Notes that survive tell us the car was driven all the way from Essex to Nardo (1558 miles at 20.6mpg) before high-speed work began. Driven by Bob Howe, Bill Meade and technician R Smith, it covered 5010.75 miles, with a highest single lap speed of 143.5mph, drinking fuel at the rate of 9.42mpg. Finally there was a significant mechanical breakdown (within the transmission), after which it was retrieved to Boreham by trailer.

Later, in June 1986, it was taken to MIRA for assessment over that establishment's fearsome Pavé tracks, where it covered 269 miles before being called in, having suffered some minor structural failures.

VIN - 053 D49 FOT

One of the original batch of road cars built at Shenstone, this RHD machine was originally sold to Hendy Ford, a thriving British Ford RS dealership in the Bournemouth area, and after spending 30 years in the hands of another person in the south-east of England it was apparently re-acquired by Hendy for its own heritage collection.

VIN - 061 C200 JJN

In 1986 this fully rally-prepared car (to full Boreham specification but maintained and repaired as needed by Mike Taylor Developments of Yorkshire) became at once the most successful non-works car, and the most notorious, by being driven throughout the year by the fiery Swedish driver Stig Andervang. This car/driver combination won European championship series, and several events outright – and in October 1986 it was also the one and only RS200 to reach India, and to compete in that nation's Rally of the Himalayas.

Although it suffered from a major chassis breakage on the last event of the 1986 season – the Lombard RAC Rally – it was completely rebuilt and sold off, to carry on a rallycross career in Sweden. Details of its tempestuous career are in Chapter 7.

VIN - 068 UNKNOWN

Although originally built at Shenstone, this car was immediately transported to the north-east of England, where it was rapidly developed into the very first successful RS200 rallycross car, driven to many victories by Mark Rennison.

VIN - 072 UNKNOWN

Following original preparation as a motorsport example, this was one of two cars supplied to Diabolique Motorsport in Portugal, intended for use by Joaquim Santos in European and world-class events.

VIN - 073 C142 JJN

Built at Shenstone at the very beginning of 1986, this left-hand-drive road-specification RS200 became a hard-working test car at Boreham, though it was never intended for competition use.

This became the second RS200 to make the long trip to Nardo for further high-speed testing, achieved in September 1986, when it completed 6398 kilometres/3976 miles before succumbing to an engine failure.

Subsequently it was restored, used for further development, before being handed over to the author for use as a normal 250bhp road car for everyday transport all around the country. It was in Graham Robson's care from April 1987 to December 1987.

VIN - 075 NOT KNOWN

Built in Shenstone in 1985/1986, then rally-prepared by Mike Little Preparations, 075 was allocated to RACE in Spain, where it was successfully used in rallies by Antonio Zanini.

VIN - 126 D631 XNO

This car was used by Bob Howe for some time as a demonstrator at Boreham, and by Bob as a road car to show to prospective customers. At the end of its useful period, it was delivered to the German race driver Klaus Ludwig, as part payment of his fees for driving Ford Sierra RS500 Cosworths in touring car racing in 1987 and 1988.

VIN - 127 E946 BNO

Handed over to Graham Robson at the Aston Martin Tickford factory at Bedworth, near Coventry, in December 1987, it was the second of four long-term 'endurance' cars he was set to use on behalf of Ford.

Early one icy morning in February 1988 the car suffered an open road accident, and was damaged by a spin. It was then returned to AMT, a lengthy repair was carried out, and in mid summer it was sold to Rick Lee, whose marketing/promotional company had links with Ford.

VIN - 134 NOT REGISTERED

This brand-new left-hand-drive machine was delivered to Ford-of-Germany in Cologne, and lives in the company's museum.

VIN - 139 UNKNOWN

According to Ford's scrappy records, and to the memories of Motorsport personalities involved in the programme, it was the very first car to be delivered to a private owner – Charles Ross, a veterinary surgeon based in the East Midlands. He used it as a regular day-to-day business car, and (because he was a vet) the structure suffered from the assault of many agricultural conditions, including chemicals that might not normally have been found on a road-going car of any type.

VIN - 161 NOT UK REGISTERED?

This car was still unsold in 1988, but was apparently rebuilt/re-prepared on behalf of Boreham (though not apparently at Boreham) for Stig Blomqvist to use in his native Sweden. Naturally it had a 2.1-litre BDT-E engine. However, it does not figure in the official list of 20 RS200s converted to Evolution cars.

VIN - 183 E994BNO

This was the third (of four) road-equipped cars used for everyday long-term transport by author/RS200 registrar Graham Robson, who collected the car in February 1988, in direct replacement for Car 127 (which had been involved in an accident). It did many miles before being itself replaced by Car 192 in December 1988.

VIN - 192 F938 MJN

This noble machine was always close to the author's heart, for it was the fourth and last RS200 he used as a long-term test 'endurance' car on behalf of Ford Motorsport. Originally thrown together in the frantic days of January 1986, just in time to be one of the 194 road cars counted by the FIA inspectors, it was initially a standard-specification 250bhp RHD example. Quite unused after that, it remained in store at Ford, or latterly at Aston Martin Tickford in Bedworth, before being totally refurbished prior to handover in December 1988.

Because the white paintwork had suffered somewhat in the intervening three years, a complete respray was offered and accepted, especially when, following an enquiry, it seemed that the new colour would be the famous Ferrari Rosso Red.

During the repreparation, this car gained the same two Recaro seats that had already featured in previous Robson RS200s, a Securicor mobile telephone was installed, and a pair of electric window lifts were added to the doors.

This car stayed in the author's possession until January 1991, by which time it had completed 48,000 miles, before it was returned to Ford at Boreham, as the RS200 programme had already ended. Apparently it was much modified by its subsequent owners, and was later quite unrecognisably different from the original specification.

VIN - 200 C117 OTW

This was the last RS200 officially built (which, effectively, means the last Shenstone-assembled car to have a VIN plate added after the rush to meet homologation had died down). A nostalgic image exists of the empty post-RS200 assembly hall at Shenstone, which had been cleared of all other equipment but with just one car still present, which was suitably carrying the '200' number on its windscreen, and was ready to be driven away. From Shenstone, it was immediately delivered to the Ford Heritage Collection at Dagenham, and remains in Ford's hands to this very day.

Technically, it was a standard-specification RS200 with 250bhp engine, and although listed in the wonderful *RS200.org* website as having right-hand-drive, it is actually a left-hand-drive model. Although it carries an appropriate 1986 registration number, it seems that it was not actually registered until 1997.

Build numbers

Below is the complete build number list of RS200s as they were initially produced from 1984 to 1986. Although authentic records no longer exist, all cars listed as 'never completed' were among those inspected on 31 January 1986, and almost certainly were then disassembled again in future months, for use as parts for the remaining fleet. The complete list of all cars disassembled for this purpose has not survived.

After Ford had completed the production run, and was selling individual machines, the proposed Hartpower 2.1-litre engine was supplied to 20 individual customers. In private life, these became RS200E Evolution cars. For the sake of administrative neatness, Ford then issued a run of 20 additional numbers – but one must emphasise that these cars were never factory-developed. In the list that follows, such cars are identified with their original and subsequent build numbers together (as an example, 101/*211).

(LHD = LEFT HAND DRIVE, RHD = RIGHT HAND DRIVE)

CAR NO	DETAIL	NOTE
001	LHD	First prototype. Crushed
002	LHD	Second prototype. Crash test car. Destroyed
003	LHD	Third prototype. Retained by Ford Heritage
004	LHD	Fourth prototype. Crushed
005	LHD	Fifth prototype. Boreham rally car. Burnt out
006	RHD	Sixth prototype. Destroyed in rally crash
007	LHD	Boreham rally car. Burnt out
008	RHD	Boreham rally car
009	RHD	
010	LHD	
011	Never completed	
012/*201	LHD	Boreham rally car
013	Never completed	
014	LHD	Boreham rally car
015	LHD	Boreham rally car
016	LHD	
017 - 019	Never completed	
020	LHD	Supplied to King Hussein of Jordan
021 - 033	Never completed	
034	LHD	Boreham test/development car
035 - 060	Never completed	
061	LHD	Boreham rally car
062	LHD	Boreham rally car
063	LHD	Boreham rally car
064	LHD	Boreham rally car
065	LHD	Boreham rally car
066	LHD	
067	LHD	
068	RHD	Original Mark Rennison rallycross car
069	LHD	

CAR NO	DETAIL	NOTE
070/*213	LHD	
071	LHD	
072	LHD	Used in Portuguese rallies
073	LHD	Boreham test/endurance car
074	LHD	
075	LHD	Used in Spanish rallies
076	Not recorded	Destroyed by Ford
077	LHD	
078	Not recorded	Destroyed by Ford
079	RHD	
080	LHD	
081/*209	LHD	
082	LHD	
083/*218	LHD	
084/*214	LHD	
085	LHD	
086/*220	RHD	
087/*204	LHD	
088	RHD	
089	RHD	
090	RHD	
091	LHD	
092	LHD	
093	LHD	
094	LHD	
095	LHD	
096/*217	RHD	
097/*205	LHD	
098/*206	LHD	
099/*207	LHD	

CAR NO	DETAIL	NOTE
100	RHD	
101/*211	LHD	
102	RHD	
103	RHD	
104	RHD	
105/*215	LHD	
106/*216	LHD	
107	LHD	
108	RHD	
109	LHD	
110	LHD	
111	LHD	
112	RHD	
113	LHD	
114	RHD	
115	RHD	
116	LHD	
117	RHD	Ford press/endurance car
118	RHD	
119	RHD	
120	LHD	
121	LHD	
122	LHD	Ford test/development/publicity car
123	RHD	
124	RHD	
125	LHD	
126	RHD	Ford-owned for test purposes
127	LHD	
128	LHD	
129	LHD	
130	LHD	
131	LHD	
132	LHD	
133	LHD	
134	LHD	
135	LHD	
136	LHD	
137	LHD	
138	RHD	
139	RHD	First private car to be delivered
140	Never completed	
141	LHD	
142	LHD	
143	RHD	
144	RHD	
145/*208	LHD	
146/*202	LHD	
147	LHD	
148	LHD	
149	LHD	
150	LHD	
151	LHD	
152	LHD	

CAR NO	DETAIL	NOTE
153/*210	RHD	
154	LHD	
155	RHD	
156	RHD	
157	RHD	
158	RHD	
159	LHD	
160	RHD	
161	LHD	
162	RHD	
163	RHD	
164	LHD	
165	LHA	
166	LHD	
167	RHD	
168/*212	LHD	
169	LHD	
170	LHD	
171	LHD	
172	LHD	
173	RHD	
174/*203	RHD	
175	RHD	
176	LHD	
177	LHD	
178	LHD	
179	LHD	
180	RHD	
181	RHD	
182	RHD	
183	RHD	Ford long-term/endurance car
184	RHD	
185	LHD	
186	RHD	
187	LHD	
188	RHD	
189	RHD	
190	RHD	
191	RHD	
192	RHD	Ford long-term/endurance car
193	RHD	
194	RHD	
195	RHD	
196	LHD	
197	LHD	
198	LHD	
199	LHD	
200	RHD	Retained by Ford Heritage

Tech Spec

Specification and performance of standard 250bhp RS200 road cars, as produced in 1985 and 1986

General layout

Limited-production two-seater sports coupé with mid/rear-mounted engine, four-wheel-drive and GRP (fibreglass) exterior body panels. Precisely 200 cars (including six prototypes) were originally commissioned. Left-hand-drive and right-hand-drive versions were available.

Structure

Monocoque centre section (including the passenger compartment), a complex assembly including some sections in sheet steel, others in aluminium honeycomb, and some in Aramid composite material, including a built-in safety roll cage. Complex multi-tubular front and rear chassis extensions supporting the suspension, engine and many additional components. All exterior body panels/lift-up sections in GRP.

Engine

TYPE Ford-Cosworth BDT
CAPACITY 1803cc
BORE/STROKE 86x77.6mm
COMPRESSION RATIO 8.2:1 (geometric), plus turbocharging to 11psi/0.75 Bar.
MAX POWER 250bhp (DIN) @ 6500-7000rpm
MAX TORQUE 215lb.ft @ 4500-5000rpm
CYLINDERS four, in line, longitudinally-mounted
CYLINDER HEAD cast aluminium
BLOCK cast aluminium
VALVE GEAR four valves per cylinder, operated by belt-driven twin overhead camshafts via inverted bucket-type tappets
FUELLING Ford fuel injection, with Ford EEC-IV engine management, Garrett AirResearch T03/4 turbocharger and air/air intercooling. Two fuel tanks, of 13.2 imperial gallons/60 litres and 6.6 imperial gallons/30 litres
ENGINE INSTALLATION mid/rear, longitudinally-mounted, driving all four wheels

Transmission

TYPE mid/rear-engine, four-wheel-drive
GEARBOX Ford/FF five-speed manual, all-synchromesh. Front, centre and rear differentials incorporating FF viscous-coupling limited-slip mechanisms. Centre differential directs 37% of torque to the front wheels, and 63% to the rear wheels
INTERNAL RATIOS first 2.692, second 1.824, third 1.318, fourth 1.043, fifth 0.786, reverse 3.083, transfer gear ratio 1.043:1. 20.16mph/1000rpm in top gear

Suspension

FRONT independent by twin coil springs, wishbones, anti-roll bar and telescopic dampers. Adjustable ride height settings on spring/damper units
REAR independent by twin coil springs, wishbones, anti-roll bar and telescopic dampers. Adjustable ride/height settings on spring/damper units

Steering

TYPE rack-and-pinion, no power-assistance
LOCK-TO-LOCK 3.0 turns.
TURNING CIRCLE 32.8 feet/10.0 metres between kerbs

Brakes

FRONT 11.2in/285mm ventilated discs
REAR 11.2in/285mm ventilated discs
SYSTEM hydraulic, with dual circuits and AP four-piston callipers. Mechanically-operated handbrake, with separate AP callipers. No vacuum servo assistance, and no ABS

Wheels & tyres

WHEELS Speedline seven-spoke cast aluminium, 8.0J x 16in
TYRES 225/50VR16 Pirelli P700 tyres

Body/chassis

TYPE lightweight composite steel/aluminium/honeycomb tub with built-in roll cage in two-door closed two-seater form. Bolt-on tubular steel front and rear subframes. Fibreglass body panels with carbon/aramid stiffening. Lift-up entire front and rear sections for access to chassis and running gear
DIMENSIONS 13ft 1.5in/4000mm long, 5ft. 9.4in/1764mm wide, 4ft. 4in/1322mm high, 8ft. 3.6in/2530mm wheelbase, 4ft. 11.1in/1502mm front track, 4ft.11.0in/1498mm rear track
WEIGHT (with full fuel tanks but no passengers) 2602lb/1180kg

Performance & economy

MAX SPEED 140mph approx
ACCELERATION 0-60mph in 6.1 secs
STANDING START 1/4-MILE 15.0 secs
FUEL CONSUMPTION 15-20mpg

Price

£49,995 at launch in late 1985

Optional rally specification

Addition of selectable two-wheel-drive/locked centre transmission shift; firmer 'tarmac' suspension springs and dampers; hard rubber bushes for engine, transmission and rear axle mountings; deletion soft interior trim and sound deadening panels; four auxiliary driving lamps in a centrally-mounted pod; works team-style diagonal rally stripes

Optional luxury specification

To be carried out after initial build of the road car: leather-trimmed Recaro seats and leather trim; Wilton carpets; colour keyed leather-trimmed steering wheel and door pockets; special paint finish (to customer's choice)